Making
   Gifts from
      Oddments & Outdoor
                  Materials

Making
Gifts from
Oddments & Outdoor
Materials

by Betsey B. Creekmore

Hearthside Press Inc.
Publishers • New York

CONTENTS

COLOR ILLUSTRATIONS

On the jacket: A "standard" topiary tree. It is made of a styrofoam ball impaled on a knitting needle, embedded in a plastic flowerpot filled with wallpaper cleaner. Air-dried dyed strawflowers (stems dipped in glue) are slipped into holes made in the styrofoam (see pages 32, 33 for details). Plastic podocarpus sprigs are threaded on needle to hide the mechanics.

CREDITS

Miss Betsey Creekmore: Color plates II, IX, XI XII, XV, XIX; black-and-white photos on pages 41, 48, 52, 137, 175.

Bill Tracy: Black-and-white photos on pages 9, 18, 25, 28, 45, 57, 69, 70, 77, 84, 100, 101, 111, 115, 116, 120, 145.

Harley Ferguson: All other color plates and black-and-white photos.

1.

Fresh Flowers and Corsages
from Cost-Nothings

Most of us are bored with mass-produced objects. Even really expensive articles, if they are seen often enough (and they are, in our affluent, instant-communication society) no longer interest or stimulate or amuse us. Shopping for gifts can be a horrendous experience because prices are high, and anyway our friends, children, mates, in-laws, etc. already "have everything". But there is one kind of gift which speaks more clearly of love and thoughtfulness than any other. James Russell Lowell says it best:

> ...Not what you give, but what you share —
> The gift without the giver is bare...

And that's what this book is all about—putting something of yourself in the gifts you give. If you're out of the habit of doing things, or never acquired the habit, I hope these pages will open the door to an absorbing creativeness; give you the pleasure of unearthing materials which can be used in making hundreds of different presents. Tin cans, cardboard tubes, candle stubs, eggs, trimmings from your fabric bag—these are some of the odds and ends from which presents can be constructed. But best of all of the usable oddments are those which Nature provides.

There are myriad gifts hidden, like seeds within a capsule, in the products of the garden, for foliage and flowers, cones and pods can be converted by craft work into "something rich and strange." This wonderfully satisfying brand of alchemy has a further advantage: during the transformation process, a gift from the garden can be made to suit the tastes and conform to the pursuits of its recipient. When we bestow such special handiwork upon the one for whom we cared enough to make it, we offer that most welcomed of all presents—a person-to-person gift.

7

FRESH FLOWER GIFTS

"A gift from the garden..." To many people, the phrase is synonymous with "dew-fresh flowers," and only the cream of the garden's crop will do. Of course the blossoms will be gathered early in the morning as they reach perfection, and it is equally important that they be conditioned before being bestowed to prevent premature withering.

CONDITIONING FRESH FLOWERS

The house-life of cut flowers will be greatly prolonged if they are conditioned immediately, before being arranged or transported, in *hot water*. Because hot water is quickly and completely absorbed, it forces out of the flower stems the air bubbles that are a primary cause of early wilting.

Fill a deep container with water as hot as it runs from the kitchen faucet — about 155°. Strip the leaves from the part of the stem that will be immersed, some six or seven inches. Then cut the stem again, slantwise, with a sharp knife and put it into the hot water immediately. This takes courage at first, but it gives the blooms a visible jauntiness and a long lease on life. Leave the flowers in the conditioning container until the water has cooled to tepid, and then arrange them in a vase filled with fresh cold water. Some flowers (poppies in particular, but also poinsettias, euphorbia, et al.) exude a milky fluid from their cut stems. Seal such a stem by searing it over a candle flame before putting it into the hot water.

Incidentally, a hot bath is a fine restorative for tired flowers. When their stems have been re-cut and placed in hot water, wilting blooms revive dramatically—even drooping florist's roses will usually perk up.

CONDITIONING FOLIAGE

Foliage, deciduous or evergreen, has a greatly lengthened life expectancy after thorough conditioning in hot water. Strip off the lower leaves, and split (with a sharp knife) or crush (with a hammer) the ends of the woody stems. Plunge them at once into scalding hot water in a deep bucket or kettle. When the water has cooled to room temperature remove the branches, cut them to the desired length, again split the stem ends, and arrange them.

Broad-leafed evergreens, which may be judiciously pruned at any time of year for all-green arrangements or for background foliage, are naturally long-lived. Condition them by the hot water method described above; give them a weekly change of fresh cool water, and they should remain un-withered for a month or more.

FORCING FLOWERING SHRUBS

In February and March, while Spring procrastinates, there is a way to rush the blooming season—by forcing flowering shrubs. This may be done as soon as the buds begin to swell outdoors on the branch, and in one to three weeks (depending on plant variety and stage of development when cut) the buds will open. Jasmine, baby's breath, spirea, forsythia and flowering quince set their buds early, while the thermometer still is hovering near the freezing point. As the midday temperature moderates, buds appear on wild plum, flowering crab apple, and ornamental cherry; the first warm rain swells the buds of apple, pear, and flowering almond.

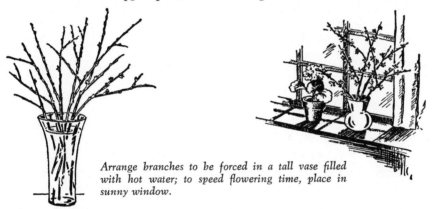

Arrange branches to be forced in a tall vase filled with hot water; to speed flowering time, place in sunny window.

As soon as you've cut branches that are to be forced, arrange them, in scalding hot water, in the tall vase in which they are to remain; much handling damages the bloom buds. Remove any buds that would be under water, and split the stem ends. Place the vase in a light, warm room; if a

Lettuce remember St. Patrick . . . a March 17 gift for a lucky Irishman includes forced branches of yellow-green forsythia and bright curly leaf salad greens from the supermarket.

sunny windowsill is available, so much the better. During the watch-and-wait period, you need do nothing except occasionally add fresh cool water to keep the container well filled.

Forced blossoms are somewhat lighter in color than those that open out of doors at their own appointed hour. Red flowering quince will have a rosy hue; cherry blossoms will be white with the merest tinge of pink.

FORCED GREEN FOLIAGE

Forced foliage, pale at first, soon deepens to a true Spring green, and cuttings from any budding tree or shrub or vine will open indoors in about a week.

Plan to present forced flowering or leafy sprays the moment the first bud opens, so that the recipient may see at close range the annual, intimate miracle of a bud unfolding or a leaf unfurling.

TRANSPORTING UNARRANGED FLOWERS

If it seems presumptuous to present a flower arrangement to someone who is a talented arranger, compliment her with well-conditioned raw materials for her own designs.

A water-filled can or bucket is all too apt to slosh as it is carried, or to tip over in a moving car, but you can safely transport fresh flowers considerable distances in coffee or shortening tins with snap-on plastic lids. First fill the can to within two inches of the brim with cool water. Snap on the lid, and punch small holes in it with an ice pick, a skewer, or a nail; hold the lid in place and make this container leakproof by sealing the rim to the side of the can with masking tape. Then push the stems of conditioned flowers down through the holes into the water; the pliable plastic will grip the stems firmly, but will not bruise them. Place the can of flowers in the center of a cardboard carton, and brace it upright with rolled or wadded newspaper.

Long-stemmed, top-heavy flowers will ride better if you insert their stems in water-filled soft drink bottles, snugly fitted back into their own cardboard carton. Woody stemmed sprays of flowering shrub or fruit tree branches travel best in a bucket of wet sand.

PLANT MATERIALS BY MAIL

To relatives and friends who have moved away, a gift of homegrown flowers or greenery is the next best thing to a return visit. Be it holly from the Pacific Northwest or bayberry from New England, camellias from Louisiana or lilacs from Illinois, well-conditioned plant materials should survive long-distance travel by air, and the extra fee for special delivery will be money well spent. If the trip is a short one of three hundred miles or less, send them by bus. They will be accepted for shipment at the freight office in your nearby bus terminal, and must be picked up at the terminal at the other end of their journey, so be sure to notify the addressee in advance that they are on the way.

PACKING MATERIALS FOR MAILING

Growers in Hawaii and Florida have hit upon a clever way to provide moisture for fresh materials in transit. After using a funnel to pour a small amount of water into a rubber balloon, they insert the stem of a conditioned flower through the balloon's neck into the water. The elastic rubber neck fits so tightly around the stem that the water does not spill.

A rigid cardboard dressbox makes a lightweight shipping carton. Inside the box, the flowers or foliage must be surrounded by a packing material that will support them without crushing leaves or petals, and will also cushion them against the shocks of handling.

FLOWER ARRANGEMENTS TO GO

Most recipients of fresh flowers will be glad to get them already arranged. However, since these days even one's local friends seldom live within walking distance, gift flower arrangements must be prepared to travel with you — over bumps and around bends.

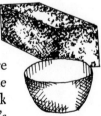

OASIS-FILLED CONTAINERS

Water is sure to spill from a vase in transit, but the answer to moisture without muss is Oasis — a solid green foam that soaks up water like a sponge — which is available from a florist. Buy Oasis in a large block — it's cheaper — and divide it yourself to fill several vases; when it's dry, you can cut it like cheese with a sharp knife. To prepare it for use, soak it in cool water for forty-five minutes, and then fit it into a container of any shape or size. You can insert flower stems into it with little force; the Oasis remains moist and the flowers remain fresh for several days.

Moist Oasis pressed into a plastic bowl is ideal for carrying pre-arranged flowers to your party hostess — all ready to slip into her own vase.

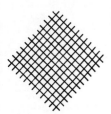

HARDWARE CLOTH AND BERRY BOXES

The best way to keep Oasis in place in a small deep bowl or an oblong shallow container, is to press an inverted plastic berry box or tomato carton down over it. For larger bowls and vases, cut hardware cloth to cover the moist foam; bend the edges of the wire mesh and push them down into the container, so close against its sides that tension holds them tight. Hardware cloth is preferable to chicken wire for this purpose because it's less limber and has smaller holes. Hardware stores stock the "cloth" in twenty-four-inch and thirty-six-inch widths, and in quarter-inch or half-inch mesh, and sell it by the foot. You can cut it like chicken wire with tin-snips or wire-cutters.

Both slitted plastic boxes and wire mesh have an added advantage: they take the place of pinholders or flower frogs, and hold the stems of flowers firmly in place.

PICTURE MOUNT AS A MEANS OF ATTACHMENT

To support an arrangement on a flat basket, an oval platter or a metal tray, give a flattish block of soaked Oasis a watertight wrapper of doubled heavy-duty aluminum foil, and anchor it in the center of the container with two or three picture mounts. These no-mar substitutes for wire-and-nail picture hangers are small flat oblongs of latex foam with adhesive on both sides. These picture mounts are similar to the sticky-on-both-sides floral foam sold at artificial flower displays, but they come pre-cut in smaller sizes, and do a much better job of sticking one object firmly to another.

ARRANGEMENTS TAILORED TO TASTE

Flower arranging, like herb cookery, is a matter of taste. Professional florists must, perforce, produce neutral designs that can be used with any decor, of flowers that won't clash with any color scheme, but amateur arrangers are hampered by no such restrictions. And when you know full well the preferences of the person for whom the flowers are intended, you may even want to make the arrangement with a specific spot in mind. For instance, if your sister always uses yellow flowers in a deep alabaster bowl on the hall console, you can make a yellow design on a foil-wrapped block of Oasis, transport it in a mixing bowl, and transfer it upon arrival to the waiting container.

However, don't just show up with your floral bounty in hand without first notifying the recipient. Sister's hall bowl could conceivably be already filled with yellow flowers received just yesterday.

TIED ARRANGEMENT

For the neighbor who likes to keep a bright posy in the blue jug on her coffee table, make a tied arrangement that can be carried like a hand bouquet and popped into the water-filled jug. Bunch blossoms in one hand, adjusting them until each one shows to best advantage. Then wrap their stems together with a pipe cleaner or a Twist 'em. (Twist 'ems are short lengths of green paper-covered wire, like the ties that come with rolls of plastic bags. They can be bought from a florist, or found at the artificial-flower counter of a variety store.) Clip the ends of the wrapped stems off evenly, and slip them into a plastic sandwich bag with a small amount of water in the bottom. Wrap the bag tight around the stems with another twist 'em, and the posy is ready to go. For car travel, insert the tied arrangement in its plastic bag in a milk bottle braced with wadded newspaper in a small cardboard carton.

ARRANGEMENTS MADE IN LINERS

You can make a line arrangement meant for a tall, columnar vase in a slender Oasis-filled tin can that will ride well braced in a cardboard box. Arrived at its destination, slip the can down inside the tall container. If the can is too short to raise the flowers above the lip of the vase, pack the vase with crumpled aluminum foil to the necessary level, and balance the can upon it.

Fill a plastic bowl that held whipped topping or sour cream with moist Oasis to support a mounded arrangement destined for display in a tureen or a wide-mouthed bowl. For its trip by car, place the small container with its spreading flowers on a shallow cardboard box lid, and brace it with rolls of newspaper.

FLOWERS FOR THE SICK

ODORLESS GARDEN FLOWERS

When someone is ill, everyone immediately thinks of sending flowers. If it's left up to the florist, flowers for the sickroom often turn out to be gladioli — his reason being that the stiff spikes last well and have no odor. It is undeniably true that strongly perfumed flowers are anathema to the very ill, but the garden offers many scentless blossoms that make beautiful, long-lasting bouquets.

Some good possibilities are: asters, dahlias, gaillardia, larkspur or delphinium, lupin, nigella, pansies, phlox, salvia, shasta daisies, snapdragon, tulip and zinnia. Garden chrysanthemums are doubtful prospects. Korean and spoon varieties are scentless, but most double mums have a slight but penetrating scent.

FLOWERS FOR THE HOSPITAL

Tall spreading arrangements do not belong in a hospital room. Their very size makes them oppressive if not downright funereal, and there is no place for them amidst the medical paraphernalia.

On the other hand, a miniature arrangement can be accommodated on a bedside table or an over-the-bed tray, and even a myopic patient gets a closeup view of it. Tiny odorless flowers are legion, and include abelia, alyssum, ageratum, bluebells, candytuft, cornflowers, daisies, fever-

"Get well" flowers should come in small containers that will not crowd the bedside table. A low-fluted candleholder (left) holds pink-and-white crepe myrtle pods, a pink-sprayed liriope stalk, blue-and-white ironweed "forget-me-nots", and one rosy strawflower. The green glass basket (right) is filled with glass flowers — rose red, blue, and pale pink campions with one white daisy and a few bits of fern.

few, forget-me-nots, gypsophila, hardy asters, the spireas, violas, and dwarf zinnias. Small spike flowers are less common, but the feathery blue blooms of mint or ajuga, and the tips of perennial salvia or veronica, are suitably sized.

The container should be small — a miniature urn, or a vase no more than four inches in height — but a minute container and minuscule flowers aren't enough; use diminutive foliage as well: twigs of boxwood, *Ilex microphylla* or *rotundifolia*, short sprays of *Vinca minor*, tips of hemlock or juniper, and feathery bits of asparagus fern.

MINIATURE ARRANGEMENTS

A good miniature arrangement looks like a full size design seen through the wrong end of a telescope. It should contain fewer flowers, however; with a reduced scale, each element of the design occupies more of the total airspace. It is a great temptation to add just one more tiny blossom, but remember the advice often given to novice flower arrangers, as it's especially applicable to miniatures: make the arrangement, and if it suits you, leave it alone. If not, take out half the flowers, and rearrange the remainder.

FRAGRANT FLOWERS

The rule of "small scentless flowers for the sick" does not apply to convalescents, who are happy to have medicinal odors masked by the perfume of roses or the light, spicy fragrance of carnations.

Anyone with failing sight appreciates sweet-scented flowers, and patients in nursing homes especially enjoy old-fashioned fragrant favorites. Daphne, lilac, mock orange, sweet shrub, buddleia, and vitex are shrubs to bear in mind, along with the incomparable roses. Old-fashioned annuals, like old friends, are sweetest: verbena, sweet pea, heliotrope, nicotiana, sweet alyssum, four o'clock, stock, and mignonette. Many hardy perennials belong in the category of fragrant flowers, among them narcissus, hyacinth, iris, peony, lily-of-the-valley, sweet violet, clove pink, tuberose and lavender. (Because the heavy scent of lilies has a reminiscent sadness, don't include them in a bouquet for the elderly or the bereaved.)

CORSAGES

For Easter or Mother's Day, birthdays or anniversaries, nothing quite takes the place of a corsage. It is axiomatic that corsage flowers will be those

that last well out of water, but they need not be orchids, camellias, or gardenias. Button chrysanthemums, roses and carnations work up well, but more unusual, and equally satisfactory, are lilies-of-the-valley, sprays of cyclamen, and rubrum or auratum lilies. Football season means house-guests, and corsages for the big game. One pompon chrysanthemum from the garden, grown extra large because you disbudded the plant, can be tied with ribbon in the college colors.

CONDITIONING CORSAGE FLOWERS

Condition a short-stemmed, heavy-headed flower by filling a half-pint plastic freezer container with hot water, snapping on its lid, and inserting the freshly cut stem through a small hole punched in the center of the plastic top with a skewer or a nail. The lid will protect the blossom from rising steam. Then wrap the stem with an overlapping spiral of floral tape that extends over its cut end to seal out air. Self-adhesive, stretchy floral tape may be bought in rolls from a florist or at a variety store.

NET SPRAYS

There is a reason for those wired net sprays that form the backing of a corsage from a florist: they support the flower at its most becoming angle and at the same time prevent petal stains on clothing. It's exceedingly simple to make such a sprig. Take a circle of nylon net, five inches in diameter, pinch it together at its center, and affix it to a short wire stem with a wrapping of floral tape; the net may be white, or a color that matches the flower. Place two or three such protectors behind a flower, and bind their wires to the wrapped flower stem with floral tape. Mask the blunt taped stub of stem plus wires by a many-looped bow of narrow ribbon that matches or compliments the color of the flower.

PACKAGING A GIFT CORSAGE

Package the corsage in a plastic freezer bag of generous size, with enough trapped air to hold the plastic up and away from the flower petals. Fold the open end of the bag three times, and pin the folds with two corsage pins before sealing the edge of the fold with cellophane tape. To support a fragile flower, insert a square of cardboard into the bag before you slip in the corsage.

CORSAGE MAKING. *1) Assemble materials: no. 24 wires (18" lengths may be cut in two); floral tape; wire cutting scissors; satin leaves; bow or ribbon; net sprays (see opposite page). 2) Wire flowers: a) Use no. 24 wires. b) Cross wiring is preferred by most florists. Insert wires as shown, then bend them gently down along stems. c) Use hairpin wiring for leaves. 3) Tape all stems with floral tape. 4) Assemble corsages: a) First wire and tape all buds, flowers and leaves. Use a small bud or leaf as top point. b) Tape on a slightly larger flower below and at an angle as shown. c) Cut off excess stem from first flower only. Tape the junction of two stems by tightly wrapping them two or three times with floral tape. Repeat, adding slightly larger flowers, cutting excess stem of next-to-last flower used, and taping junctures of stems as you proceed. 5) Adjust each flower to achieve desired design. Attach ribbon bow at corsage, last taping and interweave some of the loops and flowers. (See page 84 for flowers appropriate for birthday corsages.)*

Bridge the generation gap with a "football" chrysanthemum corsage, to be worn by a son's date at the big game.

BOSOM-BOTTLE CORSAGES

A florist will gladly sell you one or more of the glass corsage tubes he uses to provide moisture for flowers that will be worn for several hours. Each of these miniature test tubes has a tight-fitting rubber cap with a pinhole in its center, through which the stem of the flower is pushed; the hole in the cap is sealed by the pressure of its elastic edges against the stem. Such a slender tube is very little larger than a flower stem, but holds just enough water to be helpful. Masked with floral tape and topped with ribbon, it is hardly noticeable in a corsage.

In the eighteenth century, ladies of fashion wore nosegays of fresh flowers in tiny vases that were called bosom-bottles. You can retain this idea by making clever pin-on flower holders in advance, holding them in readiness for any occasion that calls for a corsage.

Buy several corsage tubes from that friendly florist, and a corresponding number of straight, inch-long metal brooch-backs from a hobby shop: you'll find these displayed with the accessories for making costume jewelry out of polished stones or shells. With Epoxy cement, attach a brooch-back (hinge at top, pinpoint at bottom) to one of your corsage tubes. Let it harden overnight; then, cover the outside of the tube and the cemented portion of the brooch-back (*don't* coat the pin itself!) with green enamel or gold paint. Come presentation time, you'll be gracefully prepared: in no more than a moment you can fill the tube with water, replace its rubber cap, and insert the stem of a conditioned flower — a Peace rose, perhaps; a "football" chrysanthemum; or an Oregon-hybrid lily.

18

NO-RETURN CONTAINERS

Gift flowers should come, like bottled drinks, in no-return containers. You can find an assortment of expendable vases of various sizes in unlikely places, and even make them yourself from throwaways.

WHITE ELEPHANTS

Most households harbor a clutch of wedding present vases that were relegated to the storage shelf because they were too large or too small, the wrong shape or the wrong color. Their ranks are thinned occasionally, when the garden club is having a plant sale or the church a bazaar, for a vase can always be donated to the white elephant table. White elephant sales are happy hunting grounds for gift vases of unusual shapes or colors — perhaps a hollow cube of pottery, inky black, to contrast strikingly with branches of crimson flowering quince, or a white china vegetable dish to hold a cool summer arrangement of white petunias and hosta leaves.

FLORIST'S VASES

Old florist's vases obviously breed in the basement, for no matter how many are donated to the PTA rummage sale, the box behind the furnace is always full. These often are attractive in shape, but usually are made of dead-white, shiny pottery that kills the colors of an arrangement, or of thick green glass that is supposed to hide stems and mechanics but does not. Last, but certainly not least in number, are clear glass bubble bowls. A quick coat of pearl gray or sage green latex paint transforms white square compotes and footed bowls into "boutique" containers. Charcoal black, verde green, or cherry red latex paint will give character to a tall glass vase. Coating the *inside* of a clear glass bubble with enamel gives its curved sides the depth and glow of a convex mirror. Pour a small amount of enamel into the bottom of the bubble bowl, slosh it around, and then distribute it over the upper sides by tilting the bowl and spreading the paint with a brush inserted at an angle.

CLAY FLOWER POTS

Those ordinary clay flower pots stacked in a corner of the garage are beautiful in their functional simplicity, and their reddish brown color is a fine foil for coarser garden blooms — zinnia, calendula, gaillardia, or nasturtium. They look (and are) better balanced in matching clay saucers, which may be bought for pennies at a garden center, and may be metamorphosed with latex paint into antique white, pale pink, or sunny yellow containers for pastel posies. To cover the drainage hole in the bottom, give a pot an instant liner — a paper cup, a disposable plastic on-the-rocks glass, or a plastic ice cream carton, depending on its size.

CONTAINERS FROM ANTIQUE SHOPS

Antique shops operate on the principle that "one generation's trash is another generation's treasure," and the front of the shop is *not* the place to look for bargains. In the very back of the room, where the light is poor, there usually is a table loaded with saucerless teacups, topless candy jars, and tureens that have lost their lids. The shelves of a dusty corner cupboard may harbor tall salt shakers that make fine bud vases. Look for little "remembrance" pitchers — the sort that have a picture of Grant's Tomb on one side, or are marked "Souvenir of Atlantic City" — that will be amusing holders for miniature arrangements.

SECONDHAND STORES

Secondhand stores, by definition, deal in discards, and their merchandise is apt to include partial sets of china. Vegetable bowls, soup plates, sugar bowls, cream or water pitchers and mugs of any material make fine flower containers, along with the water goblets, rice bowls, and pottery jars that are other possible finds.

VARIETY STORES

Variety stores offer a varied assortment of inexpensive and attractive containers: plain china bowls, glass bud vases, small mugs and pitchers, and baskets of all sizes. At the toy counter, look for a sand bucket or a doll's tea set; the former will serve to transport unarranged greenery, while the latter will provide containers for several miniature arrangements.

Salvaging secondhand containers. For leaky metal, squeeze liquid solder (bought at a hardware store) along inside seams; paint to match. For cracked china, fill cracks with Epoxy glue or waterproof cement, smooth with finger, let dry. As a temporary solution, plug cracks with floral clay. Conceal a chipped edge with leaf or flower, or shape self-hardening clay to reconstruct the missing part and paint to match. Stains on china can be soaked off in Clorox bleach. Rusty iron: remove rust with fine steel wool and spray paint (two light coats) with flat black enamel.

CONTAINERS FROM THE PANTRY SHELF

Interesting containers for short-stemmed flowers are hard to come by, and your own cupboards may be the best source of supply. Try small bright button chrysanthemums or tom thumb zinnias in a glazed pottery custard cup or ramekin; fill an individual brown beanpot with black-eyed Susans, or with nasturtiums in shades of orange, yellow, and red. Use an egg cup, sole survivor of a breakfast set, for buttercups and daisies, achillea, or feverfew. Bunch wild violets in an odd after-dinner coffee cup, and surround them with a ruff of their own leaves. Bright bold pansies, without foliage, call for a container as simple and sturdy as a mustard pot. Place clusters of spiky scillas or grape hyacinths in footed goblets. Mound pastel primroses in a sherbet glass or in an atavistic finger-bowl. Combine rock garden blossoms in a bouillon cup, offsetting the width of the saucer with the spread of the arrangement.

Small no-cost containers: a conch shell (left) holds a cured chrysanthemum and sea oats; a hairspray can top (right) is filled with styrofoam to support yellow-and-bronze straw-flowers with green feather "foliage".

CONTAINERS TO CONSTRUCT

EMERGENCY EPERGNE

In an emergency, you can make an interesting and eminently practical two-tiered container that suggests a mid-Victorian epergne from a ring-mold and a metal funnel. The lower portion must be a circular mold with a hole in the center, such as a salad mold, a scalloped Bundt mold, or an angelfood cake tin. Use a disposable aluminum foil tube pan (sold, several to the package, in housewares departments and large variety stores); it will work quite as well as a more expensive mold of rigid metal. The funnel should be a large one; if its stem is longer than the center tube of the mold, it can be trimmed to the right length with a hacksaw.

Pack the tube of the mold with (of all things!) wallpaper cleaner, which can be bought at a hardware or a paint store. (As it comes from the can, wallpaper cleaner has the consistency of modelling clay, but it dries rock-hard in time, when exposed to air. It does a much better holding job than floral clay, and is considerably cheaper. Knead it to make it more malleable; then it can be molded into any shape.)

Press the stem of the funnel down through the mastic cleaner until the flaring base of the funnel balances on top of the tube. Fill the ring mold *and* the funnel with moist Oasis to hold a lavish display of holly or nandina — the tiered container makes it possible to produce an impressively tall arrangement from short-stemmed materials. As an alternative, fill the ring of the mold with fruit, and pack the funnel with Oasis to hold a tight bouquet of flowers in the Victorian manner; add trailing sprays of ivy at the edges of the funnel.

Since both the foil mold and the tin funnel have a silvery look, they are compatible and can remain untreated. The epergne will, however, lose the makeshift look entirely if both its component parts are painted black, white, or verde green.

TIERED FUNNEL HOLDER

Two tiers are good, but three are better for making an important arrangement of insignificant flowers. Improbable though it sounds, an elegant tiered holder can be constructed of three funnels, half a curtain rod, and an oilcan.

Three pastel plastic funnels, graduated in size, are sold in one package in housewares departments. You will need a slender white metal expansion rod, of the type used to curtain a French door; this can be bought in a variety store, along with a small metal oilcan with a straight spout. Pull the rod apart, and use only half of it; the round ball at the end of this slim hollow shaft will be the top of the tiered holder. Just below the ball, there will be a hole for screwing the rod to a door. Fill this hole with a pull-open-snap-shut metal ring from a ring-binder notebook, which will give a finished look to the top of the rod and will also be a finger-ring for carrying the filled container.

Pack the tapered stem of the smallest funnel tightly with wallpaper cleaner. Force the end of the curtain rod down through the funnel until the funnel's rim is about five inches below the ring. Hold the rod upright, and adjust the funnel so that it is perfectly straight; then bind the tip of the funnel stem securely to the rod with white plastic tape. Pack the stem of the middle size funnel, and press the rod through it; the rim of this second funnel should hide the tape on the stem of the one above. Tape the second funnel to the rod, and pack the stem of the third and largest funnel with wallpaper cleaner. Unscrew the lid of the oilcan, and weight the cavity with sand or pebbles, to steady the finished holder. Replace the spout, and set the oilcan upright on a table. Force the stem of the large funnel down over the oilcan's spout until the tip of the funnel stem rests upon the curved top of the can. Straighten this funnel, and then fit the tip of the hollow curtain rod over the protruding oilcan spout, and push the rod down until it touches the can.

The tiered holder is now ready for use, but the longer it stands the harder the cleaner will become, and the steadier the funnels will be. To hold fresh flowers or foliage, each funnel cup should be filled with soaked Oasis.

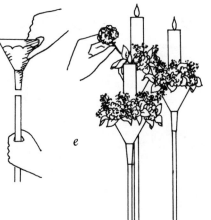

Fun with funnels for your fund-raising outdoor supper: make tiered funnel centerpieces (a, b, c, d) as described in text for each table. Then use painted funnels set on dowels to hold Oasis, flowers and candles (e); the dowels, stuck in the ground, will light the garden paths.

PARAFFIN AS A HOLDER FOR DRIED FLOWERS

This dainty tiered container is even more suitable for delicate dried flowers, and paraffin is the best holder for their fragile stems. Melt two blocks of paraffin (from the canning supplies shelf at a supermarket) until the wax is just fluid, and pour enough into the largest funnel to reach within a half inch of its rim. Wait until the surface of the wax is solid but shaky when touched with a fingertip, and then quickly fill this funnel with dried flowers. Remelt the paraffin for the middle funnel, adding another block if necessary; finish the second mound of flowers before filling the third funnel. The top arrangement should be tall enough to hide the rod to within an inch of the ring-holder. Allow the finished tiered arrangement to stand overnight before moving it, to be sure that the paraffin has completely hardened.

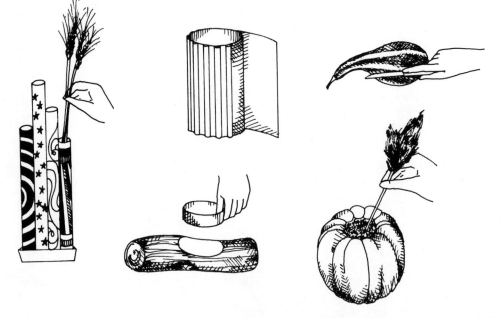

Easy-to-make containers. For dried flowers, cardboard cylinders covered with colorful papers or adhesive-backed vinyls glued together; a tall juice can covered with corrugated paper, glued on and painted; a gourd, with one side cut off, makes a bowl to be waxed or shellacked; a log with a hollow for a tuna can holding Oasis; a scooped-out pumpkin shell packed with Oasis.

2.

Ornaments from Air-Dried Everlastings

Air-dried "everlasting" flowers are as Early American as saltbox houses, braided rugs, and ladder-back chairs! Even before they left England for the New World, America's first settlers knew that certain flowers — cockscomb, celosia, artemisia, strawflowers, globe amaranth, and statice — kept all their shape and much of their color when tied in bunches

Hostess gift for the owner of a country home: air-dried wheat and "meadow wildlings" (peppergrass, boneset, teasel, and life everlasting) massed in an egg basket are shown on a butter churn. Refer to Appendix for a list of plants to dry.

and hung upside down in a warm room to dry. These dried everlastings were arranged in vases filled with sand, and used all winter long for indoor decoration. In the British Isles and on the European continent, lunaria was highly prized for winter bouquets. This plant dried naturally, out of doors. When their brown outer husks and seeds had dropped away, clusters of thin, translucent silvery disks remained on the dry stalks.

Early colonists planted these old familiar everlastings in their gardens, and added dried wildlings to their winter bouquets: pearly everlasting; goldenrod; Joe Pye weed; yarrow; cat-tails; corn, cane and sourwood tassels; plumed grasses, and sedge. For convenience, they hung flowers and weeds to dry in windowless lofts — stripping off the leaves, tying the stems together in small bunches, and suspending them upside down from cane poles laid across the rafters. Blossoms dried thus, in the dark, kept their color exceedingly well. In seventeenth century England, it was customary to dye globe amaranth and statice in strong shades of red, blue, and purple. Remembering these bright bouquets, colonial housewives colored the pallid strawy tufts of pearly everlasting with home-brewed vegetable dyes.

In the eighteenth century, many other flower varieties joined the tried and true "immortelles" in the drying room, among them scarlet and blue salvia, butterfly weed, larkspur, gypsophila, feverfew, columbine, onion, stock, and snapdragons.

METHODS OF AIR-DRYING

The traditional method of air-drying works as well in the twentieth century as in colonial days, but certain rules must be followed if the flowers are to retain their natural color. Select perfect blossoms and cut them as soon as they reach maturity. (There are two exceptions: gather strawflowers before they are fully open to prevent browning of their centers, and cut Joe Pye weed in the bud stage to preserve its rosy-purple tint.) Light-colored blooms are preferable for air drying, since dark blossoms tend to fade and streak. Gather flowers when their own moisture content is low, but not when leaves or petals are drooping — noon of a hot, clear day is the ideal time — and hang them immediately without placing them in water. To prevent mildewing, tie no more than six or eight small stems together in any one bunch, and hang large flower stalks separately. To conserve space, tie several bunches or stalks to the crossbar of a metal coathanger; then hook it over a closet rod or a clothes-

To air-dry flowers, tie them in loose bunches and hang from hooks or coat hangers in a dry dark attic, closet, or basement (see Appendix for methods of preserving flowers and foliage).

line stretched in attic or basement. The one absolute essential for successful air-dehydrating is a dry *dark* place in which to hang the plant material. Most flowers will be ready for use in ten days to two weeks, when their petals are dry and slightly brittle to the touch.

DRYING FLOWERS UPRIGHT

Our ancestors discovered very early that certain blossoms — cockscomb, celosia, Queen Anne's lace, elder, goldenrod, and lunaria — drooped in amorphous masses when hung upside down, but kept their shape (and their color) if they were dried right side up with their stems thrust deep into crocks of sand. Any flower with a large composite head and a stiff sturdy stalk prefers the perpendicular position in the dark drying room. Plumed or heavy-headed grasses and grains, placed upright in buckets of sand, dry full and fluffy; bittersweet, heather, pussy willow and scotch broom retain their graceful curves.

ARRESTING COLOR CHANGE

Some flowers change color as they mature in field or garden. If they are cut at the desired color stage, further alteration can be arrested by drying. For example, dock can retain the pinkish tan of June, the wine red of July, or the mahogany brown of August. Strip the stalks of leaves and arrange them at once in a sand-filled vase. Set them aside in a dark room until the material feels perfectly dry when rubbed between the fingers. Then the arrangement is ready to be brought forth, and its color will remain unfaded for several years.

PRESERVING POLYGONUM

Instant preservation is possible for the rosy-red wands of polygonum (bamboo, knot-bush) which must be cut as soon as the tiny disked seeds

27

are fully exposed. Strip off all the leaves, and arrange the curving sprays immediately, without water *or* sand, in the tall vase in which they are to remain. Then spray them thoroughly with colorless acrylic plastic, available at paint stores, or with hair spray. Apply three light coats at twenty-minute intervals; the spray is very nearly invisible, and the treatment will hold most of the florets on the branch for a year or more.

CORN TASSELS

The graceful beige corn tassels that dry naturally atop their stalks are at home in any period setting. Combined with beech leaves in a stoneware crock, they hark back to early colonial days; massed against a fan of red oak leaves, they have an eighteenth century formality. Crowded with plumes of pampas grass in a narrow-necked vase, they droop in the approved Victorian manner. Standing tall in a cylindrical glazed pottery container, with only cornleaves for an accent, they are as contemporary as though they had just been invented.

PAINTED HYDRANGEA

Hydrangeas, if picked when their natural colors are soft and rosy as they begin to dry on the shrub, then stripped of their leaves and arranged at once, without water, will remain beautiful for many months. And these same heavy flower heads can also take on the misty charm of a French Impressionist painting. Stand about six feet away, and frost each flower head lightly with white enamel from a pressurized spray can; at once they will seem to shade from pink to lavender and blue. Massed in a low white bowl, these will make a handsome year-round decoration for a friend's French provincial living room.

More defined color will require a heavier and more thorough spraying with paint. Use pressurized cans of enamel in any desired hue. Hold a can about two feet from a hydrangea head and spray, walking around the flower to coat it evenly on all sides. Allow this first coat to dry, and repeat if necessary to obtain smooth color. Be sure to aim the spray to reach the fuzzy center behind the florets of each cluster. A massed arrangement of hydrangeas painted in two or more shades makes a thoughtful gift for the friend with a hard-to-match color scheme.

ARRANGING AIR-DRIED FLOWERS

Air-dried flowers are less affected by light or moisture than the newer chemically cured flowers, and for this reason they make unusually long lasting floral gifts.

The strawy stems of air-dried everlastings are more fragile than the blossoms, and this makes their arrangement difficult. Colonial housewives often solved the problem by popping a tied bunch of dried flowers, just as it came from the rafters, into a posy-holder. No winter decoration could be more appropriate for a house museum that dates from the seventeenth or early eighteenth century. Use a stiff tied bunch of traditional everlastings, such as statice and globe amaranth; the container, too, should be a period piece: a tyg, a seashell, or a bottle gourd.

A simple, ancient basket would be the right holder for combined native materials such as goldenrod, pearly everlasting, corn tassels, and beech leaves. The flowers need not be arranged, but merely massed for color. Untie and separate dried bunches very carefully so as not to damage the brittle stems and blossoms. Pick up two or three stalks; thrust them together into the basket, and add similar small groupings at random until the container will hold no more and the blossoms afford each other mutual support. Separate the flowers slightly by pulling them slowly toward the sides of the basket to obtain the artless effect of an airy mound.

EIGHTEENTH CENTURY ARRANGEMENT

The more formal eighteenth-century historic house calls for a more elaborate winter bouquet, and, reflecting the elegance of the period, the container might be a low, wide bowl of Chinese export porcelain. Bright color was eagerly sought after in colonial days. An arrangement combining silky yellow celosia with red cockscomb and orange strawflowers would be an extremely good accent for a dark corner.

At Colonial Williamsburg, from November until March, magnificent masses of air-dried flowers adorn the rooms of the Governor's Palace, the Brush-Everard House, and the George Wythe House. Miss Edna Pennell, who designs these handsome bouquets, gives the following directions for making a large console arrangement:

"Fill the container with sand to give weight. For a low bowl, use a holder in the middle of the sand. Begin with a background of material, such as dried larkspur, to work out a design. If some of the spiked material is placed horizontally, the mass bouquet will gain added depth. Fill in with

Dried flowers in a brandy snifter. a) Start with a lump of floral clay in bottom; pierce with thin knitting needle to hold stems. b) Insert largest flowers around bottom, one layer deep. Leave space between for contrasting smaller flowers wired together in bunches. c) Build up design, one layer at a time, all around the glass, using progressively smaller flowers with longer stems. Work with tweezers so you won't dislodge anything. Use wired bunches of heather, wheat, grass, etc. as fillers to conceal mechanics. Place a large flat flower on top of the design, to look down upon.

other materials, strawflowers perhaps, and work into a line of design within the mass."

ARRANGEMENTS FOR MODERN HOUSES

Air-dried flowers need not, however, be sequestered in house museums. A friend whose bedroom boasts an antique cherry chest would proudly place upon it a small blue and white delft jug filled with dried larkspur, globe amaranth, and statice. A small wooden salad bowl, holding strawflowers and spikes of brown dock, would look well on the maple coffee table in a neighbor's family room. The cousin who has just moved into an A-frame house will be delighted to place before its window wall a tall columnar vase holding silvery lunaria or rosy polygonum.

Although sand is a good holder for the stiff stalks of the traditional everlastings, ordinary household paraffin offers greater security to the weak, slender stems of most air dried flowers. Melt the paraffin over low heat until it is barely fluid, cool it slightly, and pour it into a bowl or vase. When the wax becomes cloudy, begin to set the stems in place. Adjust the flowers quickly, for once the paraffin has hardened, the stems cannot be removed intact.

You can also arrange air-dried blossoms on a block or a half-round of green styrofoam bought from the artificial flower counter of a variety store. If the styrofoam does not come with a convenient adhesive pad attached, it can be anchored in the bottom of any container—metal, wood, ceramic, or basket—with a sticky-on-both-sides picture mount (see page 12). Strawy stems will shatter under the pressure required to prick them directly into the foam, so make a pattern of holes in the styrofoam with a toothpick, a matchstick, a nail, or a skewer. Dip the end of each stem in white glue before placing it in a prepared hole; this will keep the flower permanently steady, even if the stem is set in at an angle.

UNUSUAL DRIED FLOWER ORNAMENTS

FLOWER BALLS

Use dried flowers with short or broken stems to cover styrofoam balls. Small bright strawflowers, tiny Peruvian starflowers, and single florets of yarrow or statice are ideal for this purpose. First, prepare holes for the flower stems by piercing the styrofoam all over, to a depth of one-third inch, with the tines of a fork. Then dip the stems, evenly trimmed to a length of one-half inch, in white glue and insert in the holes. Insert them close together so that the entire surface of the ball is covered.

If you use flowers of several colors and place them at random, a gay "confetti" — covered sphere results. Alternating lines of color will produce stripes. For a polka dot effect, scatter circles of one color over the ball, and cover the rest of the surface closely with flowers of a contrasting hue.

Heap several floral balls in a clear glass bowl for an unusual table decoration. It's easy to attach a ribbon hanger, transforming a floral ball into a Christmas tree ornament or one unit of a mobile: tie a knot in one end of

a length of narrow ribbon; slip a corrugated wire hairpin through the knot; press the hairpin into the styrofoam ball until the knot of ribbon comes to rest on the surface.

MINIATURE "STANDARD"

Make a charming miniature "standard," just right for a dressing table ornament, from a single floral ball. Impale the ball upon the point of a twelve-inch knitting needle; select an aluminum needle in pale green, or in a color that matches the dried flowers. Fill a small clay or plastic flower-pot with wallpaper cleaner, and imbed the head of the knitting needle in the center of the pot. Camouflage the cleaner with short sprays of artificial foliage, and tie long streamers of narrow velvet ribbon around the needle just below the flower ball. As the wallpaper cleaner dries, it becomes hard and gives permanent, unbreakable support to the flower ball.

FLORAL EASTER EGGS

Styrofoam eggs, of various sizes, are sold at Easter time in variety stores. Out of season, order them from catalogs or through a retail florist, who can procure them from his wholesale supplier. Following the directions for covering round styrofoam balls with tiny air-dried flowers, you can transform these egg shapes into party favors and Easter gifts that sell like the proverbial hotcakes at a springtime bazaar. Balance large eggs, covered with a single color of minute Peruvian starflowers—blue, bright pink, or lemon yellow — in eggcups. Use smaller eggs, with matching ribbon hangers attached, to decorate an Easter tree: select a bare branch of an interesting, gnarled shape, and "plant" it upright in a pastel-painted flower-pot filled with wallpaper cleaner or with plastic wood. Tie on several flower-covered eggs, making their ribbon hangers of graduated lengths. Paint the surface of the wallpaper cleaner brown, to resemble bare earth, or cover it with a layer of white glue and sprinkle the glue with a layer of sand or small pebbles. This tree can be any size. A small branch, in a five-inch flower pot, makes an interesting table centerpiece. A tall limb, in a twelve-inch pot or a ceramic planter, can be the focal point for a picture window or a patio wall.

DYEING DRIED FLOWERS

Borrowing a leaf from the book of seventeenth century housewives, who dyed the durable but drab pearly everlasting for colorful winter bouquets, you can tint dried flowers any desired hue. In a large, wide-mouthed glass jar, dilute commercial liquid dye with boiling water, following the proportions stated on the dye label. Cool the mixture slightly, and test for color with a small piece of dried material before adding the rest. To obtain a particular color, you may have to use more than one shade of commercial dye: in small glass jars, dilute the dyes separately with boiling water; in yet another jar, mix small amounts of the diluted colors and test the mixture. When the sample of blended dye is just right, pour the component liquids into a large jar, shake to mix them well, and proceed to dye the flowers.

Hold a flower by its stem and dip the head into the steaming dye. Then lift the flower and shake it over the jar so that excess dye will not run down the stem and stain it. Set the stalk upright in a box of sand or in a soft drink bottle, and wait until the flower head is thoroughly dry before handling it. Dyed materials are lighter when dry than when wet; if the finished flowers are too pale, reheat the dye and dip them again.

Tint any flower that has lost its color during the process of air drying in this way. "Wild everlastings," grains, and grasses are fascinating to color as well. Dried pepper grass, for example, emerges from the dye bath with each minute disk aglow. Wheat and barley heads are two-toned, with hairs paler than the grains. Fluffy pampas grass, tinted in several pastel shades, makes a marvelous massed bouquet; the matted wet heads appear ruined when they are lifted from the dye, but dried outdoors (in the shade) in the wind, they rapidly regain their shape. Shaking each stalk several times during the drying period helps to hasten recovery. If the heavy heads still seem matted when thoroughly dry, a few minutes in front of an electric fan or a blowing air conditioner will fluff them.

DOWNY DUCK

Pearly everlasting takes dye exceptionally well, and can be substituted for starflowers or statice in covering styrofoam balls or eggs. Tinted yellow, it can become the down of an Easter duck that lasts from year to year. Dip the strawy tufts in bright yellow dye—the natural gray-tan of the tufts will mute the color as it dries. Using the ubiquitous wallpaper cleaner, model a small duck with lifted head and jaunty tail; knead a lump of the cleaner until it is smooth, and shape it as if it were modelling clay. Give the duckling a partially open bill by pressing two large flat scales from a pinecone horizontally into the front of the head; you'll disarrange the mastic wallpaper cleaner somewhat, and probably have to reshape the head. Make shallow holes all over the surface of the duck with a wooden toothpick. Shear the stems of the individual straw tufts one-third inch long, and dip each stem in white glue before fitting it into a hole. Cover the entire duck with yellow down, and then add two blue starflowers for eyes. As the wallpaper cleaner dries out, it gradually hardens to a rock-like consistency with minimal shrinkage.

DRIED FLOWERS IN GLASS BOTTLE TOPS

Inexpensive glass apothecary jars of various sizes become boutique containers for herbs, bath salts, or candy when their clear hollow tops are filled with bright dried flowers. Cut a circle of cardboard very slightly smaller than the neck of the top, and cover both sides of it with solid color self-stick plastic or florist's foil. Glue one large or several small dried flowers in the center of this disk. Coat the inside of the top with white glue, just above the threads that enable it to be screwed onto the jar. Turn the top upside down, and work the disk through its neck by turning it to follow the threading until its edges meet the glue. Allow the glue to dry overnight before replacing the top on the jar. The dried flowers will be slightly magnified by the rounded glass above them.

WEATHERED WOOD

Weathered wood, air-dried by nature, is the perfect accessory for an arrangement of air-dried flowers. This is not necessarily sun-bleached, sea-soaked driftwood, although salt water, sun, and sand smooth wood to a most attractive sheen. After a prolonged dry spell that lowers the water level, the shore of an inland lake or river is sure to be strewn with water-logged tree branches and sheets of bark. In winter, fallen limbs are scattered on the upland forest floor, and these often have a fascinating patina of green-gray lichen. After a deep snow or a summer thunder-storm, your own lawn may be littered with the raw material for weathered wood designs. If all else fails, see your tree surgeon. Ask him also for small hollow stumps, branch boles, or knot sections; they will make unsurpassed containers for striking line arrangements.

ARRANGEMENT ON A GNARLED BRANCH

With Epoxy cement, you can attach, permanently upright, an interestingly-shaped branch of weathered wood to a piece of weathered planking, a thick circular slice of log, or a wooden tray. You will probably need to give the balanced limb temporary support while the cement is drying; you can do this with two piles of books, narrow ones at the base of each stack and wider ones on top, so placed that they press against the branch from opposite sides.

If the shape of this skeletal arrangement is entirely pleasing, it would be a mistake to blur its outline by adding a great many dried flowers. A bright cluster of strawflowers, where limb meets base, may be enough. If the towering branch has been placed for visual balance at one side of its foundation, a flattened arrangement of strawflowers with dock or cattails extending across the surface of the board or circle will add visual weight, and help tie the vertical tower to the horizontal base.

WEATHERED WOOD CONTAINER

You can use fresh greenery or flowers in a hollow weathered wood container by filling the cavity with moist Oasis. Arrange dried flowers, grasses

To clean oil- or mud-stained driftwood, scrub with detergent and a stiff brush, and then soak in a strong solution of liquid household chlorine bleach. Here an angular branch of weathered wood holds a large fully-open artichoke and several buds, air-dried and dipped in thinned shellac. Okra pods imitate the curved wooden "antlers".

and grains on an inserted block of styrofoam, pressing their glue-dipped stems into holes made with a toothpick or a nail.

AIR-DRIED VINES

Sometimes an arrangement of fresh or dried flowers needs a new twist that can be supplied by a corkscrew spiral or a boomerang curve of air-dried vine. Bittersweet and honeysuckle have a spiralling habit of growth, and a length of vine unwound from a woodland sapling and hung by a string from a clothesline will dry in its natural shape. A straight section, however, of green twig cut from honeysuckle, bittersweet, grapevine, wistaria, or climbing rose can be trained and dried into any curve from a gentle parabola to a tortuous tendril.

First bend stiff wire in the desired shape—a straightened coathanger is fine for a short length of vine. Attach the cane to the wire by winding it, an inch at a time, with narrow masking tape; this thin tape holds well, and at the same time is more easily removed than floral, plastic, or adhesive tape. Set the curved vine aside for a month or more to allow for complete drying, and then slowly peel off the tape and separate twig from wire.

3.

Designs with Cured Flowers

In recent years, experimenters have discovered that fresh flowers buried for a time in absorptive granular material are captured in their full perfection of shape and glory of color. These new "cured" blossoms have a just-picked look that lasts for months or even, under optimum conditions, for years.

CURING FLOWERS IN SAND

Clean, dry, sifted sand, and marble dust as well were the first absorptive media to be used. Place a two-inch layer of sand in the bottom of a deep box, and settle short-stemmed flowers upright upon it. Let sand trickle slowly around and over the blooms to a depth of an additional two inches. Cover the box tightly, and keep it in a warm room for three weeks or more, by which time the flower petals are dry and rather crumbly. However, the very considerable weight of the deep covering sand layer tends to flatten the blooms beneath it, and the brittle dehydrated blossoms are difficult to remove unbroken.

CURING FLOWERS IN SILICA GEL

Newer, lighter in weight, and much more efficacious as a drying agent is *silica gel*, which literally draws the moisture out of plant materials imbedded in it. You can obtain it at hobby shops and garden centers. At a dollar a pound, it is not prohibitively expensive, for with five pounds of this chemical compound, used over and over, you can preserve hundreds of garden flowers in their succession of bloom. It looks not unlike white table salt, liberally laced with blue crystals, which turn lavender and then disappear as the chemical absorbs moisture from dehydrating flowers or from the air. Spread the gel out in a shallow roasting pan and place it in the oven at 150°; it can then be dried out for re-use, and is ready when the crystals have regained their original bright blue.

DRYING CONTAINERS

A plastic shoebox (from a variety store or a closet shop) makes just the right size drying container for five pounds of the gel, and will accommodate three large blooms, such as peonies, or a number of smaller flowers such as daisies or ragged robins. A large shoebox of heavy cardboard can be used instead. Metal fruitcake tins are often recommended as containers for silica gel, but they have this disadvantage: a tight-fitting lid will shrink during the drying process until it grips the rim of the tin in an almost unbreakable seal. Coffee or shortening cans with snap-on plastic lids are better, but many flowers seem to dry too quickly in metal; their petals are thinned to the point of translucency, and become flaccid when exposed to air.

COLORS THAT CURE WELL

Most (but not all) garden flowers can be cured successfully in silica gel. In general, flowers cure well if they have wide petals that are attached to broad central calyxes; also, the silica gel process works best for full-blown blossoms — tight buds and unopened centers have a tendency to turn brown.

Blue blossoms flout all color canons by not fading, but rather becoming brighter as they dehydrate. Yellow and orange keep their true color, but orange-reds and shell pinks darken as they dry. Bluish reds and rosy pinks are difficult if not impossible to preserve; they emerge maroon or lavender. Almost invariably, white petals turn creamy or faintly pink, but dogwood, candytuft, and spirea stay snow-white.

MOUNTING CURED FLOWERS ON STEMS

Select perfect blossoms for curing, and cut them when their natural moisture is at low ebb, in the early afternoon of a hot, clear day. (Wait two days after a heavy rain.) Many flower stems become limp when cured, while others shatter at a touch; therefore, clip off the stems of round flower forms half an inch below the bloom base. Many flower stems (zinnias', for example) are hollow. When dried, each such half-inch stub forms a natural tube into which you can neatly fit a wire stem of appropriate size. Dip the tip of the wire in white glue before you insert it. If these flowers are to be arranged on a styrofoam base in a pyramid or a mound, their stems need not be more than two or three inches long. In this case, substitute glue-dipped wooden flower picks, matchsticks, or round toothpicks (depending on the size of the cavity) for wires.

Flowers with solid stems, such as peonies or chrysanthemums, require a different mounting technique. Coil one end of a length of green florist's wire in concentric circles, making a disk three-quarters of an inch in diameter; bend and adjust the disk so that it is flat and horizontal on top of the straight stem. Cover the coil with a few wisps of cotton dredged in white glue. With scissors, snip off the flower's stem-stub flush with the base of the calyx, and settle the flower face up on the prepared wire disk. If the blossom is unsteady, bend the outer edges of the coil upward, making a shallow cup to support the calyx.

The tall stems of most spring-flowering bulbs are thick, the better to support their relatively large blooms. Cured tulips, iris, and daffodils are comparatively weightless, so from the standpoint of mechanics, a wire stem would be quite adequate. It would, however, be patently artificial, and since these flowers often are naturalistically arranged, they look better on stems the same size as their own. Green plastic drinking straws will give them instant stems: dip the end of a straw in white glue, and slip the stub of a cured flower stem inside it. The base of the blossom will rest upon the glue-covered rim of the straw and adhere to it. While the glue is hardening, stand the flower upright in a soft drink bottle. Provide stems for smaller blooms of narcissus and jonquils in the same manner, using green cellophane soda or cocktail straws.

The stiff woody twigs of flowering shrub and fruit-tree blossoms take up needless room in the drying container. Instead of struggling to fit them in, it is better to cure the blossoms individually and later, with white glue, attach them to a branch of interesting shape. Then, to complete the illusion glue single cured leaves or small foliage sprays to the flowered branch.

POSITIONING FLOWERS IN THE DRYING CONTAINER

Since flowers cure more successfully if they are rushed from garden to chemical without first being placed in water, prepare the drying container before the blooms are cut. Pour a one-inch layer of silica gel over the bottom of a clean, dry plastic shoe box. After trimming its stem to one half inch, settle a flower carefully upon the gel, face up; with the fingers, push the gel under and around the base of the blossom so that its outer petals are supported in their natural position. Then, with a kitchen spoon or a sugar scoop, trickle the chemical over the inner petals and the center of the flower. Gently lift the inner petals, and pour the gel beneath them; be sure that each petal has sufficient silica underneath it to prevent its bending backward when more gel is added to cover the flower completely. Patience pays! The flower will dry *exactly* as it is positioned, and for perfect results it must be very carefully cradled and totally covered. So that the flowers will dry more quickly and evenly, place them in a single layer in the container, and space them so that their petals neither touch nor overlap.

Roses, dahlias, chrysanthemums, zinnias, peonies, marigolds, and other round or mounded flowers all prefer the face-up position, but spike flowers take their cure lying down. For hyacinth, larkspur or delphinium, foxglove, and snapdragon, push fine florist's wire up through their hollow stems for reinforcement; then lay each spike horizontally in a shallow trough scooped in the surface of a two-inch layer of silica gel. Gradually and gently, sift more gel over the spike until all its crevices are filled and every floret is entirely buried. Even by this method, gladiolus cannot be cured as a complete stalk, but single florets dry beautifully and are splendid fillers for a large arrangement of mixed flowers. Dry individual florets of single hollyhock, single althea, mallow, and hibiscus face down. Mound the gel over a small cone of styrofoam or crumpled aluminum foil, which supports the inner surface of the blossom; fit the flower over this heap and then cover it very gradually so as not to break the edges of the petals.

Cured carnations, especially white or pink varieties, are very beautiful, but they require special preparation before being placed in the drying medium. Surround the outer petals with thumb and finger of the left hand, drawing them up and inward so that the flower appears half-open. Encircle the carnation just above the calyx with a pipe cleaner, and twist it tight to hold the petals pressed together. Place the flower face up in silica gel to dry. When the carnation is lifted from the drying container and the pipe cleaner removed, the petals will spread out in the flower's natural form.

Azaleas, lilac, rhododendron and crepe myrtle dry beautifully in silica, but for these use a smaller, deeper container such as a coffee or shortening tin with snap-on plastic lid, a wide-mouthed half-gallon jar, or a large round ice-cream carton. Place the cluster upright with its short stem thrust deep into a three-inch layer of silica gel, and then trickle in more gel very slowly. Beginning at the base of the composite flower head, cover each floret completely with the gel on which the next floret will rest. If you thus carefully layer the drying agent until the whole cluster is entirely submerged, there will be no crushing of florets or crumpling of petals.

DRYING TIME IN SILICA GEL

Once the flowers are in position, cover the container with a tight fitting lid sealed with masking tape, and set it aside for three days. By this time single roses, dogwood blossoms, daisies, larkspur, and other thin-petalled blooms will be completely cured; their petals will have a silky sheen, but will be dry to the touch. Heavier blooms or those with thicker petals — peonies, zinnias, fully double roses, dahlias, hyacinths, foxgloves, etc. — dry more slowly and should stay in the silica for five to seven days. Extra curing time will not injure any blossom, but flowers removed before they are perfectly dry will wilt rapidly when exposed to air.

REMOVING CURED FLOWERS FROM THE CONTAINER

Shake the container gently from side to side; this will raise lightweight flowers to the top of the gel, whence they may be carefully lifted. If the blossoms are large ones, slowly pour enough gel out of the container to leave them half exposed. Then carefully insert the fingers beneath a bloom and lift it, shaking it slightly to dislodge the gel between the petals. If the petals look powdery when the flower is out of the container, flick away the clinging particles of white silica with a small artist's brush.

Designed for a fifteenth (crystal) anniversary. A glass candlestick and a fluted nut dish (both from the dime store) make a handsome holder for lilies, dogwood, narcissus, mallow, and rose of sharon; all were cured in silica gel and "painted" with melted paraffin (see chapter on Waxed Flowers).

THE INCURABLES

Fleshy flowers do not cure well. For example, although cattleya orchids dry magnificently, cymbidiums usually become limber and develop brownish spots. Some flowers have such sticky petals that the gel adheres to them so that they look too dusty to be used. Among the varieties that we must reluctantly classify as incurable for this reason are: petunias, nicotiana, gloxinias, and most primroses.

REABSORPTION OF MOISTURE

Other flowers are, in a way, even more disappointing. Perfect in shape and color when removed from the drying container, they reabsorb moisture so rapidly from the air that within a few hours they droop and fade into anonymity. This group includes most of the lilies—Easter, water, and day — along with French anemones, poplar tulips, nasturtium, clematis, geranium, and evening primrose. There is a preventive method worth trying since it sometimes proves effective: the moment one of these thirsty flowers is lifted from the drying agent, give it a thin but thorough spray-coating, front and back, with colorless plastic (See Sources of Supply). This seals the petals and prevents reabsorption, but it must be done immediately; once the wilting process starts, it is irreversible.

CURING FLOWERS IN CORNMEAL-BORAX

Yet another drying agent that possesses most of the virtues of silica gel, plus a few that are peculiarly its own, is a combination of bolted yellow cornmeal and powdered borax. These components have the special advantages of cheapness and availability at the nearest supermarket. Mix five pounds of meal indistinguishably with twenty-five ounces of borax (one large package), and use any non-metallic box as a container for drying. If you dry the borax and meal mixture after each use (in the oven, at 150°, for one hour) and store it in an airtight container, it can be used again and again. While in the oven, the mix should be thoroughly and frequently stirred to prevent lumping of the borax. If lumps persist in forming, crush them with your fingers or break them with a flour-sifter.

The techniques of positioning and covering flowers are the same as those used for silica gel, but the drying time is at least twice as long: thin petalled blossoms are cured in approximately one week instead of in three days. To test for dryness, rub an inner petal between thumb and finger; the surface will feel dry and crisp if the blossom is ready to be removed. Shake the flower gently to dislodge traces of meal, and flick off borax crystals with an artist's brush.

DRYING LILIES IN CORNMEAL-BORAX

Because they dehydrate so gradually in cornmeal-borax, some of the flowers that have a reabsorption problem after silica curing can be dried with greater success in this medium. Rubrum and hybrid lilies, if you pick them the moment they are fully open and hurry them into the drying container, will usually hold up for three months or more. Even the ephemeral beauty of daylilies and Magnolia grandiflora can be captured and preserved for a time, and a thorough spraying with clear plastic will prolong the life of these and other doubtful cures.

DRYING BRANCHES OF FLOWERING SHRUB

Cure whole branches of flowering shrub in cornmeal-borax in a long, shallow grape box of heavy cardboard begged from the supermarket. If the box has cut-out handholds at the ends, cover them over (on the inside) with stiff cardboard held in place with masking tape. For shorter sprays of blossoms, a plastic blanket-storage box is even better. In the blanket box, a double quantity of cornmeal and powdered borax will suffice, but for the longer grape-box carton, you'll need fifteen pounds of meal and three large boxes of borax.

Place a two-inch layer of the mixture in the bottom of the box, and lay a limb flat upon it with the best blossoms face up. Mound the meal wherever necessary for perfect support. Trickle more meal mix over the spray of flowers, carefully covering the bloom clusters one at a time. When the whole branch is submerged, add a two-inch cover layer of the borax mixture. Put the lid on the box, and make it airtight by sealing its edges with masking tape.

CURING DOGWOOD IN CORNMEAL-BORAX

Sprays of white flowering dogwood dry to perfection in about two weeks, but pink dogwood blossoms do not keep their true color. (Wild flowering dogwood is protected in most states by stringent conservation laws, and the blossoms may not be cut or sold. Lawn specimens, however, often need to be shaped by pruning, which may legitimately be done while the trees are in bloom.)

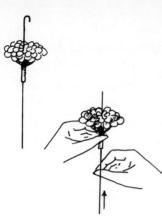

Stems of no. 24 wire may be added to flowers before curing. Push wire up through the short-cut stem to emerge in the center of blossom; bend tip of wire in a miniature shepherd's crook, then pull the stem down until the hook is hidden in the flower center.

REMOVING FLOWERING SPRAYS FROM CORNMEAL

To remove the flowering spray, pour off the covering layer of cornmeal very slowly until the tops of the blooms appear. Then, using both hands, place the fingers under the ends of the spray and lift it, shaking it slightly to remove grainy particles. Occasionally a petal or an entire blossom will have come unstuck, but you can quickly replace it with a dot of white glue.

STORING CURED FLOWERS

Whether they have been treated with cornmeal-borax or with silica gel, you can store cured flowers in lidded plastic or cardboard boxes, in a windowless closet, until they are needed. Hang a cake of dehumidifier in the closet as an advisable precaution. You can enclose large individual blooms in roomy, tightly sealed plastic bags, and imprison several small flowers indefinitely in a wide-mouthed glass jar with a screw lid.

Once you've arranged the cured materials, you must still protect them from dampness and strong light. In a house with year-round air conditioning, where temperature and moisture are constantly controlled, they should last for a year or more. Placed before an open window on a rainy day, they wilt almost immediately.

Protect cured flowers for gifts with a light but thorough spraying of clear plastic before you arrange them. If you must make the gift arrangement far in advance of its presentation day, wrap it — container and all — in a plastic dry-cleaner's bag before storing it in a dark dry closet. Seal one end of the bag carefully with masking tape. Place the bag, sealed end down, on a table, and open it by rolling the edges down from the top. Set the container inside, unroll the plastic to cover the arrangement, and secure the top of the bag with tape or wire. If you capture enough air in the bag and seal it tightly, it will look like a blown-up balloon; the air will hold the plastic away from the flowers and prevent their petals from being crushed.

ARRANGING CURED FLOWERS

Because of their fragility, cured flowers must be arranged with the utmost care. Use a half-round of green styrofoam from a florist or a variety store, anchored in a shallow container with double-sticky picture mounts; it makes a suitable holder for wire or wooden stems which you can prick into it at any angle.

MASS ARRANGEMENT

A loosely massed grouping of several round and spiky flower varieties will attest the donor's curative powers, especially if the arrangement includes flowers that bloom at different seasons. The chief difficulty in making such an arrangement is hiding the wire stems of the taller round blooms, and for this reason filler material is a must. This could, of course, consist entirely of cured green foliage, but feathery gray sprigs

"Porcelain" flowers for a twentieth (china) anniversary gift. A styrofoam ball was fitted into a lotus bowl and closely covered with cured flowers; then the completed design was sprayed with white Epoxy enamel.

of artemesia, lavender, and santolina are splendid cover-ups, as are fuzzy ageratum, wide flat Queen Anne's lace, or spreading butterfly weed and elderflower.

In making this mass arrangement, begin with large and perfect round flowers, spacing them so that they'll show from each side and from the top. Next add smaller round blooms, green foliage, and fillers with a light hand. Lastly, set in place the flower spikes that will add width, height and interest to the airy mass. In a sense, you will be making the arrangement backward, but you will be far less apt to damage the delicate spike flowers if you save them for last. Depending on its size, such an arrangement could grace either a coffee or a dining room table.

FLOWERS UNDER GLASS

During the Victorian era, our ancestors learned to protect their popular but perishable arrangements of wax or feather flowers by covering them with clear glass domes. Witness to the success of this subterfuge are the many fragile Victorian ornaments that still exist today.

VICTORIAN ARRANGEMENT FOR A HOUSE MUSEUM

For a historic house of the period 1840-1890, the most felicitous of all floral decorations would be a towering mass of cured flowers under a tall glass dome. First, measure the available dome and choose a container to fit under it. It might well be decorated, with a painted or raised floral design — it was not considered necessary in the nineteenth century that flowers repeat either the colors or the motif of the container. For the core of the arrangement, fit a cone of green styrofoam (or a white cone covered with green florist's foil) into a wide-mouthed urn, or glue it to the rim of a narrow-necked container. Cut off the pointed tip of the cone, which would be useless as a support for flower stems, leaving a flat top at least one inch in diameter to hold a single flower at the apex. The combined height of cone and container should be about three inches less than that of the glass dome. Because the cone supports the flowers, all the flower stems — be they wood or wire — can be quite short. Beginning level with the rim of the container, make a horizontal row around the cone, pricking the stems firmly into the styrofoam and setting the flowers so close together that their petals overlap. Add a second row of flowers, some large and some small, above and just touching the first; proceed in this way to the top of the cone. Inevitably there will be "vacancies" in the smooth overall pyramid, for the flowers will not fit together like pieces of a puzzle. Fill these voids with sprigs of green or gray foliage, and be sure to trail a spray of ivy or bleeding heart, a raceme of wistaria, or a nodding fuchsia over the edge of the container and down its face. Victorian arrangements did not have defined centers of interest, but a large and perfect rose was usually placed front center.

Because tall domed arrangements often were used in a niche or on a console table, they were left unfinished on the side meant to be placed against the wall. But smaller arrangements, under low domes, were sometimes placed on center tables in Victorian parlors and since these were free-standing, they were complete on all sides, and rounded to follow the curve of the glass. Decide, then, in advance, where the ornament will show to best advantage in the house museum, and design it accordingly.

The rose was so much the favorite flower during the Victorian age that no Victorian-style arrangement would be complete without one or more. Frilled and variegated flowers were very popular, too, so fritillarias, foxgloves, and honeycomb dahlias would be appropriate. Actually, you can use any garden flowers, large or small, and a great many will be required.

GAZING GLOBE

Applying the same idea to a smaller arrangement for a coffee table, a rose, a hibiscus, or a peony can take shelter under an inverted clear glass bubble bowl. A glass furniture-caster, from a variety store, will serve the dual purpose of holding the flower and sealing the mouth of the bowl. Glass casters come in several sizes, so be sure to choose one wide enough to cover the hole.

Place a small amount of liquid cement in the bottom of the caster-cup, and anchor the stem of the flower in it. When this glue has dried, cover the rim of the caster with a smooth film of liquid cement, invert the bubble bowl over the flower, and press the edges of its opening down firmly on the cement. Weight the bowl with a book until the cement has set. The rounded sides of the bowl will magnify the flower, and this ornament will be not only attractive but enduring.

Very large cured flowers can be made to pass through small openings by this method: place the stem of the flower in the center of the hole; encircle the flower with both hands and compress its outer petals upward and inward very gently as you push the stem down into the cavity.

Then lay the bowl on its side, insert a wooden spoon, and turn the flower so that its stem is toward the opening. For added importance, you can cement this gazing globe to the top of a glass candlestick. To raise the flower within the globe, fit a clear plastic pill-vial into the candle cup and touch its rim with cement. Invert the globe over it, guiding the stem of the flower into the top of the vial before allowing the rim of the bowl's opening to come to rest on the cement-covered bobeche of the candlestick.

What do you see in your crystal ball? For a lucky lady, a gift of a giant cured peony in an inverted glass bubble bowl (directions above). See also brandy snifter, page 30.

4.

Preserving Foliage and Berries

In the Spring, a number of old leaves on each broad-leafed evergreen dry on their twigs and turn brown before being pushed off by new green growth. If they are gathered up promptly, before rain and sun begin to rot them, these cast-offs constitute a veritable treasure trove. Brushed front and back with liquid wax, and wired to twig stems, they are ready to go at once into arrangements of cones and seedpods in natural shades of brown and tan. Wiped with green oil stain, they have an antiqued look that blends well with the muted colors of air-dried flowers. Painted green, they take the place of long lasting, washable artificial foliage. Sprayed gold, they form the background of holiday wreaths, swags, sprays, and table arrangements.

Look to your laurels for this self-preserved material, as well as to burfordi holly, viburnum, Magnolia grandiflora, and rhododendron. Rhododendron leaves, once they've fallen and dried, tend to roll up into cylinders; to make them pliable again, soak them in warm water for an hour; then flatten them out with your fingers, and press them in several thicknesses of paper toweling under a stack of books.

PAINTED DAISY

Paint only the front side of rhododendron, strap-leaf laurel, or magnolia leaves for this giant daisy, a flat arrangement for terrace or coffee table: select twelve to sixteen self-dried leaves that are approximately the same size and length; lay them faceup on newspaper, and brush on two coats of white semi-gloss enamel. When the paint has dried, arrange the leaves in a circle on a flat tray, around a mound of moistened Oasis wrapped in green florist's foil. Cover the Oasis completely by pricking into it small, round, short-stemmed yellow marigolds or button chrysanthemums. This arrangement will last throughout the summer, if the Oasis is unwrapped and re-soaked weekly, and fresh flowers are added. This presupposes an informed and cooperative recipient — make sure you give full instructions.

AIR-DRIED FOLIAGE

Certain other types of foliage — galax, corn, and rhubarb, for examples — dry naturally outdoors on the plants. Still others (rosettes of mullein, spears of yucca, iris, liriope, and gladiolus) air-dry well if laid flat between several thicknesses of newspaper in a darkened room. Many leaves keep their color well when air-dried while still on the branch, placed upright in a sand-filled container: red oak, white or silver-leafed poplar, elaeagnus, eucalyptus, and beech. Deep, glossy evergreen magnolia and rhododendron lighten as they air-dry thus to silvery sage green.

Any leaf is apt to wrinkle as it loses moisture; occasionally, as with the rhododendrons, one will twist into a spiral or roll up in a cylinder. Once they have been completely dehydrated, leaves can be soaked in lukewarm water for a few minutes to make them supple again. They can often be smoothed out with the fingers, but if not, they can be flattened under weights overnight.

CURED FOLIAGE

Deciduous foliage can be successfully dried in silica gel, but it also cures exceedingly well in cornmeal-borax, retaining its natural green. Cured autumn leaves keep their vibrant color. Either chemical preserves the shape of evergreen foliage perfectly, but *not* the color: the leaves usually turn brown or brownish green.

CURING FOLIAGE IN CORNMEAL

Foliage dries more slowly than flowers in cornmeal-borax. Lay short sprays or individual leaves flat on a two-inch layer of the mixture, and cover them to a depth of two inches. Rose foliage or sprays of green beech leaves dry faultlessly in two to two-and-a-half weeks. Meadow rue and ferns are especially attractive when cured in this manner, since they retain their natural curve of stem and irregularity of edge.

STEMMING SINGLE LEAVES

The woody stems of foliage sprays will, of course, require no reinforcement, but single green or autumn leaves will need stems. Place the leaf facedown on a smooth surface, and lay stiff green florist's wire along its center spine; with a covering of narrow green plastic tape, you can both hide the wire and attach it to the leaf.

PRESSING FOLIAGE

Preserving foliage by pressing is an art that has been practised since colonial days. Following the method that has remained virtually unchanged through intervening years, gather cinnamon and royal ferns as they approach maturity in late June; they can then be made to retain not only their soft green color but also their pliability. In an out-of-the-way corner of attic, basement or closet, place four thicknesses of newspaper on the floor. Lay the fronds flat upon this pad, and cover them with an additional four sheets of newsprint. Time was when pressed foliage was weighted down with wooden boards on which heavy bricks or stones were stacked, but loose boards and bricks are non-existent in twentieth-century homes. However, cardboard cartons filled with books are common to many households; use one of these for weight, or, smaller and easier to lift, cardboard six-packs of canned or bottled soft drinks that no home is without; place several of these side by side over the surface of the covering newspaper. Any interestingly-shaped leaf, especially one with deeply serrated edges, can be preserved by pressing for use as a gift package decoration or in a framed design. Poppy and peony, vitex, cleome and ginkgo, are excellent possibilities.

The incandescence of autumn leaves can be captured and saved to brighten dark winter days, for dogwood, maple, beech, hickory, red oak, sumac and sweet gum leaves respond well to this treatment. Gather these leaves as soon as they attain bright color and before the sap has left the limbs, in order to prevent their dropping off the twigs after they are pressed. Straight branches should be chosen, and trimmed to lie perfectly flat; all overlapping leaves must be snipped off.

In about three weeks, autumn foliage will be ready for use, but let green foliage stay under wraps for a month; if any moisture remains in the leaves, their edges will curl when exposed to air. Pressed leaves and foliage are indispensable background materials for fan-shaped arrangements of air-dried or cured flowers.

PRESERVING FOLIAGE WITH GLYCERIN

As noted above, most broad-leafed evergreen foliage turns brown in silica gel or cornmeal-borax, so there is no point in wasting these chemicals on evergreens. Evergreens do press well, but all pressed foliage has a distinct disadvantage for flower arranging in that it is perfectly flat.

Foliage of Magnolia grandiflora *preserved in glycerin turned glossy chocolate brown. The creamy blossom was removed, cured in cornmeal and powdered borax, sprayed with colorless acrylic plastic, and glued back on. (Arrangement by Mrs. George T. Fritts.)*

Fortunately, broad-leafed evergreens have their own appointed chemical preservative, glycerin, which a pharmacist can get you if his drugstore does not stock it. Rhododendron, laurel, holly, viburnum, eleagnus, and magnolia respond especially well to this one-step method of preservation.

PRESERVING EVERGREEN BRANCHES

Treat evergreen branches in the late summer, after the new-growth tips have stiffened and become woody. Don't cut the leaves when they are wilted after a prolonged drouth; gather them on a clear, hot day. For best results, use sprays no more than twenty-four inches long. Do not wash the leaves with water, but clean them by wiping with a ball of cotton dipped in glycerin. Then strip four inches of bark from the base of the branch, and cross-split the stem end. In a tall, slender container (an old florist's vase or a milk bottle) place one cup of glycerin; add two cups of boiling water, and stir vigorously with long-handled wooden spoon to blend the liquids thoroughly. While the mixture still is hot, plunge the stem into it, making sure that the scraped end is completely covered. Keep the container where it will be seen daily, for it is interesting to watch the leaves change color as the glycerin slowly seeps along their veins. Remove the branch from the solution as soon as the color change reaches the edges of the top leaves; this full absorption usually takes place in five to seven days. Rhododendron leaves take on a deep bronze sheen, while magnolia foliage turns milk-chocolate brown. To keep a green tinge, leave the spray in the glycerin mix for two days only; then hang it upside down in a dark basement or closet for four days more to complete the cure.

PRESERVING SHORT FOLIAGE SPRAYS

Submerge galax leaves, ivy and vinca minor sprays, and boxwood or azalea twigs in a mixture of equal parts glycerin and boiling water. Use a flat, shallow container — an oblong roasting pan is ideal, but protect it with a liner of aluminum foil — and weight the leaves with small clean stones to keep them beneath the surface at all times. Ivy's green deepens, and a spray is ready for removal in six days. Galax turns mahogany red in ten days. Other materials turn brown by the time they are ready for use.

DECIDUOUS FOLIAGE

Some deciduous foliages — oak and beech leaves in particular — cure very well in a mixture of one part glycerin to two parts boiling water, taking on a shiny greenish brown. Dogwood flouts all rules by turning a deeper, richer green. For permanent preservation, keep a dogwood branch upright in the glycerin solution for two full weeks.

TURNING BROWN LEAVES GREEN

You won't prevent foliage from turning brown by adding half a cup of bright green liquid dye to the glycerin-and-boiling-water mix, but you will add a greenish cast to its hue. Also, try rubbing brown treated leaves with the green oil stain made for wooden shingles for a pronounced and very pleasing overglow. "Green wax," made by adding cold liquid dye to self-polishing liquid wax, is another effective coating for brown leaves.

SMOOTHING WRINKLED LEAVES

Occasionally, leaves wrinkle or twist as they absorb the glycerin solution. Smooth them with an electric dry iron set for synthetic materials, using one sheet of waxed paper under one layer of newspaper as a "pressing cloth."

WALL HANGINGS WITH PRESERVED FOLIAGE

Wall hangings, reminiscent of medieval banners, are popular replacements for pictures on panelled or painted walls. For a man's study with dark panelling, make this masculine design in shades of brown and tan. Begin with a three-foot length of broomstick handle; cover its cut ends by gluing over them brown-painted plastic pill bottle caps for finials. Hem a thirty-six-inch square of natural colored burlap, incorporating six curtain weights at intervals in the bottom hem, and stitch loops of wide brown cotton tape to the top hem, six inches apart. With brown thread, sew glycerin-treated leaves of various shades and sizes — magnolia, beech, laurel, holly, boxwood — to the burlap in a pleasing montage; pliable glycerined leaves will not split if the needle is slowly pressed through near the center stem. Thread the wooden rod through the tape loops, and with the banner, present two large brass cup hooks for attaching rod to wall.

For the painted wall of a master bedroom, a hall, or a breakfast room, use an inexpensive hollow brass curtain rod with knobbed ends to support a long rectangle of black, dark green, or deep blue velveteen on loops of matching velvet ribbon. Weight the bottom hem of the material with lead beading (from a cloth shop or an upholsterer). Spray both sides of colorful pressed autumn leaves with colorless acrylic plastic and let them dry thoroughly. Then glue the leaves to the material in a graceful spray or an airy elongated oval.

IRONED LEAVES

Late in the nineteenth century, students of botany were taught to prepare leaf specimens for mounting by placing them between sheets of waxed paper, laying a single sheet of brown paper like a pressing cloth on top, and ironing them with a heated sad-iron. Warm wax from the paper was transferred to the leaves, forming a protective coating on both sides. As soon as the leaves were cool, they were lifted from the papers and pressed overnight between the pages of a heavy textbook.

This academic device works well for coleus, hosta, scarlet maple, and caladium leaves, none of which respond well to other methods of preservation, and is also successful with green grasses and tiny wild flowers. Use an electric dry iron, at the setting for synthetic materials.

SKELETONIZED LEAVES

Victorian ladies managed to preserve leaves by reducing them to their elemental structural form. This process was called "skeletonizing," and it involved boiling the leaves in lye and scraping away all fleshy pulp. Then the leaves were soaked in buttermilk and bluing, and bleached in the sun. Such skeletonized foliage was arranged with waxed flowers and placed under a glass dome. Skeletonized leaves are once again in vogue; the process is rather tedious, but the finished leaves are reduced to architectural blueprints and are fine accents for functional furniture in a friend's contemporary house.

METHOD OF SKELETONIZING

Bring one quart of water to a boil in a porcelain (not a metal) kettle, and add two tablespoonfuls of granular lye, which will be found among bathroom cleansers at the supermarket. Immerse several freshly plucked green leaves in the lye bath, and simmer them for forty minutes. *Do not touch the caustic liquid.* Remove the leaves with the handle of a wooden spoon, and dispose of the cooled lye by pouring it into a toilet. Rinse the leaves several times in cool water before handling them. Then lay a leaf flat on a wooden breadboard, and with the dull edge of a tableknife carefully scrape away the fleshy pulp; turn the leaf over, and scrape the other side. This will leave a brown framework of veins connected by a film of tissue so thin that it is translucent. Whiten the leaves by soaking them in a solution of household chlorine bleach: two tablespoonfuls of strong liquid bleach to one quart of cool water. One hour in this solution will produce creamy beige leaves; to turn them snowy white requires two hours or longer. After you lift them from the bleach, rinse them gingerly in cool water and dry them between paper towels; then place them between fresh paper towels, and press them beneath a stack of books for twenty-four hours.

PRESERVING BERRIES

THINNED SHELLAC

Bright berries are extremely attractive additions to flower, foliage, or dried arrangements, but shrivelling and shattering are second nature to them. You can break short berry sprays of these disconcerting habits by dipping them into a mixture of equal parts of white shellac and ordinary rubbing alcohol. A small bowl, protected by a liner of heavy-duty aluminum foil, can hold the liquid. This thinned shellac will be well-nigh invisible on berries or stems, and the treatment is a great help to holly, bittersweet, nandina, bayberry, barberry, hawthorn, cotoneaster, and privet. (It also works well on magnolia pods, holding their bright red seeds in place for weeks, and on cattails, keeping the pods unsplit and the white fluff unscattered.) Such fleshy berries as pyracantha, bush honeysuckle, eleagnus and mahonia will not be so well preserved, but should last at least a week.

For someone born under the sign of Leo (July 23-August 22), an amusing lion made of braided and raveled rope, with a wooden head and legs. "Hearts-bustin'-with-love" is the common name of the unusual plant (*Euonymus americanus*) whose twigs were dipped in thinned shellac to hold their pendant seeds.

ACRYLIC PLASTIC

Protect long, graceful berried branches by spraying them with transparent, colorless acrylic plastic. This is available at paint stores in pressurized cans.

PAINTED PRIVET

After a cold, wet Spring, holly may not bear any berries at all, and other shrubs may be very sparsely settled, but privet never seems to have an off-season. Cut the privet berries green, and air-dry them hanging upside down. Generously fruited privet branches look well with needled evergreens or with autumn leaves. Left on the shrub, they turn navy blue, and their color is striking against cured broad-leafed evergreens that have been spray-painted bone white.

Sprigs of privet berries sprayed with Chinese red paint can serve as stand-ins for absent holly berries in a wreath or a Christmas arrangement. Long, full, red-sprayed trusses of privet berries closely resemble nandina.

Frosted or completely covered with gold spray-paint, these chameleon berries are fine accents for holiday gift arrangements: combine them with

57

cured foliage sprayed white, gold, or silver. Use a short spray to top a package wrapped in bright red foil. At Thanksgiving, trail a long raceme of gilded berries over the edge of a compote filled with fruits, or spill several bunches from a gilded cornucopia and add accents of lady-apples and seckel pears.

LEAVES AND BERRIES DIPPED IN LIQUID FLOOR WAX

In autumn and winter, when their sap is down, you may effectively preserve fresh evergreen leaves by brushing self-polishing liquid floor wax on both sides and then dipping the stems in the liquid wax. Ivy, burfordi holly, laurel, ligustrum, vinca, and creeping euonymus are leading candidates for this treatment, and will remain green and glossy for several months. The leaves gradually lighten to sage green, and eventually turn bronze, but are attractive in all their color stages.

Hard-skinned berries, too, can be preserved for months by being dipped in liquid self-polishing wax. Hawthorn, holly, nandina, mahonia, bittersweet and privet are best suited to this easy means of preservation. All except bittersweet and privet will eventually turn brown.

Since the color change of leaves and berries is so gradual, evergreen foliage and berries for holiday package toppers, gift door swags, and candlestick sprays can be cut and waxed before the last-minute Christmas rush begins.

WASTEBASKET WITH WAXED PRESSED FOLIAGE

Inexpensive metal wastebaskets, round or oval in shape, can be very effectively decorated with pressed ferns or autumn leaves and self-polishing wax. Paint a basket, inside and out, with two coats of white enamel. Glue to one side a spreading cluster of pressed fern fronds, and when the glue is perfectly dry, brush self-polishing liquid floor wax over ferns and painted surfaces. Finish the basket with wide green braid or several rows of green rickrack glued around the rim. Or, paint the basket sage green and glue a montage of colorful pressed autumn leaves on one side. Cover leaves and painted metal with floor wax, and glue sage green velvet ribbon around the rim of the basket.

5.

Pictures, Prints and
Pressed Flowers

Preserving plant materials by pressing is a technique long known and used by scientists as well as artists, and the method remained unchanged for several centuries. Leaves were placed between several sheets of newspaper, covered with boards, and weighted with stones or bricks, but since flowers and their stems contain much more moisture than tree leaves or ferns, they could not simply be placed beneath weights and forgotten for a fortnight. For the first two days, it was necessary to change the papers that surrounded the flowers every twelve hours; after that, fresh papers were needed every day. Depending upon the fleshiness of their petals and stems, flowers were pressed for eight to fourteen days, until their petals looked papery and felt dry.

These flat blooms, glued to mounting paper in a "botanical specimen" or a floral design, were framed and given a glass covering that fitted close against the glued materials to hold them firmly in place and to seal out moisture. Even so, after two or three years, most red and blue blossoms had faded to pallid gray, for light rather than air is the enemy of color in pressed flowers.

A NEW METHOD OF PRESSING FLOWERS

A new method of pressing flowers, which actually is a combination of pressing and chemical curing, sets color permanently by adding one step to the preservation process.

Gather the flowers with long stems, but cut each stem off flush with the base of its blossom, and remove all leaves from the stem. Place the flowers, face up, on a one-inch layer of silica gel in a plastic shoebox, and add the stems and leaves, laid flat. Sprinkle more silica over the plant materials until they are completely covered, and allow the materials to remain in the drying container for no less than eighteen and no more than twenty-four hours. They will then be slightly limp. Transfer blossoms, stems and leaves to newspaper, sandwiching them between the halves of a thick folded section of the daily paper; separate them so that they do not touch or overlap. Use only the black print section of a newspaper; colored inks will stain the flowers. Lay the folded paper flat on a hard surface — an out-of-the-way table, or a corner of a closet floor — and weight it with a box of books or with several cartons of soft drinks. Leave the flowers undisturbed for seven days; by then they will be ready for use.

FLOWERS THAT PRESS WELL

Your selection need not be limited to naturally flat blossoms, like pansies, for pressing, but it is necessary to choose flowers with small calyxes that when flattened, won't lose their clear and recognizable outline. Violets, pinks, columbine, larkspur, bluebells and pink dogwood are among the flowers that profile to perfection. Individual florets of geranium are colorful additions to pressed flower designs; this dual method of preservation works beautifully for them, although they do not cure well if left full time in silica gel. Other flowers that wilt from moisture re-absorption after curing can be stabilized at the moment of perfection; lilies press best if they are cut in half, lengthwise, after the partial curing and before being placed under weights.

Listed below are flowers that press well, with the length of time that each should remain under weights after partial curing in silica gel:

Acacia (pubescens) — press yellow blossoms separately — seven days
Ageratum — press in small pieces — five days
Ajuga — seven days
Albizzia julibrissi (mimosa) — press flowers and leaves separately — seven days
Alyssum — five days
Alyssum saxatile (basket-of-gold) — five days
Anemone (windflower) — press flowers and leaves separately — ten days
Aquilegia (columbine) — flowers separately — five to seven days
Aster (Michaelmas daisy) — flowers separately — seven days
Astilbe — five to seven days
Baby's breath (gypsophila) — flowers separately or as a spray — three days

Black-eyed Susan — seven days
Buttercup — five days
Calliopsis — five days
Candytuft — five days
Celosia — press small tufts — seven days
Clematis — press flowers separately — ten days
Cleome — flowers and foliage separately — six days
Clover — white, seven days; red, ten days
Cornflower (Centaurea cyanus) — seven days
Cosmos — seven days
Daisy — six days
Delphinium (and larkspur) — seven days
Dianthus (pinks) — five days
Feverfew — seven days
Forget-me-not — seven days
Forsythia — florets separately — five days
Gaillardia — seven days
Geranium — florets separately — five to seven days
Golden glow — flowers separately — six days
Goldenrod — small pieces — six days
Heather — five days
Heuchera (coral bells) — seven days
Hydrangea—florets separately — five days
Korean chrysanthemum — seven days
Lavender — five days
Liatris — seven to nine days
Lily — split lengthwise after partial curing — ten days
Mertensia (blue bells) — ten days
Mullein — flowers separately — seven days
Pansy — four days
Poinsettia — seven days
Potentilla — five days
Primrose — flowers only — nine days
Queen Anne's lace — five days
Rose (single) — seven days
Salvia — seven to nine days
Shasta daisy (single) — seven days
Snow-on-the-mountain (Euphorbia marginata) — foliage only — five days
Squill — six days
Statice — five days

Stock — flowers separately — seven days
Sunflower (small single) — ten days
Tansy — six days
Verbena — flowers in small clusters — five days
Zinnia (single) — seven days

MOUNTING PRESSED FLOWERS

Mount these thin and fragile pressed flowers with patience and extreme
care. Lift the sturdiest specimens with tweezers to brush white glue
lightly on their undersides. But the more delicate petals and stems
will crumble under the pressure of tweezers or fingernails; for these,
apply white glue directly to the mounting paper and let it stand until
tacky. Then lift the pressed flower by touching it with the moistened
tip of a forefinger, and gently lay it upon the sticky surface.

BOTANY PRINTS

In the eighteenth century, botanical explorers from afar, like Swedish
Peter Kalm and French André Michaux, explored America's meadows
and mountains in search of new plant varieties. There was no camera
to record their finds in natural color, but they discovered that by pressing,
they could preserve entire plants — root, stem, leaf, flower, pod and
seed — for further study. It was fashionable to take an interest in this
subject that concerned the intellectuals of the day, and the mounted
pressed specimens of returned explorers were examined and admired
by amateur "botanizers," who soon began to imitate them, treating
small plants from the garden or a nearby woodland as botanical specimens
and mounting them to show their complete growth cycle. Some could
be pressed intact, but more often stems, leaves and even petals were
pressed separately and reassembled by being glued individually to white
mounting paper. The total design was light and airy against its background of white; the completed composition was given a wooden backing
and a narrow frame, and a protective glass that fitted flat against the
pressed materials.

"Botany prints" are no longer considered "philosophical," but they have
never lost their popularity as wall decorations. Most plants do not produce
blossoms and seeds simultaneously, so the pressing of a plant must continue
over a period of several weeks; however, you will not harm the blooms
and stems by leaving them folded in newspaper until you've prepared
the rest of the plant. The roots, pods, and seeds, being naturally rather

A small shadow-box frame contains a three-dimensional grouping of cured violets, narcissus, azalea, and blooms of mountain blueberry.

dry, need not be cured first in silica gel, but should at once be placed between papers and beneath weights. Cut one seed pod in half before flattening, to show its inner structure, and split the thick seeds carefully with a sharp knife before mounting. In reassembling the plant on a white mat (or on white blotting paper), follow in sequence its natural pattern of growth. Be sure that the mount is large enough to accommodate the whole plant without crowding; a long, narrow panel may be more appropriate than a square, but this depends upon the spread of the plant. Very often the design is more pleasing if the plant is presented in bloom, while the seed capsule and seeds are relegated to a lower corner.

PRESSED FLORAL DESIGNS

Floral designs of pressed flowers can be extremely colorful and charming, and are perfect gift accents for a bedroom furnished with early American or Victorian pieces. Early American pressed flower pictures were light and bright in composition; the background was white, and the frame narrow. Nineteenth-century pressed flower designs were more often mounted on black broadcloth or black paper, and usually were given oval gold frames. For either type of design, it is wise to buy the frame first, at a secondhand store or a variety store, or from a picture gallery, and to fit the picture to it.

63

Wreaths of mixed pressed flowers and foliage, very popular in the eighteenth century, are extremely effective. Drawing around a large tray or a dinner plate with a pencil, trace the outline of a circle on mounting paper that you've cut to fit the purchased frame; the paper need not be white, but should be very light in color. First, glue on short sprays of pressed foliage as a background for the flowers, but arrange all the foliage to your satisfaction *before* beginning to glue it. Then lift the sprigs one at a time, brush white glue on their backs, and replace them. When all the foliage is in place, cover the mount with a layer of paper toweling and weight it overnight with heavy books. This will keep the foliage from curling and dislodging flowers glued on top of it. Place the large flowers first, in groupings of three or five, and glue them; when you have settled a flower on the mount, cover it with a sheet of white typewriter paper and gently press it down by going over it with a kitchen rolling pin. Fill in the design with smaller blossoms; if necessary, you can cover broken petals or stubby calyxes with single pressed leaves.

Remove the glass from the frame. Spread a narrow band of glue around the outer edges of the mounting paper; fit the glass over the paper, pressing its edges down to meet the glue. To be sure the glue holds as it dries, weight the glass overnight with heavy books. Then return the glass, with the mounted design attached, to the frame. Pad the back, if necessary, with one or more sheets of cardboard, and press down the clamps that edge the inside of the frame. Cut a sheet of heavy black or brown paper to cover the back of the frame, and glue it in place.

Egg sous cloche: a blown eggshell decorated with pressed flower petals and cedar sprigs, encircled with gold braid, and topped with a tiny Venetian glass bluebird, is suspended beneath a keepsake dome.

An oval frame lined with black velvet holds a miniature Victorian bouquet of pressed violets, phlox, potentilla, spirea and lilac florets, with green-and-white fringe-tree blossoms for foliage.

VICTORIAN PRESSED FLOWER PICTURE

In the Victorian era, pressed flowers often were mounted in a mixed bouquet "tied" with ribbon; instead of their own stems, wheat straws usually were used.

For such a design, an oval frame is most appropriate — either an antique or a reproduction. Remove the glass and lay it on a sheet of cardboard; trace its outline on the cardboard and cut. Then, using the cardboard as a pattern, cut a covering for it of black broadcloth or felt, allowing a one-inch border of cloth all around. Stretch the cloth over the cardboard and glue it to the back; slash the edges at frequent intervals and overlap them, to make the cloth lie flat and smooth. Draw the outline of the floral design on the cloth in white chalk, and begin by gluing on the stems. Each straw must be quickly dipped in glue and laid in place, and the group of straws should fan out slightly at the bottom. Outline the edges of the bouquet with bits of lacy pressed fern and then place the flowers, beginning at the center of the design with single roses, evening primroses, or lilies. Add smaller round flowers, and angled spikes of larkspur or bluebells extending over the background fern. Last of all, glue on flat pieces of ribbon, in the shape of a bow with streamers, to hide the juncture of bouquet and stems.

Flowers pressed, after partial curing, in airtight frames will retain bright color for many years if they are not exposed to an overabundance of light. They should never be hung in direct sunlight, nor should they be placed where strong electric light will often shine upon them.

MOUNTING PRESSED FLOWERS ON GLASS

A more unusual type of picture, and one that is visible from both sides, is achieved by sandwiching pressed plant material between two sheets of clear glass that are exactly the same size. Thin (16 weight) glass can be cut to any size and shape by a glazier listed under "Glass, retail" in the yellow pages of the telephone directory.

Pressed flowers and leaves should be attached to glass not with glue, which would show on the reverse side, but with albumin. Beat the white of an egg slightly, just until it begins to foam; use a new artist's brush to apply it to the glass in a thin layer. Egg white dries very rapidly, so apply only enough at a time to hold one flower or leaf, and set the plant material in place immediately. The albumin will be invisible when dry, and will hold the weightless flowers steady until the covering layer of glass is added.

Lay the second glass very carefully over the pressed materials, matching the edges of the two sheets. Flatten this glass sandwich as completely as possible with a heavy paperweight. While the weight is still in place, take a wooden tongue depressor and, using special clear glass cement available from a glazer, go around the outside edges of the two glass sheets, exerting sufficient pressure to close up the thin crack between them. Leave the picture under weights overnight to be sure that the glass-glue is firmly set. This rimless picture lends itself to several possibilities: it can be placed on a small easel or on a plate holder; it can be cemented to its own permanent base — a glass-slab paperweight, or a narrow strip of black lacquered wood: after you measure and mark carefully, glue the picture upright onto its base with Epoxy cement; brace it on either side with a stack of books, and leave it overnight before moving it.

If the mounted picture looks unfinished without a frame, glue on inch-wide velvet ribbon or cloth tape to cover its edges, side and top, in imitation of Victorian passepartout. Brush the back of the tape with glue, center the tape on the crack between the two sheets of glass, and press it down on the edge of both sheets; then bend it onto the flat surfaces of the two sheets, and press it firmly between the fingers to smooth it.

PRESSED FLOWER TABLETOP

A pressed flower design on a glass-topped table makes a handsome top. Choose, preferably, a table whose metal rim extends at least half an inch above its own glass. Remove the tabletop and take it to a glass company;

This impressive autumn gift is easy to make. Pressed leaves of crimson dogwood, pale gold bittersweet and coppery tulip poplar are glued on sky blue poster board (from an art supply store) cut to fit under the glass top of a coffee table.

have them cut a piece of exactly the same size but of the thinnest weight. Clean both sheets thoroughly with detergent, and polish them with a soft cloth. Glue the pressed material to the original tabletop, add the lightweight glass, and seal the outer edges of the sheets with glass cement. Allow the glue to set for twenty-four hours before replacing the top in the table frame.

For a terrace or porch table top, a grouping of ferns or autumn leaves is not only more effective but more practical than an arrangement of pressed flowers. Caution the person who receives this handsome table not to place it in direct sunlight, which would fade the plant material very quickly.

DYEING PRESSED PLANT MATERIALS

Actually, the only way to be absolutely sure of preventing fading is to reinforce the colors of the pressed materials with dye. Dip ferns and deciduous foliage, after pressing them, in green liquid dye diluted with boiling water; do the dipping while the dye still is slightly steaming.

Then dry the foliage between paper towels and press it again, between white blotters or several thicknesses of paper toweling, for twenty-four hours.

Stabilize autumn leaves, laid flat on paper towels, by painting over their own colors with matching hot, dilute, liquid dye. For parti-colored leaves, prepare two or more shades of dye in small containers such as custard cups, and brush them on alternately, allowing the second tint to overlay the first slightly and thus blend the colors.

Color flowers, on the other hand, only *after* they are mounted. Use a very small camel's hair artist's brush, with so light a stroke that its tip barely touches the surface of the petals. Use only a small amount of dye, let it dry, and then add a second coat of color. It is not necessary to re-press these delicately dyed blossoms, since they already are glued flat to their mount, but they *must* dry for twenty-four hours before glass is placed above them.

PRESSED FLOWER DECOUPAGE

A new use for pressed flowers, and one that protects them as successfully as the most careful framing and glazing, is an adaptation of the increasingly popular technique of decoupage.

In eighteenth-century France, decoupage was the do-it-yourself substitute for rare and costly Oriental lacquer. A trimmed, hand-tinted print, or a motif cut from handpainted Chinese or French chinoiserie wallpaper, was pasted to the surface of a painted tray. There was an obvious difference of texture and height between the painted background and the mounted paper, and the problem was to blend the two into a smooth and unified surface. This was done with layer after layer of clear lacquer, each coat allowed to dry for twenty-four hours and sanded before the next coat was applied. As many as fifty or sixty coats might be required to sink a thick wallpaper motif completely. The original Oriental motifs soon were supplanted by French pastoral scenes and delicate floral designs as the craze for cut-and-paste spread to England and to America.

Using a modified version of this technique, twentieth-century craft enthusiasts decorate wooden boxes and plaques, metal trays and wastebaskets with cut-paper motifs or with decals. They often meld these appliqués and their backgrounds not with clear varnish (which darkens and yellows the colors it protects) but with the new colorless plastic finishes developed especially for decoupage work.

Pressed flowers make much more unusual and interesting decoupage designs than blossoms cut from paper or applied as decals. Far from harming the delicate flat blooms, clear plastic finish seals them beneath a hard and glassy surface that protects them indefinitely. In the center of a metal tray painted with three coats of black enamel, a spray of pressed pink dogwood blossoms and green leaves is startlingly beautiful; twigs and stems can be indicated with brown or gray enamel. On a wooden wall plaque, a tall and slender botany print takes on a new dimension. If you like, enamel the flat top surface of wood to contrast with the plant material and to match a color scheme, leaving the plaque's bevelled edges untreated; the clear plastic will give the wood an attractive finish.

Whether you use wood or painted metal as the basis for a decoupage of pressed flowers, it is important that you plan the design in detail before the first flower is glued. Pressed materials are damaged by handling, so they cannot be moved about like pawns on the tray or plaque until they fall into a pleasing pattern, nor can their position be changed once they are glued to the surface. Draw slightly smaller outlines, with white chalk that wipes away with a damp cloth, of each flower form, and erase and adjust the outlines until the design takes shape. Do not plan for the flowers to overlap. In the first place, their petals are translucent-thin, and there would be blurring of color. Second and more important, several more coats of plastic would be required to smooth the surface over this extra petal layer. Indicate pressed stems, if you have them, with chalk on the outline design. If stems are to be painted on, do them first and allow them to dry thoroughly before beginning the gluing process.

Cover the flower outlines with white glue, thinned with a few drops of cool water to make it flow easily from an artist's brush, and wait until the glue is tacky to the touch of a finger. Lift a pressed blossom with tweezers or with a moistened fingertip, and lay it gently over its sticky outline. Lay a sheet of white typewriter paper over the flower, and apply light pressure — with fingers, with the flat of a book, or with a doll-size rolling pin. Lift the paper, and immediately wipe away with the edge of a slightly dampened cloth any glue that has oozed from beneath the blossom. When all the flowers and/or leaves are in place, cover the whole design with white typewriter paper and weight it overnight with a large and heavy book.

Plastic decoupage finishes, with directions for their use, are available in hobby shops and wherever artist's supplies are sold. They come in two types: spray, and brush-on. Because the passage of the brush might dislodge or break the edges of the pressed flowers, colorless plastic in a pressurized spray can is preferable for this work. Holding the can about eighteen inches away from the decorated surface, move it slowly from side to side while applying a light but even spray coat. This first coat must be entirely dry and smooth to the touch before a second coat is applied. You can protect the project from dust by covering it, between coats, with a large overturned cardboard carton. It usually takes seven to ten sprayings to level the flowers and their background. If, however, the arrangement has been made on a tray intended not for display but for actual use, apply a good twenty spray coats to ensure complete protection. The plastic coating will be shiny as a sheet of clear glass; if you prefer a matte finish, add a last thin coat of white liquid wax, and buff it very lightly.

INEXPENSIVE PRESSED FLOWER GIFTS

NAPKIN RINGS WITH PRESSED FLOWERS

Dainty napkin rings decorated with pressed flowers are attractive accents for a luncheon table, and a set of four or more makes a much appreciated hostess gift. Small rolls of adhesive tape have outer protective rings of white metal that are perfect for decorating; some rolls of cellophane tape have circular plastic cores that also can serve. White rings encircled with pressed violets are extremely effective. You can glue florets of pink or blue hydrangea, lilac, phlox, geranium, or sweet William at intervals around a white ring for a multicolored design. On red or green plastic tape-cores, pressed white hydrangea or spirea florets make a striking contrast. For a holiday gift, ornament red rings with pine needles or cedar tips; use red geranium, phlox or sweet William on green circlets. In any case, apply the pressed flower decorations with white glue, and allow the glue to harden overnight. Then cover the decorated ring with a strip of clear self-stick *plastic* tape to keep the flowers in place and protect them from dampness.

PLACECARDS WITH PRESSED FLOWER DECORATIONS

Anyone who entertains often will find placecards useful, and these unusually pleasing ones are surprisingly quick and easy to make. Cut bright blue, green or yellow craft paper in four by three-inch rectangles, and fold each down the middle to make an easel-card four by one-and-a-half inches. In the upper left hand corner of one side, glue a single pressed white hydrangea floret, a white fruit tree or berry blossom, or three tiny white spirea florets. Over each blossom press a square of clear plastic tape. Present a dozen placecards with a small bottle of white ink for writing the names of party guests.

DECORATED NOTEPAPER

In similar fashion, apply pressed white flowers to a box of pale grey or blue notepaper sheets and matching envelopes. Center one or three florets one-half inch below the fold, to the left of course, and cover with clear tape. Use bright pressed florets for a box of white informals, a different color for each folded sheet.

Notepaper is an especially thoughtful gift for a new mother, and in this instance use blue or pink flowers on white paper. Several boxes, assorted as to color, are nice to have on hand for baby presents so that you are prepared for either exigency. White flowers on blue or gray paper, or assorted colors on white, are splendid home-from-the-hospital gifts for convalescents.

DESK SET WITH PRESSED FLOWERS

Expanding the old idea of the tin can pencil caddy, make a decorated desk set with holders for pencils, stamps, and paper clips from three cans of various sizes and a large round plastic lid. For pencils, choose a slender can of the fruit-nectar type; a squat mushroom or Vienna sausage can will hold a generous supply of paper clips, and a potted meat can will accommodate a roll of stamps. Paint both sides of the plastic lid and the cans, inside and out, with two coats of flat black enamel, and gild all the rims with gold paint and a very small artist's brush. Glue a cluster of small pressed flowers to one side of each painted can, and add a few pressed green leaves. Cover the cans with self-adhesive clear plastic, to protect the flower montages. Then fit·the cans attractively on the painted lid and cement them in place; the flowered side of each can should of course face outward. This really practical accessory keeps supplies at hand on the home desk, and takes up a minimum of space.

WOODEN KEY CHAIN DISC

A large flat wooden disk, with key chain attached, is easy to find at the bottom of a crowded purse, but costs several dollars in a boutique.

Such a disk is even more attractive when ornamented with pressed flowers than when decorated with painted designs or decals, and makes a marvelous all-occasion gift for college girls as well as for their mothers and grandmothers. A two-foot strip of thin plywood thirty-six inches wide will yield as many as forty four-inch circles. If there isn't a jigsaw enthusiast in your neighborhood, you can have the disks cut, for a fee, at the builder's supply store where the plywood is purchased. Each disk also must have a hole bored near its rim, through which you can thread a short self-lock key chain (from a hobby shop). (Large boys' clubs and senior citizens' centers often have woodworking shops, and in return for a donation toward club supplies, someone might be willing to cut and bore the plywood for you.)

Smooth the rim of a disk with sandpaper, and give both sides and edges of the plywood two coats of enamel — white, black, sage green, bright blue, or Chinese red. Glue a single large pressed flower, a cluster of small blooms, or a pressed autumn leaf to each side of the disk. Pink dogwood blossoms are striking on black disks, as are yellow pansies; fan-shaped yellow ginkgo leaves look well against sage green paint. Cover both sides of the key disk with clear self-stick plastic.

SANDWICH TRAY COVER WITH PRESSED FLOWERS

Your relatives and friends who entertain will find abundant use for a tray cover decorated with pressed flowers that keeps sandwiches or cookies fresh until all the guests have gathered. Cut a circle pattern from wrapping paper or cardboard, twelve inches in diameter for a medium-sized round tray. With pinking shears, cut a circle of white felt the size of the pattern; then cut two circles of clear plastic material, which can be bought at a variety store or salvaged from the unprinted portions of dry-cleaner's bags.

Glue colorful pressed flowers — all one color and variety or an assortment of shades and shapes — to the felt. The pressed blossoms can be scattered at random, or grouped in nosegays, or arranged in a wreath; a few small pressed leaves will enhance the composition. Cover the circle with white paper or white sheeting, and weight the flowers overnight with several heavy books. Next day, sandwich the decorated felt between the two layers of clear plastic, and machine-stitch the circular edges of the materials together, using a loose-tension setting and a basting-

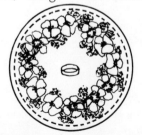

length stitch. Then attach a white plastic curtain ring in the center of the cover to serve as a lifter. Use double white thread and sew through all three layers of material. The plastic will not stick to the cookies, and if it becomes smeared, it can be wiped clean with a damp cloth.

BOOKMARK WITH PRESSED FLOWERS

A smaller but similar pressed flower gift is a bookmark made of black or colored felt and clear plastic material. Cut a strip of felt eight inches long and two-and-a-fourth inches wide, and one matching strip of clear plastic material; if you like, the ends of the strips can be pinked or scalloped. Glue a vertical motif of tiny pressed flowers to the felt, cover with white paper, and weight overnight with a heavy book. Then fit the clear plastic over the decorated felt, and machine-stitch the materials together with thread that matches the felt. This is a good "small remembrance" for a reader of any age and of either sex.

For a housewarming gift, make a felt slipcover for a hearth broom; glue on pressed flowers or small shells.

6.

"Glass" Flowers

Flowers dried by chemical methods are not really cured of decay, but are only arrested cases. Air-dried everlastings have a longer life-span, yet they, too, eventually return to dust. There are, however, other ways of preserving plant materials not for months or for years, but for a lifetime.

"GLASS" FLOWERS

The very popular, Italian-inspired "glass flowers" sold in boutiques and specialty shops are in fact molded of plastic. It is possible to create "glass" flowers that are not only more unusual than these but also far more authentic by coating real blooms with clear plastic. One must begin with air-dried or cured materials, for fresh flowers are eaten alive by the acid that is the hardening agent for liquid plastic.

The easiest, though not the most permanent, way to apply the plastic to the flowers is with a pressurized spray can of the same colorless coating plastic used to strengthen cured flowers before arranging them. Many thin but thorough coats are required to build up a thick but transparent glassy shield, and it is wise to practice on a sturdy strawflower before going on to more delicate and difficult cured blooms.

Balance the strawflower faceup on the rim of a juice glass — a chipped or cracked one will do as well as any other. Holding the spray can about a foot away, spray the surface of the flower. Wait until the petals are completely dry and smooth to the touch, then add a second spray coat. Add more sprayings, allowing adequate drying time between,

Cured bronze chrysanthemums acquired amber color and translucency when glazed with plastic spray. Given clear plastic drinking straws for stems, they are arranged with "glass" ivy leaves in a dime store bud vase. (In the language of flowers, chrysanthemums say "you're a wonderful friend".)

until the buildup on each petal is clearly visible. The petals are now rigid and can support the flower's weight, so you can safely remove the flower from the juice glass and place it facedown on newspaper. Spray coat the back of the blossom as carefully as the face, to ensure permanent protection.

Obviously these coated blooms are heavier than they originally were, and they will need rigid stems. Sections of bamboo dipped in hot green liquid dye will do, as will stiff green florist's wire. Much more esoteric are hollow clear glass or plastic stems — hospital drinking straws or laboratory pipettes which may be bought either straight or curved at a surgical supply company. Cover the rim of a pipette with clear household cement and insert the stub of a glazed flower's stem; the calyx of the flower will rest upon and be bonded to the rim.

BRUSHED-ON PLASTIC COATING

Patience and a steady hand are needed to glaze flowers with plastic applied with a brush, but only one coat (or at most two) will be required. The coating material is colorless plastic resin, called casting plastic, which is sold in hobby shops and from mail-order catalogs. (See Sources of Supply). As it comes from the can, the resin is a viscous liquid; the label will have detailed instructions for adding the catalyst or hardener that comes with it in a small plastic squeeze bottle. As it hardens, casting plastic generates heat and emits a penetrating though not unpleasant odor; use it *only* where ventilation is good, and preferably out of doors.

Measure one ounce of liquid plastic, pour it into a paper cup, and squeeze into it three drops of catalyst from the plastic bottle. Use a flat wooden popsicle stick to stir the plastic; do so gently so as to create as few bubbles as possible, but thoroughly. Place a flower faceup on a sheet of household plastic wrap laid over a pad of newspaper. With a plastic picnic spoon, dribble the coating resin over the flower's entire surface; spread the resin evenly with the popsicle stick, and separate the petals with a wooden toothpick. (One ounce of resin will coat the face of one large flower or three small ones.) Let the plastic dry thoroughly — to be on the safe side, allow about four hours for this. Then lift the plastic wrap and peel it away from the edges of the flower; turn the flower over. Mix half an ounce of resin with two drops of hardener, and with it coat the back of the flower. After three hours it should be smooth, well glazed, dry and ready to be attached with liquid cement to a clear glass stem.

The heat generated by the plastic during its curing process will cause the thin petals of some flowers to become translucent. This only adds to their attractiveness, for they seem actually to be made of glass.

USES OF GLASS FLOWERS

GLASS FLOWERS TO TOP GLASS OR PLASTIC BOXES

Glass flowers make very attractive toppers for wrapped gift packages, but can be used much more effectively to decorate clear glass or plastic boxes. As a present for a gifted needlewoman, buy a flat plastic thread box at a sewing center. With liquid household cement, attach to the box top one or more glazed flowers or a spray of leaves cured in silica gel and brushed with casting plastic.

GLASS POINSETTIA PLANT

Looking to the future, let this year's Christmas poinsettia provide next year's holiday gift plant. While they still are fresh and jaunty, cut the blooms and the leaves from each poinsettia stalk. Cure them in silica gel for seven days, and glaze them with brushed-on casting plastic as soon as they are removed from the drying agent. Let them stand in open air for twenty-four hours, and then seal each blossom and leaf in an individual plastic bag, and store them in a cardboard box. As the holiday season approaches, wrap a five-inch clay flower pot with green florist's foil, and fill it with wallpaper cleaner or ready-mix concrete. Force a single slender bamboo or polygonum cane down through the center of the filler, and paint the surface of cleaner or cement brown to look like soil. Cement several glazed leaves along the vertical stem. Then cover the top of the stalk with liquid cement and upon it balance a glass poinsettia bloom. If your original plant was a large one, it may yield enough leaves and blossoms to make several such gifts, which are suitable for patients in nursing homes as well as for friends who tend to kill live houseplants with kindness.

CANDLEHOLDERS DECORATED WITH GLASS FLOWERS

An unusual and attractive wedding present is a pair of clear glass candleholders with glazed flowers encased in their bases. For these, you will need two footed juice glasses — preferably those with hollow flared bases — plus two small glass salad plates, from a variety store. In the center of each plate, cement a round glazed flower of mounded shape: a half-open rose, a honeycomb dahlia, a chrysanthemum. Brush glass cement around the rim of a juice glass and invert it over the flower, pressing it down upon the plate to ensure bonding.

If the base of the glass is hollow, you can fit a candle into it with no further effort. If, however, the base is flat on the bottom, use glass glue to attach a clear one-and-a-half ounce shot glass (also from a variety store) to its center; the rim of glass base that surrounds this candle cup will serve as a drip-catcher.

COSTUME JEWELRY FROM GLAZED FLOWERS

GLASS FLOWER EARRINGS

Among their jewelry findings, hobby shops offer inexpensive earring-backs of pierced, clip, or screw types, and these are the bases of pretty glass flower earrings that make delightful gifts. Any small cured or dried flowers, glazed front and back with plastic, spray or casting, can be attached with household or Epoxy cement to the metal disks of button or drop earring-backs. Good possibilities for this purpose are dried star-flowers or strawflowers, and cured tom thumb zinnias, wax button ranunculus, or feverfew. Glazed four-petalled single florets of cured pink hydrangea look like miniature dogwood blossoms.

MEDALLIONS WITH GLAZED PRESSED FLOWERS

At costume jewelry counters in department (and variety) stores, plain disks of gold- or silver-colored metal are sold on long chains. These are meant to be monogrammed, but pressed flowers and casting plastic will turn them into pop art medallions that will please coeds or career girls. Using white glue, attach one pressed flower of medium size to the center of a large disk and allow it to dry overnight. Then, cover it with a thick coating of casting plastic applied with a brush. The flower could be a wild rose or a daisy, nasturtium, columbine, delphinium or windflower blossom from the garden. Half an ounce of resin mixed with one drop of catalyst will be quite enough to coat the disk; pour a small amount of the mixture over the flower and spread it out to the edges of the disk with a small artist's brush. Allow the plastic to harden overnight before the disk is handled. A montage of smaller flowers may be used instead of a single blossom; lilac, spirea or abelia florets and blossoms of phlox, sweet William, or primrose are all effective possibilities.

FLOWER DISK FOR A CHARM BRACELET

By the same method, a plain silver disk can become a unique bracelet charm to delight a fellow gardener. Two flowers, one glued to either side of the disk, will double its attractiveness, but the first flower's coating of plastic must harden for twenty-four hours before you glue the second blossom to the other side of the charm. Depending upon the size of the disk, select larkspur or bluebell florets, violets or yellow violas, forget-me-nots or baby's breath.

FLOWERS ENCASED IN GOLD

Boutiques and better catalogues offer attractive, Austrian-made pins that are actual rosebuds or holly leaves plated with gold. With liquid plastic and fused gold, you can acquire the Midas touch and turn cured flowers into golden costume jewelry.

Among the jewelry findings at hobby shops are straight and circular brooch-backs and earring-backs to which cured flowers can be adhered with Epoxy cement. From the costume jewelry display at a variety store come inexpensive "gold" circle pins that will make fine brooch-backs for large round cured blossoms. You can buy fluid fused gold in one-ounce bottles where artists' supplies are sold, or by mail order. (See

Sources of Supply.) The metallic dust, from a separate packet, must be mixed with its accompanying liquid resin just before it is used.

In a paper cup, mix one ounce of clear casting resin with ten drops of catalyst. The double amount of hardener will cause the plastic to cure very rapidly; its heat will destroy the color of the cured blossom it coats, but since the flower is to be gilded, this does not matter.

Pick up a cured flower — a daisy, perhaps — with tweezers by the stub of its stem and hold it face up in the left hand. Using a small artist's brush, coat the center of the blossom and then the petals with the liquid resin. Be sure that every bit of the surface receives a thin, even layer of the plastic. Still holding the stem with the tweezers, turn the daisy over and paint the back of its calyx and petals with resin. By the time the back of the flower is covered, the plastic on the flower's face will have begun to harden, so if any straightening or separating of petals is necessary it must be done immediately with a wooden toothpick. After ten minutes, it is safe to lay the flower faceup on kitchen plastic wrap, where it should remain overnight. If the petals are then the least bit limber, mix half an ounce of liquid resin with six drops of hardener, and repaint only the back of the daisy. Again allow twelve hours' drying time before going on to the next step. Clip the uncoated stem of the daisy off flush with the base of the calyx.

Apply a small amount of Epoxy cement to a circular brooch back; wait two minutes, and settle the daisy face up on the glue. Let the Epoxy

Two popular gifts for Christmas fund-raising. The blossom (left) is a real narcissus which has been cured in sand, coated first with casting plastic and then with fused gold, and cemented to a pin-back. At the right is a pin made of tiny casuarina cones bound with fine gold cord.

cement harden undisturbed for twenty-four hours to effect a permanent bond.

Now mix the metallic powder with its resinous liquid, hold the flower by its pin, and brush the fused gold onto the face of the daisy. Do the center first, using a small camel's hair artist's brush, and then each petal separately from center to tip. Apply fused gold smoothly and accurately, as you can't retrace the brush strokes without leaving a raised streak.

Cap the fused gold tightly and wait six hours for the gilded face of the flower to dry thoroughly. Then stir the gilding liquid and coat the back of the flower; brush the back of the metal pin as well as the flower surface. After six hours, the daisy encased forever in gold will be ready for presentation.

Narcissus, anemones, single roses, individual leaves or short flat foliage sprays respond to the golden touch of a brush, but tight rosebuds should be dipped in fused gold. The excess must be brushed off immediately, with long even strokes, from the base to the tip of the bud.

IMBEDDING FLOWERS IN PLASTIC

Flowers can be forever captured, like flies in amber, in clear plastic resin. Liquid casting plastic, with catalyst added, takes on the shape of any mold into which it is poured, and hardens into a glass-hard transparent solid mass. Flexible, reusable polyethelene molds are sold along with the resin at hobby shops and by mail order, but any hollow container of glass, rigid plastic, wood, china or metal can double as a mold provided it has smooth sides and is larger at the top than at the bottom. A hardened casting can easily be removed from the flexible polyethelene by bending the mold. With any other material, a mold-release coating must be used. Commercial mold release is available where plastic supplies are sold, and is absolutely necessary for wood or metal containers; heavy mineral oil works just as well for glass, china, or plastic containers.

Only cured, pressed or air-dried plant material can be cast in plastic. The moisture in fresh flowers, turned to steam by the heat generated during the plastic's hardening process, literally cooks them from the inside.

DOME PAPERWEIGHT

When it comes to casting, it's wise to start modestly, before entrusting the cream of your cured-flower crop to this medium. Begin with a glass

custard cup and one flower, a tom-thumb zinnia, to make a dome-shaped paperweight. Gauge the capacity of the custard cup by filling it with water and pouring the water into a measuring cup. Dry the custard cup carefully, and coat its inner surface generously with mineral oil. Pour out the excess oil and turn the cup upside down on paper towelling to drain for forty-five minutes.

Measure one-third as much casting resin as the cup will hold, and pour the liquid plastic into a paper cup. Following the directions on the resin can, add the correct number of drops of catalyst to the paper cup — five drops of hardener usually are recommended for each ounce of liquid plastic. Stir slowly with a wooden popsicle stick or a plastic picnic spoon; mix in the catalyst thoroughly but try for as few bubbles as possible. Lift the spoon, wait for bubbles to rise to the surface, and puncture them with a wooden toothpick. Slowly pour the mixture into the prepared custard cup mold.

Allow the plastic to cure to a jelly-like consistency. This will take from fifteen to thirty minutes, depending upon the depth of the casting and the temperature of the air. To be sure that the plastic is ready to receive its embedment, touch the surface with a wooden toothpick. If the pick pushes in easily but the plastic peaks as its tip is withdrawn, the consistency is right.

Pour a second batch of liquid resin into the paper cup, the same quantity as before. This time, add only *three* drops of hardener per ounce of resin, and mix well.

Using tweezers, lift the cured zinnia by the stub of its stem and lower it slowly into the paper cup until it is just submerged in the plastic. Lift it carefully and place it at once, upside down, upon the gelled plastic in the mold. Pour the rest of the liquid resin slowly over and around the flower. Use a wooden toothpick to settle the petals and to probe beneath the flower for air bubbles. This second layer of the casting, with a smaller amount of catalyst in it, will harden more slowly. Test it frequently with a toothpick, and add a third batch of resin as soon as the layer has gelled.

For the third and final layer of the casting, you needn't fill the custard cup; just cover the back of the zinnia to a depth of one-fourth inch; one ounce of liquid resin probably will suffice, and it should once more be mixed with *five* drops of catalyst. Allow the whole casting to harden completely before attempting to remove it from the mold; a properly cured plastic casting makes a clicking sound when struck with the edge of a wooden popsicle stick. Turn the mold over and tap it lightly; the clear dome with its imbedded zinnia should slide slowly out.

Occasionally, plastic will not cure click-hard, even after several hours; its surface will remain slightly sticky. Should this happen, place the mold in the oven at 150° for thirty minutes; remove it and run the tip of a paring knife around the edge of the casting. This unmolding trick works for all except polyethelene molds.

If the casting *still* does not come out when the cup is turned upside down and tapped with the handle of a tableknife, set the mold in the freezing compartment of the refrigerator to shrink the plastic away from the sides of the mold. After this freezer treatment, the casting will be cloudy when it emerges from the cup, but fifteen minutes at room temperature will restore its pristine clarity.

HOW IMBEDDED FLOWERS LOOK

Miraculously, lilies of the valley and daisies that turned creamy when chemically cured are restored by the casting process to snowy whiteness; leaves lose their thin and dusty look; colors brighten, petals plump, and flowers look dewy-fresh. Furthermore, this time, the freshness lasts!

FLOWER BUTTONS AND BROOCHES

Clear "glass" buttons with tiny real flowers imbedded in them, perfect for a sweater, a blouse or a summer dress, are unexcelled as gifts for the home dressmaker or knitter. You can buy sets of reusable half-round polyethylene molds, three-fourths inch or one inch in diameter, at hobby shops. Larger cabochon castings, for pins, can be made in individual glass salt dishes. Button shanks and pin mounts are among the metal jewelry findings available at hobby shops.

Cured tiny "wax-button" ranunculus, feverfew, cinquefoil blooms and individual florets of lilac, spirea, hydrangea or salvia are good miniature embedments.

Six three-fourths-inch buttons require one ounce of liquid resin with five drops of hardener, and in such small quantities plastic sets very quickly. No sooner is the first layer poured into the six molds than it is time to prepare the second batch of plastic; use one-half ounce of resin with only two drops of catalyst. Dip each flower carefully, with tweezers, into the liquid resin and place it upside down in a mold, and then pour the remaining resin over the flowers — it should fill the six tiny molds. As soon as this layer has gelled, place a button shank upright in the center of each mold, with the stem imbedded in the plastic and its ring just touching the surface. When the miniature castings have dried click-hard, turn the multiple mold upside down and twist its edges slightly to dislodge the buttons.

The method of making a convex flower pin in a saltcellar differs only in that the glass must be coated with mold-release or mineral oil. A half-ounce of resin with three drops of catalyst will make the first layer; when this has jelled, mix another half-ounce of resin with two drops of hardener, dip the flower, and place it in the mold. Pour enough of the resin into the saltcellar to fill it to the brim, and when the surface is gelid lay the metal pin mount across it. The cabochon casting will come from the mold with its pin already attached.

IMBEDDING IN RIMMED BUTTONS

Shank-type buttons with raised rims enclosing solid color surfaces can be bought at sewing centers, and each such button can be embellished with a single tiny, flat white flower — a spirea, viburnum, tea-olive, euonymus or pyracantha floret. Since you will not want to remove this miniature casting from the button-well, do not use mold release. Mix one ounce of liquid resin with three drops of catalyst in a paper cup. Lift a floret with tweezers, dip it in the plastic, and center it faceup on a button — it is easier to do this if the buttons are left on their card, which holds them level and steady. Dip a plastic picnic spoon in the resin and cover the flower by dribbling resin over it; use enough to fill the button cavity to the top of the rim. One ounce of resin will fill at least a dozen three-quarter-inch buttons.

MOLDING FLOWERS IN PAPERWEIGHTS

Any transparent hollow glass or plastic container can become a one-time mold, a permanent holder for a flower casting. Plastic dome molds for paperweights can be bought at hobby shops or by mail, but paperweights need not be mound shaped. The glass funiture-cups sold at variety and hardware stores are perfect for small flat paperweights; each will hold a single medium-sized flat flower, such as a daisy, a cosmos, or a Korean chrysanthemum. An office supply company is a good source of clear glass paperweight material: rectangular oblongs designed to hold paper clips and rubber bands; round sponge bowls; flat glass-slab paperweights with raised edges; square cigarette boxes.

A most unusual and highly personal wedding gift can be made in a cigarette box or a paperclip holder. Ask the mother of the bride to give you a spray or two of lily-of-the-valley from the bride's bouquet; cure the flowers in silica gel and imbed them faceup in casting plastic with a pressed four-leaf clover. Follow the directions for layering a casting in a custard cup, but use no mold release. Add enough resin for the final layer to fill the glass mold to the very brim.

A flat glass slab becomes a millefleur paperweight by the same method used to add single florets to raised rim buttons. Use any small flat colorful cured blossoms and/or leaves: hydrangea florets in pink, blue or white; phlox, geranium or sweet William florets; pansies, violets, bluets, johnny-jump-ups; cinquefoil, strawberry, blackberry, or wild rose blooms. After dipping them in resin, arrange these blossoms facedown on the clean dry glass slab, and pour more resin over them to the top of the rim. One-and-a-quarter ounces of resin plus four drops of hardener will fill one slab; leave it undisturbed until it is smooth, hard and dry. When the paperweight is turned over, the flowers are magnified as they are seen through the thick glass.

FLOWER-OF-THE-MONTH BIRTHDAY PRESENTS

A flower-of-the-month paperweight is a very personal and thoughtful birthday present for man, woman, or child. The list of monthly flowers varies from one authority to another, but in most parts of the country the following garden-grown blooms would be appropriate:

> January — snowdrop or carnation
> February — pussy willow or primrose
> March — daffodil
> April — violet, sweet pea or lily
> May — lily-of-the-valley
> June — daisy or rose
> July — larkspur or delphinium

August — zinnia or gladiolus
September — aster
October — dahlia or calendula
November — chrysanthemum
December — holly

Make such a paperweight in any mold of appropriate size and shape: June's daisy in a flat glass furniture caster; February's pussy willow in a shallow oblong; October's dahlia in a dome; December's holly in a cube.

FLOWERS IN DRAWER PULLS

Metamorphose small round glass percolator tops, which are sold separately at variety and department stores, into flower-filled pulls for drawers or cabinets. You will need a shallow pan full of sand to hold the tops steady during the imbedding process, and a quarter-inch stove bolt one-and-a-half inches long for each drawer pull you plan to make. The same tiny white or colored flowers listed for millefleur paperweights will be right in size, as will wax-button ranunculus and feverfew.

To make eight drawer pulls, measure three ounces of resin and add ten drops of catalyst. Hold a blossom with tweezers, dip it in the resin, and place it face down in the cavity of a percolator top; center the flower and settle its petals with a wooden toothpick. Pour in resin on top of the flower, filling the cavity to the point at which its bulbous surface narrows to a short neck, and allow this plastic to harden completely. Then mix one-and-a-half ounces of resin with eight drops of hardener. Fill the neck of each percolator top two-thirds full, wait five minutes, and place a stove bolt, head down, in the center of each neck, pressing the head of the bolt down upon the surface of the solid first layer of plastic. As the resin hardens, the bolt becomes an integral part of the drawer pull. Slip it through the drilled hole in a drawer front and tighten it, with its nut to hold the pull in place; if the bolt is too long, cut it short with a hacksaw.

A set of drawer pulls in white, pastel, or assorted colors makes a marvelous house present. They can be used on kitchen cabinets or on nursery chests of drawers, and are especially nice for medicine and bathroom storage cabinets.

LAMP FINIALS

Small percolator tops filled in this way with tiny flowers make fine finials for table lamps. From the lampshade display in a department store, buy a shade-riser for each finial; these brass tubes are about an inch and a half long. One end is hollow and threaded to screw on the harp of the lamp; the other end is solid, and threaded to receive a brass knob. Pour enough resin into the neck of a percolator top to fill it two-thirds full, and stand a shade-riser, solid end down, in the center of the neck. When the plastic has hardened, you will have a brass finial ending in a flower-filled glass globe, and it will screw into the harp of any lamp. A pair of these makes a fine shower gift or birthday remembrance, and they look very charming atop dressing table lamps.

FLOWER-EMBEDDED DOORKNOBS

Make dandy doorknobs from large-sized percolator top replacements with embedments of cured ragged robins, daisies, button chrysanthemums, tom thumb zinnias, dwarf marigolds or asters. At a hardware store, buy the sort of two-piece metal doorknob shank that screws together in the middle to make a rod. After you've embedded the flowers in the cavities in two large percolator tops, fill them with resin to the point at which their necks begin and let this plastic harden completely. One-and-a-half ounces of plastic, plus five drops of catalyst should be sufficient. Mix another ounce of resin with five drops of hardener; insert one half of the doorknob shank in each neck, and add enough resin to fill it to the brim. It will be necessary to brace the shank-half upright until the resin hardens.

These doorknob sets are especially attractive for closet, bedroom and bath. The two portions of the shank will slip inside the metal sleeve that lines the hole through the door, and the glass knob will fit against the original knob's backplate.

DECANTER STOPPER

One large glass percolator top, with a single flower embedment, can be a decorative and practical stopper for a decanter or a wine bottle — an all-occasion gift for a man or for a couple. Combine one ounce of casting plastic with three drops of hardener, dip a cured flower in the mixture, and place the flower facedown in the hollow glass cup. Fill the cavity and the neck of the percolator top with resin and allow it to cure until it is gelid. Insert the head of a one-and-a-fourth-inch pointed wood screw

For birthday or shower gifts, flowers preserved forever in plastic. The glass furniture-caster paperweight holds a daisy, the flower for June; a decanter stopper, made of a large glass percolator top, encases a bright blue ragged robin; the curved glass dome mold magnifies hemlock cones, cedar sprigs, and bittersweet berries.

into the neck of the percolator top, straighten it, and brace it upright until the plastic is click-hard. Then work the screw slowly and carefully down into a cork that is one inch in diameter at the top.

LAMINATING PLANT MATERIALS IN PLASTIC

Anything that is laminated is put together in layers, and you can permanently preserve pressed leaves, flowers, or flat foliage sprays by laminating them between thin layers of clear plastic. The resulting "sandwich" has a wide variety of uses. It can be of any size from coaster to room-divider panel: trivets, place mats, trays, wall hangings, door or window-panes, and square lamp shades are only a few of the many possibilities.

PANEL CASTING

The first step in panel casting is to create a frame the exact size and shape of the desired finished sheet. You can make this frame of wood or metal strips, but it is constructed much more easily of heavy-duty aluminum foil.

To make a six-inch square trivet with a red maple leaf in it, you will need a strip of foil twenty-six inches long and six inches wide. Lay the strip flat on a table and fold the edges in lengthwise, butting them

87

together at the center. Now fold this long strip in half lengthwise, pressing the layers of foil firmly together with the flat of a ruler, to obtain a firm but flexible metal strip one-and-a-half-inches wide, that can easily be bent to any shape. Bend the strip into a six-inch square, and tuck one end behind the other at a corner. Coat the inner surfaces of the frame with mineral oil, and allow the foil form to drain on paper toweling for forty-five minutes.

On a smooth flat surface (a glass tabletop is ideal) spread a sheet of Mylar from a hobby shop that sells plastic materials; ordinary kitchen plastic wrap *can* be used for this eight-inch square protective sheet, but Mylar is much better for the purpose.

Center the metal frame on the plastic film. Cut a six-inch square of fiberglass mat (also available where casting plastic is sold) to fit inside the mold. This fiberglass, which is used for lampshades as well as for laminating, is white and opaque, but it will disappear completely during the curing of the panel.

In a paper cup, mix four ounces of liquid resin with twenty drops of catalyst, and spread a thin layer of the liquid plastic on the Mylar within the frame. Smooth the plastic with the edge of a wooden tongue depressor, and fit the fiberglass neatly into the frame on top of the layer of resin. Flatten the fiberglass with the tongue depressor, pour a second layer of the resin over the mat. and spread it out. As the liquid resin soaks into it, the white fiberglass will gradually disappear. Look carefully for air bubbles, and prick them with a wooden toothpick.

After fifteen minutes, when the surface of the casting has barely begun to gel, mix three ounces of liquid resin with nine drops of hardener in an aluminum pie tin. Lift the autumn leaf with tweezers and dip it, flat, into the plastic in the pie tin; then center the leaf facedown on the square casting and smooth it out carefully with the rounded edge of the tongue depressor. Pour the resin remaining in the pie tin slowly over the leaf, and spread it carefully out to the edges of the mold with the edge of the tongue depressor. Again watch for, and pop, any air bubbles, with a wooden toothpick. (If the leaf insists upon floating on top of the resin instead of remaining properly submerged, anchor it with a second square of fiberglass mat and another ounce of resin with five drops of hardener.) Now lay a six-inch square of Mylar on top of the resin, and allow the casting to harden for two hours. Remove the foil mold, and peel off the top and bottom layers of Mylar to reveal the thin flat transparent trivet with the maple leaf glowing at its center.

Smooth any irregularities of the trivet's edges with dampened sandpaper, which you also can use to round the corners slightly for a neater finish.

LAMINATED TABLETOPS

Transparent tabletops with pressed flowers laminated in them are especially attractive wedding gifts and are actually easier to make than the trivet just described. Select a table whose metal rim extends at least three-eights of an inch above its own glass top, which will be the base of the casting.

First wash the glass and dry it carefully. Mix resin and hardener as before, using enough to cover the surface of the glass. Do not cover the glass with Mylar, but pour the resin directly on the glass and smooth it out to the metal table rim. You will not need to reinforce this casting with a fiberglass mat, since the rigid glass tabletop will be a part of the finished panel.

As soon as the surface of this first layer of resin begins to gel (eight to ten minutes) mix twice the first amount of resin with hardener — three drops per ounce — in an aluminum pie tin. Lift a pressed flower or leaf with tweezers, dip it flat into the resin, being sure to coat both sides, and lay it right side up on the tabletop. Continue until all the flowers and leaves are in position. Pour the remaining resin very carefully over the flowers and smooth it with the edge of a tongue depressor. Add a top sheet of Mylar cut to fit the tabletop, and only remove it after the casting has cured and hardened for two hours.

LAMINATING WITH SHEET PLASTIC

A showy but far more simple method of laminating pressed flowers or leaves is to seal them between two thin sheets of clear plastic (Plexiglas). It goes without saying that the two sheets used should be exactly the same size. Large hobby shops usually stock small-sized sheets of Plexiglas and the transparent cement made especially for bonding plastic to plastic; large sheets, or special sizes cut to meaure, may be obtained from firms listed under "Plastics Suppliers" in the yellow pages of the telephone directory. Sheet plastic is available in various weights; for this purpose it should be no more than one-eighth inch thick. This lightweight, flexible material is unsuitable for unsupported tabletops, but makes stunning and eminently practical trivets, place mats, screens, and room dividers.

Lay a sheet of clean dry Plexiglas flat on a table, and plan a design of pressed blossoms or foliage for it. A design that's too large in proportion to the total area will be less attractive than an uncrowded one. Three small flowers, a few bamboo leaves, a single fern frond — enough is enough. Beat the white of an egg until foamy, and use an artist's brush to paint the albumin on the back of a fern frond; position the frond immediately on the panel and press it down. Lay a sheet of white typewriter paper over the fern and apply pressure with a book or with a rolling pin. For small flowers, brush the albumin not on the flower but on the plastic, and lay the flower at once upon it, using tweezers or a moistened fingertip to lift the blossom. Wait three hours for the eggwhite to dry.

Following the directions that come with the special plastic cement, apply this glue in a quarter-inch stripe around the outer edge of the decorated panel and fit the edges of the two sheets very carefully together. Weight the plastic sandwich with large heavy books extending over its edges, and leave the books in place for twenty-four hours.

7.

Pinecones: Flowers That
Wooden Grow

This lucky earth is generously endowed with trees, and, in accordance with the Master plan, each brings forth its fruit in season. Bloom follows bud; fruit swells where flower fades; seeds fall from fruit's protective covering to start the cycle over. Cone-bearing evergreens follow this design for living, but they do so with a difference: their blooms look like fleshy fruits, and their wooden fruits have petals!

Within a conifer's petalled fruits are wooden blossoms that have the permanence of plastic flowers without the stigma of artificiality. They are washable and unbreakable; they can take on all the hues of the rainbow, and their colors do not fade. Flowers can be made from any size cone, from half-inch hemlocks to twenty-four-inch sugar pines, and the best cone to use is the kind most readily available. Search the ground around a feathery white pine for long slim finger-shapes; pull the squat, light brown rosettes from a Scotch or Mugho pine; gather two-inch oval oblongs beneath a scrub pine, or fat eight-inch cylinders under a long-leaf pine; look for miniature full-blown beige roses on the limb of a larch.

As you collect the raw materials for these naturally permanent blossoms, reject only the gray cones that are brittle with the dryness of age, and the black cones that are soft and rotted at the stem from lying half-buried in damp ground. Immature gray-green cones with undeveloped scales will be valuable "buds" in future flower arrangements. Bright brown cones with tightly closed scales can be made to open up — left uncovered in a heated room, they may do so unassisted, but even stubborn specimens will respond to treatment. Arrange them in a single layer on a cookie sheet, and toast them in a slow (225°) oven for an hour. Their scale petals will spread out and down; their tiny winged seeds will be loosened, and will fall out in response to shaking.

MAKING FLOWERS FROM PINECONES

Only three tools are required to turn cones into coneflowers: a pair of long-handled pruning clippers (the "gooseneck" type) for cutting large, tough cones; wire-cutters or tin-snips for severing slender cone-cores; a pair of long-nosed pliers for twisting off individual scales.

CUTTING A MEDIUM-SIZED CONE

Choose a medium-sized cone to practise on, and examine it; its woody scales will be attached in circular rows to a stiff center stalk. Count up five rows from the base of the cone, and insert the blades of a pair of tin-snips between two rows of scales. If the scales are too close together to admit the blades, remove one row: grasp each scale with the tips of a pair of pliers, and twist it off the cone's stem. Push the tin-snips in as far as they will go, so that the center stalk is at the blades' dividing point, and snip. The detached base of the cone will have a flat top, and from its core a corolla of scales will ray out like petals from the center of a daisy.

If the top section of the cone contains at least three more rows of flattish petal scales, cut another slice by the same method. If there is not another "daisy" there, use the pliers to pull scales from the bottom of the segment until only six or eight tilted tip scales are left; these angled petals will resemble a half-opened bud. You can instead pull off all but the top four scales; these stubby, rounded prickles will have the look of a forsythia floret.

CUTTING A LARGE CONE

Even a large, seemingly impermeable cone is not too difficult to cut. If there is no room for the pruning clipper's blades between its scales, remove a row of scales around its equator. Pull out one scale with pliers, twisting to separate its base from the center core. This should give sufficient space to insert the tips of the tin-snips, and their sharp blades will readily cut through a circle of scales near the cone stem. Now fit the pruning clipper's blades around the core and quickly pull the handles together, hard; if the stem does not snap under this first assault, press the blades firmly into the cuts already made, and try again. Laying a tough cone on the floor, on its side, may give you extra leverage as you work the clipper from above it. This cutting process is much less difficult than it sounds, and is certainly easier (and safer) than sawing the cone in two.

A large cone should yield at least three flowers. If its petals are recurved at the base, the first slice from the bottom of the cone will resemble a chrysanthemum rather than a daisy if you make the base of the cone the face of the coneflower. From the mid-section of the cone you can expect to realize two huge daisy shapes, each having three rows of petals, and in addition there should be an opening flower bud from the top of the cone.

FLOWERS FROM SMALL CONES

The tough, pointed rosette of the Scotch or Mugho pine will yield at most two flowers. Halfway up, this cone has a flat plateau; in the top portion, the stiff scales are attached to the stem at a 45° angle. With the tips of a pair of pliers, press opposite angled scales together, upward and toward the stem. Move the pliers around the cone, crunching its top into a tight bunch. Now, holding the pliers horizontally, grasp the bunched scales firmly and twist off the top of the cone. If your cone is old, this will be easy. Fresh cones (bright brown and glossy) will give more trouble; protect the hand that holds the rough cone base by wearing a glove. Don't throw away the top you twisted off; chances are a forsythia blossom can be salvaged from those crumpled scales. The base of the cone, with its flat top and pointed scales, is remarkably like a Tom Thumb zinnia.

Use this method to halve cones of the slash-and-jack-pines, also. Old cones will snap apart in response to the twisting pressure of the pliers; fresh cones have stringy stems that fray as they are twisted in two. This is good, for it creates a different flower — one with a fuzzy center. The long, slim, flexible cone of the white pine (strobus) has rounded scales almost as thin as the petals of a living flower, and its soft center stem is easily cut with tin-snips. Each cone will furnish a spiky tip plus three or four flattish flowers.

Larch cones are soft — leathery rather than woody — but these mounded two-inch roses keep their shape for years. There are two kinds of midget hemlock cones. Those from the more common Canadian hemlock are only half the size of their Carolina cousins, and simulate tiny roses with no treatment at all. Leave some as they are, for use in miniature arrangements, and turn the rest into fruit-tree blossoms. With pliers, twist out the top half of the cone and discard it — pressure will have crushed the delicate scales. Then, working from the bottom, carefully pull off scales one by one, with the fingers, until only two rows are left; the diminutive cuplike flower that remains is like a pear blossom or a buttercup.

STEMS FOR CONEFLOWERS

Now is the time to give each coneflower a wire stem. The variety store's hardware counter will offer coils of single-strand aluminum or copper wire, and of hair-fine aluminum wire. A heavy green wire precut to short lengths is available from your florist; its stiffness makes it harder to work with, and it is needed only for the very heaviest cones. Of course, the larger the blossom the stronger its stem should be, and the size wire you select will depend upon the size and weight of your coneflowers. For a medium-sized daisy, use single-strand all-purpose wire. Cut a twelve-inch length from the coil with wire-cutters. Hold the daisy upside down and wrap the wire around its center stem above the lowest row of petals. Pull the wire taut and twist it securely together, leaving a free end at least eight inches long. Little hemlock cone roses or buttercups are almost weightless, and the nearly invisible hair-wire is best for them. It is the right type, too, for spiky cone tips and for very small daisies destined to be bunched into nosegays.

WOOD ROSES

The Cedar of Lebanon is a decorative tree, and is often chosen for planting because of its Biblical and historical associations; its cousin, the deodar cedar, is a graceful and shapely evergreen that is favored for specimen planting. Both grow tall. Cones form on their topmost branches — fat brown globes that open their scales as they mature during their second winter. They shatter as the winds of March worry them free and blow them clear of the lower branches, and each cone peels like an artichoke as it comes apart. The loose lower scales are flat, fan-shaped, and about two inches wide. Scales further up the cone are first slightly and then sharply curved, and smaller. Gather the scales into a paper bag, and keep searching. That lump, almost buried under the needles at the base of the tree by the force of its fall — pick it up and examine it. The top inch of the cone has remained intact, in the form of a perfect full-blown rose!

If cedar wood roses are brought into the arid atmosphere of a heated house, the lower petals may dry and fall off. To prevent this (and to keep the flower perfect for years to come) squeeze plastic wood from a tube into the hole left by the cone's center stem. If the stem has broken off at the base of the rose, a coating of plastic wood over the center back of the flower will hold the scales in place. Plastic wood lightens as it dries to a pale straw color, and hardens to a permanent bond with the woody cone. Once it has set, you can easily attach a stem to the rose by passing a length of wire above the outer ring of scales and drawing it tight with a twist; since the rose is heavy, use lightweight green florist's wire.

CEDAR CONE BASE

Occasionally you may find a twig bearing the unshattered base of a cedar cone. It will have several rows of scales gummed tight together, and rising from its middle will be the pointed spike that was the cone's center stem. Squeeze white glue or liquid cement around the stem to hold the petals invisibly to it, attach a wire to its base, and set this strange object aside for future reference. If its rows of scales are flat, it suggests an anthurium; if the scales curve upward, it looks like an oriental poppy.

CONSTRUCTED FLOWERS

Now turn your attention to your collection of loose outer cedar scales. Fit five of the largest, flattest ones together in a circle, pointed bases touching in the center: a wild rose. In the circle of your thumb and forefinger, fit four or more of the curved scales from the mid-section of the cone: a tulip. How can you fasten these petals together in a permanent flower form? Glue will not hold them, nor will liquid household cement, but plastic wood will. Plastic wood is available at any hardware or paint store, and at variety stores; be sure to buy it in a tube rather than in a can.

SINGLE ROSE

On a sheet of heavy-duty aluminum foil, place a few drops of salad oil and spread it into a circle with a fingertip. Cut a twelve-inch length of all-purpose aluminum wire, and twist a loop half an inch in diameter at one end. Squeeze a quarter-sized "coin" of plastic wood in the center of the oiled circle, making it at least one-fourth inch thick. Lay the loop of wire on the plastic wood, and press it down until it is well imbedded. Now arrange five fan-shaped petals, centering them over the sunken wire loop. Press their sharp, recurved base tips deep into the soft mastic, letting it rise between and around the points.

Plastic wood requires several hours to harden completely, so it is best to leave these flat flowers on their foil backing overnight. To remove one, pick up its stem and lift, holding the foil flat with the other hand. Transfer the flower to a paper towel and allow the film of oil adhering to its back to be absorbed.

LARGER FLOWERS MADE ON A SINGLE ROSE BASE

This flat five-petalled single rose also is the basis of other, more complex flowers. For a semi-double rose, fit another five scales (smaller this time, and very slightly curved) above the original flower. To anchor this second layer of petals, use another, smaller, coin of plastic wood in the center of the basic flower and wedge the tips of the new petals between the existing points. Gardenias and camellias may be made by the same method, using scales that curve downward at the outer edge; three rows of these imbricated petals, each row a little smaller than the one on which it rests, will do the trick. For peonies and magnolia blossoms, use three rows of upward-curving petals — the innermost row should consist of three scales, and they should stand almost erect. Allow the plastic wood ten minutes drying time before setting these upright petals in place, and hold them steady with your fingers for a few seconds to allow the plastic wood to take a firm grip on them.

TULIPS AND POPPIES

Tulips and poppies require a different technique. A cardboard egg carton makes a handy holder for several of these during the drying

The coneflowers shown in Color Plate XV (opposite) are: cone-tip "forsythia", Scotch pine "zinnias", cedar scale "iris" and "tulips", jack-pine "carnations", "marigolds" and "daisies", white pine "narcissus" and "flowering quince", long-leaf pine "chrysanthemums", "peonies", "dahlias", and "rudbeckia", cedar-cone base "anthuriums", cedar scale "poppies", single and semi-double "roses", "dogwood", "anemones", "camellia", and "gardenia", cone-tip "wistaria". The self-preserved magnolia foliage was rubbed with green oil stain (page 49).

I. Above: *Left to right. Easter eggshell ladies wearing dried strawflowers. A fireman and sailor of shellacked simling gourds. China nest egg lass with a plastic-basket hat and starflower corsage; one with a minktail boa and a plastic shoebuckle hat (see pages 179-180).*

II. Above: *Enameled lunchboxes decorated with canteloupe, pumpkin, squash and green pepper seeds, half-round split peas, round okra, radish, mustard seeds and berry sprays. The white compote is "hobnailed" with barlay. Directions on page 130.*

III. Below: *A "decoupage" of pressed flowers and leaves on a wooden plaque. Red dogwood, red and pink azalea, pink oxalis, lavender creeping phlox, and yellow sorrel are protected by many coats of clear plastic spray; see page 68.*

IV. Above: *Flower buttons (see page 82). In the long box, cured cinquefoil blooms in half-round button molds; in the other, spirea florets in orange buttons with raised rims.*

V. Right: *China nest eggs colored with nail polish and "jeweled" with seeds; on the red calico egg, pepper seed petals surround green split-pea centers (see page 177).*

VI. Left: *Mother-and-daughter Christmas packages. One holds a full-blown Cedar of Lebanon "rose" and a bow of velvet ribbon. The plaid-wrapped box is topped with a coneflower and a shiny satin bow.*

VII. Right: *For a housewarming — drawer-pull gifts made of glass percolator tops and metal bolts, with embedments of cured wax-button ranunculus. The tiny flowers are magnified by the curved glass that surrounds them (see Chapter 6).*

VIII. Left: *Seedpods of unusual shape make a whimsical bird package-topper (page 211) and a mini-mosaic to decorate a desk. The latter is a large waterlily pod with dried starflower inserts.*

IX. Below: *Two summer carryalls. The lid of a white basket holds miniature flowerpots filled with tiny painted podflowers. The brown split basket with yellow-center pinecone "daisies" cemented on top.*

X. Right: *A tiny tree for a friend's small apartment is made of a large pinecone mounted on a flat plastic lid. Short sprigs of juniper fitted between the cone's scales hold tiny glass ornaments and sugar cube "packages" wrapped in gold foil. A gilded gum-tree pod stars the top (page 196).*

process, while a wineglass or a demitasse cup will do for just one. Line the wineglass with oiled aluminum foil, and squeeze a thick coin of plastic wood in the center of the bottom. Press the loop of a stiff wire stem into the plastic wood and bend the wire upward to follow the side of the cup. Stand four curved scales upright in the center of the glass, their pointed bases fitted together and touching in the bottom. Remove your steadying fingers and allow the scales to settle toward the sides of the glass and lean against its rim. If these petals are sufficiently large and curved to overlap, you may not need to add others. The chances are, though, that your tulip will be more lifelike if you give it an inner row of four petals, fitting their points between those of the original four and pressing their tops firmly back against the outer petals. After an overnight hardening period, remove the flower from the cup by lifting out the foil liner. Gently peel off the foil, transfer the tulip to a paper towel, and straighten its stem.

IRIS

By combining large recurved scales for the falls and smaller up-curved scales for the standards, you can construct an iris. This is quite a challenge, and you may make several before achieving one that pleases you. First make the falls. Select three large backward curving scales and balance them in the bottom of a foil-lined teacup with their points touching. Squeeze plastic wood on top of the points, and press a loop of wire stem firmly into it — you're making this part of the flower upside down, so the stem should stick straight up. When the lower half of the iris has set, use its stem to lift it out of the cup. Turn it over and pull the wire to one side so that this portion of the flower balances, right side up, on its downcurved petals. The next step is to fit three upward curving standards on top of it, leaning them inward so that their tops almost touch. An iris has six petals, three up and three down, so each standard should appear to be growing between two of the falls. Select one of the three small scales and coat its sharp tip generously with plastic wood. Set it upright, with its tip wedged between two down-curved falls; hold it steady for a moment until balance and the grip of the plastic wood keep it in place. Repeat the process for the remaining two standards of the iris, and evaluate their stance. With a light touch of a fingertip you can adjust their position without dislodging them. After a suitable hardening interval, pick up the finished iris and straighten its stem.

NARCISSUS

Cedar cones are not an absolute necessity in making flowers from scratch. By the same method, daffodils or narcissus can be constructed of petal-shaped scales from white pine or long-leaf pine cones. Pull (with pliers) or cut (with tinsnips) the flat scales from the stem of a cone, and trim the base of each to make the petal rather short in proportion to its width. Fit six petals together in a circle on a coin of plastic wood with an imbedded loop of wire. When this portion of the flower has set, add a dot of plastic wood where the petals join in the center, and press a large acorn cup down on it to form the trumpet.

ARRANGING BROWN CONEFLOWERS

In their natural state, cones run the gamut of browns from greenish beige to almost-black, and the most attractive coneflowers are soft sepia or bright chestnut in color. Make a gift arrangement of different varieties in a pottery bowl, and reserve some, too, for Christmas wreaths. These unpainted blooms will last for years if they are given a protective coating — you could dip them in clear varnish or in white shellac, but either treatment leaves them obtrusively shiny and does strange things to the paler shades of grayish brown. A better treatment is a spray coat, front and back, of colorless acrylic plastic, available at paint stores in pressurized cans. Your florist has a similar preparation (no better, but more expensive) specifically designed for use on plant materials.

If your brown arrangement seems monotonous, try tipping the edges of the largest flowers with gold. You can touch on gold paint with a small artist's brush, or apply gold wax to a petal edge with your fingertip, but whichever method you choose, use it with restraint. Let the gilt-edged accents stand overnight and look at them critically. You can always add more gold, but it is almost impossible to remove an excess.

CONEFLOWERS ON A WOODEN BOX

An especially handsome gift is a wooden box with a decoration of wooden flowers on its lid. Well made unfinished boxes, ranging in size from small square cigarette to large oblong photograph containers, are sold at hobby shops and intended to be decorated with decoupage. For this purpose, the box should not be painted or antiqued, but should be finished with a light oil stain which will allow the grain of the wood to show through. To outline the coneflower design, glue a narrow picture frame of natural or gilded wood flat to the box lid. If no ready-made frame

Coneflowers and deodar roses, in natural shades of brown and tan, are grouped around a large beige "poppy" (the base of a Cedar of Lebanon cone) to form a three-dimensional picture on the lid of a wooden box. Leaf-shaped milkweed pods serve as foliage, and ironweed pods add an edging of "forget-me-nots".

of the correct shape is available, use four strips of narrow half-round molding, cut to size, and mitred at the corners at the builder's supply company where they are purchased.

Group several large cone flowers of various types — a rose, a poppy, a camellia, a giant dahlia — in the center of the frame like a three-dimensional picture.

Smaller cone daisies and sprays of ironweed-pod forget-me-nots are good for edging, and leaf-shaped milkweed pods can substitute for foliage. Each of these materials can be permanently bonded to the box top with a coin of plastic wood. Spray the completed design with acrylic plastic for a desirable sheen and a dust-resistant finish.

COLORING CONEFLOWERS

It is obvious to anyone who has ever leafed through a seed catalog that black-and-white pictures show only the form of flowers, while color

From the decorations chairman to all the members of the women's club or the patriotic society: a permanent arrangement that can stand on a lectern or in the center of the speaker's table at a luncheon. An eagle-topped wrought iron stand holds miniature clay pots filled with red-and-white coneflower "carnations" and artificial ivy.

photographs bring the blooms to life. Appealing as cone-flowers are in their natural monochromatic shades, they are even more pleasing when they wear the bright hues of their living models. Before you metamorphose your wooden blossoms, decide which natural flower forms they most resemble, and then give them the colors of their live counterparts.

Certain quite different garden flowers have the same basic shape — marigolds and hardy carnations, for example: each has a ring of flat petals enclosing a fluffy center. This year's cones whose centers splintered as they were twisted apart have just such a ring of flat scale petals surrounding a frayed central mass. Paint one solid yellow or bright orange for a marigold; paint one white, and tip its edges with red, for a carnation. Pear blooms are white and peach blossoms are pink, but each is small, five-petalled, cupped. Hemlock-cone cup flowers will simulate any fruit tree blossom, so paint some white and some shell pink. Try white with a pale pink overcoating to achieve the flush of apple blossoms. For a real change of pace, give some a bright yellow color and they will be buttercups. Bright yellow spiky cone tips are remarkably like forsythia florets, but painted white or purple and wired together in a drooping raceme, these same cone tips become wistaria. Flat daisies of all sizes — made from slim white pine cones, from long-leaf giants, from Scotch pine rosettes or slash-pine ovals — need not be white with yellow centers although they are nice that way. Tinged with pale yellow, they masquerade as marguerites. Give them a deeper, brighter yellow tint and

100

call them coreopsis; then paint their centers dark brown and turn them into black-eyed Susans. Brush them with bright pink or with cerulean blue to bring out their resemblance to *Anemone blanda.* Color them red, pink, orange, yellow and lavender, and gather up a bright bouquet of zinnias.

SPRAY-PAINTING CONEFLOWERS

There are three ways of coloring cones with paint: by pressure-spraying; by dipping; with a brush. If you are impatient to see results, or if you have a great many flowers to paint and want them all the same color, by all means use a spray. Spread several thicknesses of newspaper on the floor of a porch, a garage, or a well-ventilated room. Arrange the coneflowers in a single layer, upside down, as close as possible without having their petals touch. Vigorously shake a pressurized can of enamel, hold it about two feet above the flowers, and move the can slowly back and forth as you spray the blossoms until they appear well coated. Allow two hours for the paint to dry. Some cones, particularly those that are old and dry, soak up this first layer of paint and present a blotchy appearance, but a second coat will cover. When the backs of the flowers are perfectly dry, lift them by their stems and bend the wires to one

This elegant oval design (made on a styrofoam wiglet stand from the dime store!) would be an equally appropriate gift for a golden wedding anniversary or for a Victorian house museum. Cedar of Lebanon "roses" were dipped in dull gold enamel (pages 94-95); coneflower "daises", poplar "tulips" and mallow pod buds (Chapter 8) were sprayed with shiny gold paint.

side so that you can place the cones flat on the newspaper, face up. Give their faces the coat or coats necessary for complete color coverage. When they dry, dip a very small brush in yellow enamel and touch it to the center of each coneflower.

This method works best on flat, daisy-like flowers, and is useful for applying the undercoat to a parti-colored blossom. Spray-paint is relatively expensive, though, and the color choice is extremely limited.

DIPPING CONEFLOWERS IN ENAMEL

Coloring coneflowers by dipping them in enamel is an alternative to spray-painting, and the method is simplicity itself provided that a basement, a garage, or a utility room may be devoted to the project. A clothesline is another must. From a quart of white and a half-pint each of red, yellow, and blue semigloss enamel, you can create all the colors of the rainbow; but before opening the paint, spread a thick pad of newspaper underneath the clothesline and extend it several feet on both sides to catch spatters.

Pour two or three inches of white paint into a wide-mouthed glass jar or a clean, empty number two tin can. Add red paint with a plastic picnic spoon, and stir with another spoon — the iced tea length is handiest. Add more red until you have the shade of pink you like. Too rosy? Dribble in a drop or two of yellow, but don't overdo it. Too bright? A bit of blue will tone it down.

Holding a flower by its wire stem, dip its head down into the jar; lift it and hold it above the surface of the paint until it drips only occasionally. Now quickly hook the wire stem over the clothesline, and clip stem to line with a clothespin. The flower will drip-dry overnight. With a little practise, you can dip two or even three flowers at a time, and you'll discover the quick flick of the wrist that dislodges the greatest amount of excess paint as the flowers are withdrawn after immersion.

The level of paint in the jar goes down very quickly. You may want to vary the shade when you add more, or to change color entirely. By adding more and more yellow, you arrive at salmon, peach, apricot, orange; more and more blue will yield dusty rose, lavender, violet, and purple. The range of color is as wide as your fancy, and if the tint of a finished coneflower does not please you, the blossom can be re-dipped. Deeper or lighter flushes, stripes, or variegated effects can be added with a brush.

The obvious advantages of this method are its speed and thoroughness — there is really no other way to get into every crack and crevice, and dipping is a must for cedar roses. Its disadvantage is its messiness. Better wear a coverall and plastic gloves, and be sure the layers of newspaper underneath the clothesline are thick enough to absorb all the dripping paint.

DIPPING CONEFLOWERS IN DYE

A variant of the dipping method colors coneflowers not with enamel but with liquid dye. Dilute the dye with boiling water, and immerse a flower, leaving it in the solution for three minutes to allow the liquid to penetrate the wood. Then lift the flower, shake it over the dye container, and clip it to a clothesline to drip dry. Dyed cones have a different, deeper color texture, and rich dark shades are more successful than pastel tints, which are somewhat muddied by the brown hue of the wood.

BRUSHING PAINT ON CONEFLOWERS

Lacking the space or the inclination to dip your coneflowers, you can sit comfortably at a table (protected with plastic cleaner's bags spread over a newspaper padding) and paint them with a brush. You'll need two or three soft half-inch brushes and one very small stiff artist's brush; all should be of the cheapest brands, from a variety store. Provide yourself with some small flat tin cans (deviled ham type) or heavy paper baking cups, and with plastic spoons for dipping and stirring. Brush painting uses far less paint than the dipping method — a pint of white and a quarter-pint each of red, yellow, and blue enamel will suffice for fifty small flowers. Hold a blossom by its wire stem, and paint the underneath side first; set it aside to dry while you go on to another. After fifteen or twenty minutes, it will be safe to pick up the flower and hold it right side up to paint its face. It will be a temptation to hold the cone just above the can and to slather paint upon it in imitation of the dipping method, but the flower is then very messy to handle and will stick to any surface on which it is laid to dry. Taking up a brushful of paint and forcing it between the layers of scale petals may be tedious, but it is undeniably neater.

CASEIN PAINT

For those allergic to (or merely repelled by) the odor of enamel, there is an alternative in casein paints. These come in tubes, and may be found where artists' supplies are sold. A large size white plus three small tubes — one bright yellow, one deep bright blue, and one clear red — will afford the same range of color obtainable with enamels. Casein paint is thick, and must be applied with a brush. On a tabletop, protected by a plastic bag, lay out some paper baking cups, several clean brushes, and a cup of water. Squeeze a large dollop of white casein into a paper cup, add a small squeeze of red, stir with a brush until well blended, and apply pink paint to a cone. If the brush becomes clogged with paint, dip it quickly in the cup of water. Do not, however, thin the paint with water; watery paint will not cover well, and will be flaky when dry. If you *must* thin, use a drop or two of milk.

Casein color has a different texture from enamel, and is especially suited to flowers with thick, non-shiny petals such as gardenias or magnolias. Its one great fault is that it tends to flake or chip at the edges of the petals, but this is not an insoluble problem. Reach once more for the pressurized spray can of colorless acrylic plastic. Casein-painted blossoms should be given a thorough coating, fore and aft, of this clear plastic as soon as they are dry and before they are subjected to handling. Casein-coated plastic-sprayed flowers are less shiny than cones painted with enamel, and their petal surfaces have a moist look that is extremely lifelike. The greatest advantages of casein paint are its quick drying time and the fact that brushes and hands will wash clean with soap and water.

The newer acrylic artists' paints also are quick drying and water-based, but their colors are harsher and do not combine as well as caseins to form shades and tints.

Cone scales differ in texture from smooth and shiny to velvety. In fact, Cedar of Lebanon scales are smooth on top and positively furry on the underneath side. The fibre variations persist after color is applied, no matter what method or what medium is employed, and add verisimilitude to the finished flower. Velvety scales may look a trifle streaked, but so do velvety flowers. The same shade of paint dries a little lighter on shiny surface areas, and this slight change of color is natural and pleasing.

TAPING WIRE STEMS

There is one more step to take before the blossoms are finished: something must be done about their stems. Your largest, heavy-headed coneflowers will not need further attention, since they already have green stems of florist's wire, but all the rest should have a coating of green over their aluminum or copper wires. You will need a roll of green floral tape, from your florist or from the artificial flower display at a variety store, some green wooden flower picks from the same source, and a package of green plastic soda straws, which usually are sold in supermarkets.

All-purpose aluminum or copper wire stems should be sheathed with floral tape, and there is a trick to winding the tape smoothly. It is easier to learn on a short piece of wire without a flower head. Lay the end of the wire at a slant across the end of the tape. Fold the small triangle of tape-end over the wire, cross the long piece of tape over this and wind it around the wire. Pull the tape as you wind, to stretch it and make it taut, and press the layers of tape together with your fingers to make them stick to each other. Then twist the wire slowly with one hand while holding the tape stretched and taut with the other hand; spiral the tape along the wire in barely overlapping turns. Smooth the finished stem with your fingers. Now try a wired cone daisy, beginning at the base of the flower. A small bump of tape is almost unavoidable at the starting point, but is no cause for concern; real flowers, too, have a green swelling where the calyx joins the stem.

For daffodils, tulips, and iris, there is a different and easier way to sheathe a stem. Simply insert the attached wire into a green soda straw, and bind straw to wire just below the flower head with a quick twist of floral tape.

If you plan a cluster arrangement, or a pyramid built upon a cone of styrofoam, don't bother to wrap any of the coneflower stems. Merely wire each blossom firmly to a wooden floral pick and it will be ready to be pricked in place. Fruit-tree and shrub blossoms need no stems at all, for they should be attached with liquid cement to real branches of attractive shape.

ARRANGING PAINTED CONEFLOWERS

Since pinecones in their original state are coarse and woody, it would seem logical that flowers made from them should be arranged in heavy containers of wood, pottery, or copper. Large and weighty coneflowers do look best in such materials; huge daisies from sugar pine cones, given strong bright color in imitation of sunflowers, dahlias, or rudbeckia (black-eyed Susan, etc.) are tremendously effective massed in a metal bowl or mounded on an interesting driftwood shape. For a dramatic terrace accent, spill these gigantic flowers from the pockets of a clay strawberry jar.

On the other hand, small delicate coneflower forms are quite appropriate for containers of alabaster, silver, or porcelain. Here's a chance to fill a bowl of unusual color by painting flowers to match or compliment it; now is the time to use an antique Parian vase that does not hold water, or an alabaster urn that would be stained by real flower stems. Candelabra can be decked with sprays of flowers that will not fade; plaques of painted coneflowers can add a touch of color to a panelled room; garden figurines can dress for a party in wreaths or leis of bright weatherproof blossoms. In short, painted coneflowers take on the character of the real blossoms they represent, and should be given a suitable setting.

FRUIT TREE BLOSSOMS AND SHRUB FLOWERS

For verisimilitude, tiny hemlock fruit blossoms should be glued in clusters to real leafless fruit-tree twigs. A dead limb amputated by the wind would be an ideal basis for them, as would suckers or drooping branches pruned from a tree. Arrange three or five branches of "plum blossoms" in a tall white vase — instant Spring!

Yellow painted cone-tip forsythia blooms will look astonishingly real if you cement them to curved canes cut from a straggling shrub. White pine cone-florets, painted bright, clear pink, come to life as flowering quince blossoms when they are glued to thorny branches, and incidentally, prunings from a hawthorn tree will serve quite as well as canes from a japonica shrub.

Left to right: *Coneflower "iris" with real iris leaves; coneflowers and driftwood with real leaves; coneflowers on real tree branches look like fruit tree blossoms.*

ARRANGEMENTS IN PARAFFIN

For lightweight flowers made of hemlock, larch, or Mugho cones, paraffin is the best holder. Heat a block of the white wax slowly, in an old saucepan until it liquefies. Rinse a small container with very hot water, and pour in enough melted wax to fill it almost to the brim. Allow the paraffin to stand at room temperature until it becomes cloudy and its surface has congealed. Then arrange the flowers quickly, standing by to adjust them if necessary until the wax has hardened. A posy is the easiest type of arrangement to make in paraffin. Gather the flowers together in one hand, shifting and straightening them until the grouping suits you, and secure the stems in position by wrapping them with wire. When the wax in the container is semi-solid, insert the tied arrangement and balance it by bending the wire stems of the outer flowers down until they touch the rim of the vase. This is a splendid way to utilize small painted florist's vases or little containers from your no-return collection, and the finished arrangement makes a most suitable hospital gift. Furthermore, it can be transported anywhere without spilling a drop of wax or unseating a single flower.

ARRANGEMENTS IN WALLPAPER CLEANER

Heavier coneflowers will need a weightier holder for balance, and for these, wallpaper cleaner is the best solution. As it comes from the can, ordinary wallpaper cleaner has the consistency of stiff putty; exposed to the air, it dries and hardens over a period of time into a rock-like mass. Knead a lump of cleaner into a ball, and press it down firmly upon the bottom of a container. Use enough cleaner to cover the flowers' wire stems to a depth of at least three inches — more if the stems are very long or the coneflowers very heavy. Make the arrangement, and be sure it suits you before you leave it; as the surface of the wallpaper cleaner dries, it shrinks slightly and grips the flower stems. It may take a month or more for a large lump of cleaner to dry out completely, but the moment its surface is sealed, the arrangement will be as unchangeable as the laws of the Medes and the Persians.

ARRANGEMENTS ON STYROFOAM PLASTIC

Green styrofoam plastic serves well as a holder for changeable arrangements. It comes in a variety of shapes — blocks, thick sheets, cones, half-orbs — and is sold at the variety store's artificial flower counter. Since styrofoam has little weight, it must be anchored to the bottom of the container. One way to do this is by pressing a block of the plastic down on the points of a heavy needle holder; this makes it possible to transfer an arrangement undisturbed from one container to another. Florists use an extra-sticky green substance to attach plastic foam to containers, and are willing to sell several inches off the large commercial roll. This sticky tape is handy for balancing a cone of styrofoam in a compote or atop a candlestick, but still better for such a purpose are picture mounts of thin foam rubber with adhesive on both sides.

FOLIAGE FOR CONEFLOWER ARRANGEMENTS

Before beginning an arrangement, consider what type of foliage would be most becoming to your coneflowers. Real foliage is certainly a possibility, with the outline of green living material established first, in water, and sparked by accents of painted wooden flowers. For example, form a fan-shaped background with iris spears for a grouping of cone tulips, iris, and narcissus. Peony foliage is an ideal foil for heavy peony blossoms made from deodar scales. Bring fresh ligustrum branches into bloom by wiring on cone camellias or gardenias. Evergreen sprays of rhododendron or magnolia welcome coneflower centers of interest.

Coneflowers in permanent arrangements, however, are best complemented by lifelike artificial foliage — podocarpus, rose leaves, pine branches, ferns, or philodendron. Most sprays of artificial foliage are made up of leaves molded separately and added later to the stem. Usually each leaf grouping has a round hole at its base; the hole has been fitted over a bulbous-tipped protuberance on the plastic twig, and a sharp tug will pull it off. You can make coneflowers grow their own leaves by slipping a wrapped wire stem through such a leaf hole — a twist of green floral tape will hold the foliage in place.

For an arrangement on a green styrofoam cone or a white cone covered with green florist's foil, cover the pyramid with foliage before the flowers are added. You can attach single leaves or longer foliage sprays in a trice, by pressing the point of a small wire hairpin (or an electrician's brad) through the stem hole into the plastic. Try attaching flat circles of leaves having a hole in the middle with wooden kitchen matches. The red or blue match head makes an unobtrusive but effective colored "bud" in the center of the circlet, and holds the foliage firmly when the stick of the match is pushed deep into the plastic foam. Once the foliage is in place, the coneflowers can be added very quickly. Their own wire stems, cut short, usually will hold steady if pressed into the plastic at a downward angle, but very heavy blossoms such as roses should be wired to wooden picks that are then pricked into the cone. It is often effective to wire two, three, or five small flowers to a pick instead of pricking them into the arrangement one by one.

Since coneflowers are of natural material, glycerin-treated broad-leafed evergreens are exactly right for arranging with them — brown leaves for uncolored cones, green-dyed or green-waxed foliage for dyed or painted flowers.

CARDBOARD TUBE CONTAINER

Three giant coneflowers painted in neon colors make a congenial accent for a teenager's room; the more so if you present them in this tall "slim jim" container made of three cardboard tubes (paper towel size). Paint one tube to match each of the three flowers, and glue the tubes together end to end; cover each joint with a narrow strip of green plastic tape. As a base for the tall vase, remove the bottom of an empty thirty-six-ounce juice can with its rim intact, by inserting the can sideways into a wall-type can opener. Paint the metal circle green, to match the plastic tape, and cement the joined tubes upright in its center. Give each coneflower a long stem of heavy green wire, twist the three stems together, and insert them in the top of the tube. Bend the stems until each flower shows to best advantage.

DECORATED TOTE BASKET

For a young mother, a compulsive knitter, or anyone who often travels by car, a large rectangular tote basket is a much-appreciated gift. Plain baskets can be bought at department stores and needlework shops, and are not expensive, but decorated totes command a fancy price in boutiques and basket shops.

Most basket totes have a strip of openwork near the top through which wide green ribbon can be threaded. In the center of one long side, knot the ends of the ribbon around the stems of a generous bunch of bright pinecone zinnias. Line the bottom and sides of the tote with green quilted self-stick plastic, gluing each corner for security.

PENCIL CADDY

Tin can pencil caddies are not new, but here is one that is different. Remove the top of a soft drink or beer can smoothly, with a wall-type or electric can opener, leaving the rim intact. Then remove the bottom of an empty thirty-six-ounce tomato juice can with its rim; again insert the can sideways. Cover the sides of the topless can with green-and-gold adhesive plastic, and cement the covered can in the center of the gold inner surface of the large lid. To the rim of the lid that extends beyond the base of the can, glue sprigs of small flat artificial foliage in a ring. Then glue to the foliage clusters of gilded hemlock cones that look like roses, and finish the decorative wreath with a flat bow of narrow green velvet ribbon glued on at an angle.

TIN CAN BANK

In a similar manner, construct a decorative holder for small change from a can that comes with a snap-on plastic lid: chocolate sauce, ready-to-serve puddings, and ready-to-spread frostings come so equipped. Remove the label and wash the can thoroughly; then cover it with red self-stick felt. With the heated tip of a paring knife, cut a slit for coins in the center of the plastic lid. Cover the lid with felt, and slit the felt above the hole in the plastic. Put the lid on the can — the layer of felt will hold it firmly without gluing, but it can be prised off to remove the coins. Now glue the bank in the center of a large rimmed metal can-top covered with red felt, and trim the lid with white pinecone daisies and a bow of white ribbon.

YARDSTICK HOLDER

Any friend who likes to sew will welcome a yardstick in a handy holder that hangs from a hook on the wall. Use two strips of colorful burlap as the basis of the holder. One strip for the back should be thirty-eight inches long and four inches wide, while the front strip should measure four by thirty-seven. Put a shirt-tail hem in the top strip edges, and sew a brass curtain ring in the center of the longer strip's hem. With green thread, sew a procession of pinecone zinnias by their green wrapped wire stems up the middle of the shorter piece. Match the bottoms and sides of the two strips, and machine-stitch them together one inch from the edges. Fringe the edges by pulling threads. Insert a yardstick (from a hardware or a variety store) in the long narrow pocket, and the gift is finished.

COLOR CONES

First-year chemistry students learn in the laboratory that copper sulphate burns green, lithium sulphate red, calcium chloride orange, sodium chloride yellow, and potassium chloride violet-purple. All pipe-smokers are familiar with the bright blue flame (and the brimstone odor) of burning sulphur, for this chemical is used to tip wooden matches. Treated with these substances, pinecones become "color cones".

If you confide your purpose to your pharmacist, he can obtain the chemicals you need, in powder form, from a wholesale drug company. Pure powdered sulphur (called "flowers of sulphur") he probably will

A gift to warm the heart and hearthside of your holiday hostess — "color cones", dipped in liquid wax and sprinkled with chemicals (as described below) to burn red, yellow, green, blue and purple.

have on hand, and you need not ask him for sodium chloride, which is ordinary table salt. You will also need liquid floor wax from the supermarket — the cheapest brand will do as well as any other — and a large kitchen saltshaker.

Spread newspapers on a table and on the floor around it. Pour liquid wax into a clean, empty number two size tin can, and fill the shaker with one of the chemicals. Dip a cone in the wax, shake it over the can until it stops dripping, and place it face up on newspaper. While the wax still is wet, sprinkle the surface of the cone with chemical from the shaker. When you have enough cones of one color, empty the shaker, wash and dry it well, and fill it with another chemical. When all available cones have been treated and their wax coating has dried, they are ready to be gift packaged. Place one or two of each color in a clear plastic bag, and tie it with bright ribbon — these cones deserve a see-through package, for they appear to have been polished and then dusted with particles of color. For a hearth-centered home, heap a selection of cones in an attractive basket that can stand beside the fireplace or ornament the mantel. In either case, include a list of the chemicals and the colors they produce.

PINECONE BIRD FEEDERS

For the ornithologist on your gift list, for the shut-in who sits by a tree-shaded window, even for a child just old enough to be fascinated by the flash of wings and the trill of song, a pinecone bird feeder makes a matchless birthday present.

Choose a large cone, with well-spread, flat scales — from a big-cone, long-leafed Jeffrey, or Ponderosa pine — and prepare it for mounting on a tree limb by winding a two-foot length of all-purpose aluminum or copper wire around its central stem above the lowest circle of scales. Twist the wire tight against the cone stem, leaving both ends long, and fill the cone by either of the following methods:

1 — Melt butcher's suet over low heat until it liquefies, and strain it into a bowl. When it has cooled slightly, add enough sunflower seed and/or wild birdseed mix (from a garden shop) to make a stiff paste. With the flat blade of a tableknife, force the seed-filled suet between the scales of the cone; when you've finished, all the spaces should be filled, and the cone should be a solid pyramid. If the mixture becomes too stiff to spread before the cone is filled, set the bowl in a pan of boiling water until the suet is slightly softened.

2 — Empty a half-pound jar of crunchy peanut butter into a bowl, and place the bowl in a pan of boiling water until the spread becomes runny. Stir into it two cups of parakeet or wild birdseed mix, and use this stiff combination to fill a large cone.

Package each cone in a clear plastic bag, and identify its use by topping its ribbon closure with a tiny colorful bird.

8.

Presents from Pods,
Seeds, and Nuts

Winter is the ideal time to appreciate shape unhampered by the distractions of color. The sycamore is trimmed with a ball-fringe of small globes on slender, pliant stems. The gum tree is decorated with a multitude of spiky orbs like tiny, many-pointed Spanish stars. Paulownia's pods are black bunches of magnified grapes, growing upside down. Oxydendron's clustered fronds spread like old-ivory fan sticks. Golden chain tree is covered with inverted miniature Japanese lanterns. The Chinese chestnut's burrs look like baby porcupines, and hickory nut hulls shatter into curved flower petals that are black on the outside and yellow within.

Nature is no haphazard artist. In preparation for summer's gigantic color masterpiece, she sometimes sketches from memory a detail in sepia. Look up into the leafless branches of a tulip poplar tree to see pale spectres of last season's bloom. Look closely at your shrubs before you prune. In the woody remnants of frost-blackened seedpods, the seeing eye discerns flower shapes — a souvenir of blossoms past and a promise of bloom to come. Mockorange twigs are thickly studded with brown seedpod crosses. A lilac's bare canes are topped with upright trusses of pygmy pods. Vitex wears spires encrusted with pearl-size seedballs. Crepe myrtle's branches end in bouquets of little serrated cups as perfect as minute chrysanthemums carved from wood. Althea (and her double first cousins, hibiscus and mallow) has clusters of half-opened wooden flower buds.

Two shrubs of the same species, growing side by side, bear seedpods slightly different in color and size; there are even minor variations in

A light-hearted decoration for a teen-ager's Halloween party. The scarecrow has a styrofoam-ball head, straw hair, apple-seed eyes, and a strawberry corn-kernel mouth. An acorn-cup beret is perched on his head; a bundle of straws tied around a wire core forms arms that are sewn inside burlap sacking. One hollow bamboo leg was fitted over a spindle to hold the figure upright on the slice of tree limb; the head is pressed on the point of the spike. The bird has a pinecone body, pod head, and wings of feather-shaped maple seeds.

shape. Each shrub produces exactly the same pods year after year, as individualistic as human fingerprints.

UNTREATED SHRUB PODS

The branches pruned from your garden's dormant shrub border will provide ready-made and really permanent flowers. Some are attractive in shades of tan and brown. Some have black exteriors and centers of pale beige. Washed and lightly coated with clear acrylic plastic spray, these are ready to be Hogarth-curved in a tall vase, or angled in a line arrangement with a bright brown coneflower as the center of interest.

PAINTED SHRUB PODS

Some shrub pods, like lilac, rhododendron, and mockorange, are attractive in form but even after washing are dull and drab. Closely clumped pod-flowers at the end of a twig take kindly to dipping in enamel. Try lavender or purple paint for lilac pods, lavender or blue for vitex. Pods scattered

114

along a branch should have color brushed on, leaving the bark brown or black for contrast. Use white for mockorange; try light, clear yellow or salmon pink for althea. For maximum effect, dip crepe myrtle's sharply indented cups — give them chrysanthemum colors and set them aside for use in miniature arrangements.

PAINTED TREE PODS

Poplar tulips dip well, but paulownia grape clusters are so large that they must be sprayed. One heavy cluster, given three spray-coats of gold paint, makes a splendid center of interest for a Christmas gift arrangement of large gilded leaves or needled sprays. The lighter and more graceful golden chain tree pods take naturally to a frosting of sprayed gold, and combine well at Christmas with silvered broad-leafed evergreens. Halves of chestnut burrs, frosted with black spray-paint, make interesting centers for large flat coneflowers, turning them into lifelike sunflowers and rudbeckia.

FLOWER SEEDPODS

After the orange pods of Chinese lantern have been gathered, and the slender fluted pods of okra have been cut, there still are phantom pod-

Landscape in a dish. A spray of triangular beige begonia pods rises like a stunted tree above grouped chunks of blue-green copper ore. A beige snail shell nestles in a crack, and "growing" on a small stone is a large mushroom that dried rock-hard in silica gel.

flowers in the garden in late fall. The onion-shaped pods that succeeded the blooms of daylilies and bulb iris have opened into tiny tulips. Liriope's brown spikes are studded with small bronze balls. Look for hardy begonia's graceful sprays of miniature orchids. Columbine offers minute open-throated lilies, and salvia's diminutive bell-shaped pods arranged in circles imitate bluebells.

PAINTED FLOWER PODS

Begonia "orchids" have a bronze sheen, and are interesting in their natural state. However, if you need a drooping stem of small blossoms for a color arrangement, touch them lightly with a brushful of white or lavender enamel.

Dip or brush-paint the flower pods that so closely resemble pygmy tulips and lilies in the colors of their namesakes, using a very small artist's brush to give them the black or yellow centers that complete their disguise. Add crepe myrtle's small-scale chrysanthemums and iron weed's full size blue forget-me-nots or white baby's breath, and you have all the essentials for perfect, permanent miniature arrangements.

A branch of laurestinus — the prunings from any broadleafed or needled evergreen would be equally long-lasting — with magnolia pods glued on, makes a handsome gift for Christmas or for a silver wedding anniversary. The pods were sprayed silver and sprinkled with diamond dust glitter, and the branch was planted in ready-mix concrete with a topping of sand.

MINIATURE SEEDPOD ARRANGEMENTS

Tiny arrangements in egg cups are great fun to make and to give at Easter time. To brighten a neighbor's breakfast table, use a solid color cup and saucer container for painted pods. Make several nosegays in cheap small vases to have on hand for hospital gifts. Construct a pod-flower crescent or a miniature mass bouquet for an aunt who suffers from hay fever — these bright blossoms will be more than welcome where pollen-heavy fresh flowers are taboo.

DRIP-CATCHER FOR A FESTIVE BOTTLE

No decoration is more suited to a festive gift bottle of champagne (or, for that matter, to a tall bottle of cologne) than a drip-catcher wreath of painted podflowers.

For the basic wreath, cut a circle three inches in diameter from a colorful plastic kitchen sponge that is only half an inch thick; the sponge will cut easily with shears. From the center of this round, remove a circle one-and-a-half inches in diameter, leaving a sponge doughnut. Trim the wreath with tiny hemlock cone roses and very small pastel painted podflowers — daylily tulips, ironweed forget-me-nots, and columbine lilies — attached with hair-fine wire threaded through the circlet of sponge near its outer edge.

Mold the bottle in silvery aluminum or colorful florist's foil, making no attempt to disguise its shape, and tie narrow velvet or grosgrain ribbon around the neck in a bow with long flowing streamers. Fit the flowery wreath over the neck of the bottle and let it come to rest above the ribbon; it can then be slipped off easily, and replaced once the bottle is unwrapped.

This sponge drip-catcher does an efficient job of preventing wine stains on linen or perfume scars on furniture, and the painted wooden pods are unharmed by alcohol.

NAPKIN RINGS SEEDPOD DECORATIONS

Colorful napkin rings add a festive touch to the daily dinner table, and a set of decorated rings — one for each member of the family — makes a fine housewarming or anniversary gift. Cardboard cores of wide rolls of plastic tape are the right width and circumference for napkin rings. With a saw or a serrated kitchen knife, cut the heavy cardboard center of a roll of paper towels into five circlets, each two-and-a-fourth inches wide. Measure the width and the circumference of a circlet, and cut a strip of adhesive-backed felt or burlap corresponding in circumference, but twice as wide. Center the sticky strip on the cardboard, and fold its edges under to meet in the middle of the inner surface. Glue a spray of small artificial leaves to one side of the ring, and add a cluster of tiny painted pods. Dip whole trusses of lilac or rhododendron pods in enamel and allow them to drip dry; then cut off the individual pods for gluing to the rings.

For the Christmas dinner table, cover the rings with dark green felt and use red painted pods. For a springtime gift, begin with pastel burlap, and paint the pods in pale colors or white. For Valentine's Day, trim red felt-covered rings with tiny nosegays. Cut a circle of white cotton lace two-and-a-half inches in diameter and glue it to the felt. In the center of the lace, glue a red painted hemlock cone rose, and encircle the rose with blue ironweed pod forget-me-nots.

WEEDS

Along country roads, where the purple ironweed and the goldenrod wore complimentary colors in early autumn, pale feathery ghosts of goldenrod blooms are ready for winter picking, safe even for hay fever sufferers. Be on the lookout for the tall ironweed, each stalk bearing many clusters of minute flat wooden flowers — each is a perfect forget-me-not, an exact replica in shape and size. Look for patches of pearly everlasting's dry stems topped with clumps of stubby straw tufts. Gray mullein spikes, like exclamation points, and beady brown dock are well worth watching for. The odiferous jimson weed wears prickly sputniks, and the husks of milkweed pods are shaped like pointed leaves. Here are the makings of long-lasting winter gift bouquets.

Like ageing rakes, summer's wicked weeds turn virtuous in the end. The bushy heads of blown goldenrod, sprayed crimson or pale yellow with paint or dye, closely resemble celosia. Pearly everlasting's strawy tufts, spray-painted dark blue, take on the look of ageratum; sprayed yellow, they can be glued to flat coneflowers to make realistic centers. A cluster of leaf-shaped milkweed pods, green painted, becomes the foliage for a dried or pod arrangement.

ARRANGING DRIED WEEDS

Coming as they do with stems attached, these weedy everlastings need no wiring. Their skeletal stems are, however, extremely fragile — much more so than the vestigial blossoms they support. A kneaded lump of floral clay in the bottom of a vase makes an excellent holder for them, since the stems

A make-believe bonsai uses preserved polygonum (knot-bush) to simulate a stunted tree: the ends of short curving sprays (see pages 27-28) were dipped in glue and forced into a hollow forked stem. The miniature planter's filling of plastic wood is concealed by pebbles. (Bonsai trees also can be made of dyed, cured monkey grass, pine needles, or cedar sprigs.)

may be inserted with little pressure. An alternative to floral clay is a block of green styrofoam, and a foam-based arrangement has the advantage of being transferable from one vase to another. When you use plastic foam, prick holes into it for the stems with a toothpick or a small nail. Dip the tip of each stem in white glue; then, with little danger of breakage, you can guide the delicate stalks into the styrofoam holes.

GOURDS

Gourds, the inedible seedpod cousins of pumpkins and squash, were used by America's ingenious and thrifty pioneers for bowls and dippers, bottles and baby rattles. Then as now, small bright-colored or interestingly warted varieties were grown especially for decoration — one packet of mixed ornamental gourd seed will produce the raw materials for many an attractive gift.

PRESERVING GOURDS

To last well, the shells of ornamental gourds must be dried and polished. Hammer a small nail into the top of each, near the stem, and make a similar hole in the bottom — take advantage of the thin spot in the center

119

of the blossom end. Lay the gourds on newspaper in an airy, shady place — a garage, a breezeway, or an attic. Each morning, turn them over and with a soft cloth wipe away the moisture that has condensed on their shells. The shells will dry in ten days to two weeks, depending upon their size and thickness. A coat of clear shellac is a good preservative, but it leaves the gourds excessively shiny; the same is true of the three thin coats of colorless acrylic spray required to seal their surfaces. Self-polishing liquid wax, applied with a brush, will protect them well and give them a matte finish.

ARRANGING DRIED GOURDS

Baskets and gourds go together as well today as they did in the seventeenth century. Present one large and handsome "king's crown" on a raffia paper plateholder. Heap small smooth orange, red, and yellow globes in a round lacy basket without a handle. Mix slender white pine cones with gourds in a fruit basket.

Gourds need not, however, be confined behind wicker bars. Heap several small gourds of the same color — orange, perhaps — in a wooden salad bowl interspersed with autumn leaves. Middle-sized red warted gourds are stunning mounded on a white compote and topped with a bunch of large, white-painted artificial grapes.

Those holes punched in their shells before they were dried make it easy to add gourds to an arrangement, or to wire them together in a long, colorful wall hanging. Press the blunt end of a wooden flower pick into the hole in its blossom end, and a gourd is instantly prepared to be pricked into styrofoam. Make a hanger for the stem end by pressing together the sides of a stiff wire hairpin and pushing its points down into the hole until the

Plant ornamental gourds along a fence when weather is mild (about the time tomato plants are set outdoors) and follow the directions in the text to preserve them for many years. Present them, perhaps, to an early-American house museum: shown on a sugar chest are yellow gourds in a wooden bowl; in the background, a little brown bottle gourd holds a posy of dyed wheat and air-dried celosia.

top corrugations of the hairpin are level with the rim of the hole. Once you release the pressure of your fingers, tension will hold the hairpin steady, and you can wire its rounded top like the hanger of a Christmas tree ornament. A yellow-brown arrangement of gourds, cones, and cotton or honey-locust pods, wired together like a long and narrow plaque, will make a handsome wall ornament for a friend with a pine-panelled playroom.

GOURDHEAD DOLL

Small beige ovoid simling gourds (which also are called "nest eggs" or "darning eggs") make splendid heads for male character dolls. Choose one that is lightly freckled for a Huckleberry Finn, a darker blotched gourd for a sea captain or a farmer, and paint features on one side. Buy a small wire armature (where artist's supplies are sold), or make one yourself by bending two lengths of coat hanger wire, one long and one short,

Doll collectors would treasure this unique farmer seated on a miniature wooden chest. He has a simling gourd head and chopped brown wool for hair, eyebrows and whiskers. The body was made on a wire armature (drawings follow).

together at the middle. Wrap the four wires tightly at the bend with plastic tape to create a one-inch neck; spread the two short wires outward for arms, and tape the two long wires together for four inches to form the doll's body. Then separate the long wires into legs, and bend their tips at right angles into feet. The finished armature has the look of a stick figure without a head. Pad the limbs and the body with cotton batting secured with overlapped plastic tape; cover the feet with black plastic or tire tape, for shoes, and the neck and hands with tan plastic tape. Dress the doll before attaching its head.

Enlarge the hole at the blossom end of the simling gourd by scraping its edges with a serrated paring knife. Cover the top of the armature neck with white glue, and fit it into this hole. Then finish the head of a farmer or a sea captain with hair and whiskers of lamb's wool, absorbent cotton, or steel wool glued to the top of the gourd to cover the hole in the stem end. Give a freckle-faced boy-doll short red hair: first cover the hole in the top of the head with a bit of plastic tape; draw a hairline with a pencil, and coat the surface within the outline with white glue. Cut rust-colored yarn, with scissors, into snippets so small that they are fuzzy, and sprinkle the chopped wool over the wet glue. Top the head with a hat or a cap, and give the figure an appropriate stance by bending its wire arms and legs. Present it to the doll collector, child or adult, on your Christmas list, secure in the knowledge that she will not have a duplicate.

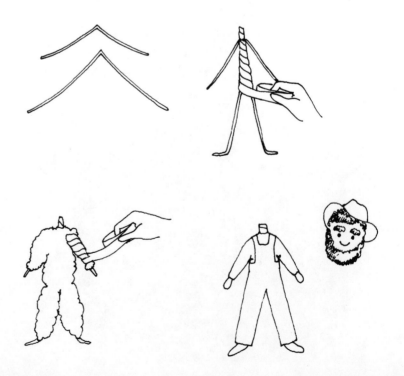

CORN

ORNAMENTAL EARS

Corn is not only good to eat but also good to look upon. Since colonial days, tiny oval ears of strawberry corn, each kernel a shiny red bead, have been grown for ornamental use. Pull the strips of husk back from the ears and dampen them; then, smooth and curve each strip by pulling it across the dull edge of a tableknife; it will resemble a tuft of foliage. Using plastic hair rollers, you can also convert these same pulled-back and dampened strips of husk into yellow-beige flowers. Four or five flower-topped ears of strawberry corn, in an individual wooden salad bowl, will look well in a panelled den; a cluster of the small ears, their tufted tops sewed together with a darning needle and crochet thread, can trail over the edge of a nut bowl filled with ornamental gourds. Sewed together in a long raceme and topped with a "bow" of cornleaves dampened and bent into loops, strawberry ears make a fine wall hanging. Wire the looped leaves to straight leaf streamers, and then wire the bow to the top of the corn string.

Slender yellow-beaded ears of popcorn are equally decorative, and you can create a most colorful ornament for the wall of a wood-panelled kitchen by stringing ears of popcorn and strawberry corn together, with a rug needle and heavy red or yellow yarn.

Large ears of Indian corn, mottled with red, yellow, orange and black kernels, need the support of all-purpose aluminum wire when hung upon the wall. The husks of Indian corn should be split and separated, but not pulled up into a flower or a tuft; the colors of the kernels show up well against the straw-colored husks. Although these ears make attractive wall hangings, they are at their best when arranged on a tray or in a basket with ornamental gourds.

INDIAN NECKLACE

Indians in the Southwest make necklaces of varicolored corn kernels, stringing them on deerskin thongs; you can adapt this idea, minus the thongs, to creating colorful ropes or chokers to be worn with slacks and sweaters. This gift will be appreciated by high school and college students for its timely Indian vogue as well as for its practicality. Dye the large, white shield-shaped kernels of field corn and string them on doubled nylon thread. Of course, the dried outer shells of the kernels are too tough to be pierced with a needle, but they can be softened and colored in one fell swoop. The full procedure is as follows:

In a large saucepan or a kettle, mix half a cup of liquid dye with two cups of boiling water; place the pan over low heat. Add two cups of shelled white corn, and simmer gently for fifteen minutes. Remove the pan from the heat, and let the corn stand in the dye ten minutes longer. Rinse under cool running water until no more dye washes off. Then, with a sharp darning needle and a thimble, make a hole through each kernel lengthwise, beginning at the rounded end and going toward the point. This must be done as soon as the kernels are rinsed, before they dry out and harden. Soft pastel colors are produced by this method; yellow dye colors corn best, but blue-green and shell-pink necklaces also turn out well. Longer boiling time would be required for deeper shades, but might split the shells of the grains. String the dyed corn kernels on matching doubled nylon thread. A rope necklace will need no clasp, but inexpensive metal clasps for chokers are sold separately in hobby shops and at jewelry counters in variety stores.

CORNSHUCK DOLLS

In pioneer days, toys of any sort were a luxury and a rarity, but little girls who longed for dolls found a way to make wide-skirted ladies out of cornhusks. The method is still much the same, and a shuck doll would delight a child or an adult doll fancier.

Remove fresh cornhusks from the cob, separate the strips, and bleach them in the sun until they are completely dry. Then soak the shuck strips in warm water for ten minutes to make them pliable. Place three long strips one on top of another, and fold them in the middle; wrap all-purpose aluminum wire around the bundle, one-and-a-half inches below the fold, pull the ends of the wire very tight, and twist them together securely. The folded shucks will bulge into a rounded head above this wire neck, which should be hidden with a narrow strip of cornshuck glued or tied above it. Separate the tied bundle of husks below the neck, and insert a slim six-inch roll of shuck to form the doll's arms; tie the roll near each end with a strip of shuck which will be a wrist. Fold three more shuck strips, and insert them between the halves of the first three; push the fold firmly

*This bustling doll is fashioned entirely·of cornshucks, as are the tiny flowers in the basket.
Her cornsilk hair was air-dried in darkness to retain its yellow color and smooth texture, and
the chignon is caught up with a cornshuck bow. Features (not shown) were painted on as
described in the text.*

against the arm-roll to hold it tight against the tied neck. Now, at the doll's waistline, wrap and tie the bundle of six folded shucks with wire and cover the wire with a belt made of a strip of shuck. Trim the flaring ends of the husks evenly, into layered skirt and petticoats. Glue cornsilk hair to the doll's head, and paint features with watercolors. Add a sun bonnet and an apron, cut from strips of shuck and glued in place, to make this a traditional shuck doll. For a gift that is truly unique, reproduce the panniers and kerchief of the eighteenth century, the high-waisted slim skirted Empire look, a bustle, or leg-o'-mutton sleeves from strips of shuck.

CORNSHUCK FLOWERS

From this same "worthless" material, you can make very sophisticated and long-lasting flowers. Petals cut from fresh green shucks are wired together into flower forms, and then allowed to dry. The pale green husks of white sweet corn bleach to cream color in the sun, while darker husks of yellow sweet corn fade in the shade to a greenish silver. The petals wrinkle as they dehydrate, and the flower actually seems to wither; once the shucks are completely dried, soak the whole flower in warm water for ten minutes to restore flexibility. Then smooth the petals with your fingers or flatten them with an electric iron at the setting for synthetic materials. Curve petal tips by rolling them over a round wooden toothpick, and curl whole petals by winding them on plastic hair-rollers.

Flat flower forms, like French anemones or opened tulips, are built around a center made by folding three short shuck strips in the middle and wiring them tightly below the fold to form a flattened ball. Cut a rounded petal from the thick, smooth base of a husk, giving it a straight stem one inch long and half an inch wide that will serve to attach it. Arrange five or six such petals around a prepared center, and wrap wire around their stems and the center's tail of shuck. Bend the petals back to flatten the flower, and allow it to dry. After it has been soaked, reshaped and dried again, trim the wired petal stems evenly and cover them with a spiral of green floral tape in the semblance of a calyx.

Fanciful lilies are made of longer and more slender petals with pointed tips; they do not require a center. Wire the stems of five petals together and adjust them: one straight upright petal for the top of the flower; two petals flaring outward for the sides, and two curving sharply downward at its base.

Stylized carnations are made of short, inch-wide shuck strips, their ends cut with pinking shears to indicate the characteristic jagged petal edges. Bunch twenty strips in one hand, and wrap them tightly together with aluminum wire; they will bend above the wire as it is pulled tight, and will form a flaring fluff. You probably won't need to reshape this flower after drying it, but trim the strip ends evenly below the wire and wrap them with floral tape.

Make curly chrysanthemums of thirty very slender pointed strips, their bases firmly wired together. After drying and soaking, curl several petals at a time by winding them toward the flower center on small plastic hair-rollers. Let the flower dry for three hours, and remove the rollers; the husks should still be slightly damp. Separate the petals, and reroll or straighten them with the fingers until the flower takes form.

"A rose is a rose," and a cornshuck rose is surprisingly lifelike. Cut three cardboard petal patterns, of graduated size, in the shape of a heart with a shallow cleft at the top; extend the point of the heart into a straight stem one inch long and one-fourth inch wide. Using the rougher and more pliant upper portions of shuck strips, cut three petals from each of the three patterns. Beginning at one corner, roll a two-inch square of shuck into a cylinder; encircle the three smallest petals around it, and wrap the petal stems to the cylinder with a wire pulled tight. Add the three medium sized petals, placing them over the gaps in the first row and wiring them tightly to the cylinder. Cover the gaps in this circle with the three large petals, and wire their stems. Dry the rose, and soak it in warm water. Smooth and straighten the petals between thumb and finger, and curve their upper edges by rolling them over a round wooden toothpick. Trim the base of the rose, and cover its wired calyx with green floral tape.

All these flowers are extremely handsome in their cream or silver-green state, but they can also be dyed in natural or psychedelic colors. Make flowers of cream-colored husks, and dry them. Then soak them for ten minutes, not in lukewarm water, but in hot diluted liquid dye. Rinse each flower under cool running water, shape it, and let it dry again. The petals probably will be slightly streaked, but so are those of many fresh flowers.

You could add stems of stiff green florist's wire to the stubs of the petals before they are wrapped with tape, but it is more amusing to give each flower a "cornstalk" for support. Use a straight, slender shoot of green bamboo, or a curving spray of polygonum — both are jointed and hollow like their cousins corn and cane. Simply cover the end of a shuck flower's taped calyx with white glue, and slip it into the open end of a stem. Bamboo shoots will dry shiny and yellow, while polygonum stems will turn mahogany red.

SEEDS

Despite the descriptive adjectives that the word connotes, a seed is not necessarily small and brown. Some are large and flat; some are round, ovoid, or kidney-shaped; and some resemble flower petals. Most seeds are muted in color: white, tan, brown, black, and gray. Some, however, are striped, mottled, or contrastingly edged, and many retain bright color even when hard and dry. In the large legume family, seed peas dry green or yellow, and lima beans pale green or white. Seed string beans follow the spectrum of color from black to white with blue-black, purple, magenta, carmine, orange-red and yellow varieties. Amazing maize produces not only flat horseshoe-shaped white and oval yellow kernels, but the tiny red beads of strawberry corn and the red, orange, and black grains of Indian corn. Minuscule Oriental poppy seeds are blue, while the equally small seeds of collard are deep red. The daisy-petal seeds of canteloupe, pumpkin, squash, and gourd are orange, yellow, cream-colored, and white. Sunflower seed are striped in black and white; white cushaw seed are rimmed with yellow. Some peas and beans have black, brown, or yellow eyes, while many beans are striated in black, brown, or white. Bell pepper's small white seeds are like the round, ruffled petals of a tiny flower, and beet seeds are infinitesimal tan wood-roses.

Children will have fun making these seed gifts. Left: a house cut from styrofoam and mounted on a sheet of cardboard has windows, doors, and trim of corn and shells attached with special styrofoam glue. Right: Pumpkin, sunflower and squash seeds and black beans are mounted on a cardboard mat with white glue that dries transparent — the plain picture frame is also seed-decorated. Opposite: Pumpkin seed flowers with poppy seed centers are made on circles of brown wrapping paper (slashed to center, slightly overlapped, and glued to form a shallow cup) with a wire stem hooked through the cup center. "Ferns" are made from lengths of florist's wire bent to shape, with seeds glued on at an angle.

XI. Left: *A mosaic wall hanging made from corn, popcorn, beans, peas, peanuts, pumpkin, canteloupe, collard, okra and sunflower seeds. The forked stick perch casts a poppyseed shadow; the background is parakeet feed (see page 129).*

XII. Right: *Real hydrangea heads, dried and spray-painted to match upholstery fabric (page 28) will last for years.*

XIII. Right: *"Sculptures" for nature-lovers: styrofoam eggs covered with dried starflowers, and a duckling modeled of wallpaper cleaner, with yellow-dyed pearly everlasting "feathers" and two pinecone scales for a bill. Directions on page 32.*

XIV. Below: *Wise Man from the East, with a styrofoam-cone body and a dried apple head (see page 200).*

XV. Right: *Coneflowers, see list on page 96, were painted to match their real counterparts.*

XVI. *Package toppers. Above: Merry Chris Mouse has a wreath of dried, dyed boxwood leaves on a rubber jar ring. Miniature lapelpin wreaths (page 213-214) are in the sleigh.*

XVII. *Right: The bow is made of dyed curled cornshucks (page 209); the bottle trim is a sponge dripcatcher wreath with painted hemlock-cone "roses" and small pod flowers (page 117).*

XIX. *Below: Dried starflowers, cured blooms of bishop's weed, and spraypainted pearly everlasting in a funnel container (see page 23).*

XVIII. *Above: Gardener egghead (page 181).*

SEED MOSAIC

The very popular seed mosaics are made by gluing seed to a rigid backing; this could be a wooden plaque, a sheet of heavy cardboard, a rectangle of fibreboard, or a framed cork bulletin board. The simplest mosaics are geometric designs filled in with colored popcorn, which comes dyed in all the colors of the rainbow, but with such a wide range of naturally colorful seeds available, one can disdain dyed materials and select seeds for shape as well as for color.

Department stores, hobby shops, and mail order catalogs offer flat rattan wall hangings in a variety of motifs: flowers, sunbursts, human and animal figures, birds, and butterflies. For anyone who cannot invent and draw original designs, these serve as ready-made outlines for seed mosaics when glued flat to wallboard or to a cork bulletin board.

Decide on a pattern of color; then, consider texture. The seeds need not be arranged in rows within the frame, but can be swirled or circled; they need not lie flat, but can be turned on end or on edge. Fitting the seed into the assigned space is rather like assembling a miniature jigsaw puzzle: for a small space, a small seed; for a larger void, a wide seed or two narrow ones. It takes time to glue each one individually, but this extra effort is well worth the trouble. Hold a seed between thumb and finger, dip it quickly into white glue to moisten only its back, and set it in place at once.

If the mounting material is attractive and its color appropriate, it can be left bare. If, however, the design is made on fibreboard or cardboard, you will want to cover the background completely with tiny seeds. Consider black lettuce-dust, gray celery, gray-blue poppy, brown cumin, yellow or white mustard seed. The proper complement for a bird motif would, of course, be birdseed!

Since these seeds are too small to be set in place one by one, treat the background by brushing white glue over one small section of it at a time, and sprinkling seed over the glue while it still is wet. When the whole mount is covered and the glue is thoroughly dry, turn the mosaic over and tap it lightly to dislodge any seeds that have not bonded to the surface. Brush the resulting vacancies again with glue and fill them in with a second sprinkling of seed.

Seed mosaics are great gifts for gardeners, and appeal especially to men.

SEED FLOWER PICTURES

Featherweight flat seeds glue as easily to paper as to a rigid backing, and small framed seed-flower pictures make attractive and desirable gifts. At a variety store, select a small oblong or oval picture frame with a protective glass. Open the back of the frame; remove the cardboard liner, and glue white or colored kraft paper to it.

Draw or trace the outline of a simple floral design — a tight grouping of a few small flowers, or a more elaborate arrangement in a basket or a compote. If you include a container in the design, cover it with small seeds before constructing the flower forms. Dill or caraway seed will simulate the woven texture of a brown basket, while rice or barley will give a look of white hobnailed china to a footed compote. Dip a small artist's brush in white glue, and paint within the outline of the container. Sprinkle the seeds on the wet glue, adjusting them with the tip of a wooden toothpick to follow the straight or curved edges.

Melon, squash, and pumpkin seeds are indispensible for floral motifs, for they form the pointed oval petals of flat daisy flowers in white, yellow, or orange. Round, ruffled white pepper-seeds, encircling a green or yellow split-pea center, make tiny fruit blossoms. Sprays of "berries" substitute for background foliage in such a design, and are made of mustard, radish, collard, or poppy seed; these round seeds, along with pointed black okra globes, also form the centers of the daisy flowers. Four-petalled dogwood blossoms, made of large white cushaw seeds, should be given beet-seed centers. Buds can be made of yellow popcorn, barley, or white rice.

Place the daisy petals first, dipping each seed in white glue. Angle the several petals around a small open space that will receive the seed center. Add tiny pepper-seed petals after the split-pea center is in position: squeeze dots of glue from the bottle tip onto the paper, encircling the center, and drop a pepper seed on each dot, maneuvering it into position with the tip of a toothpick. Make sprays of berries by squeezing out a line of glue and sprinkling it with round seed.

Allow the glue to set overnight. Then lift the picture, turn it over, and tap it. Re-attach any errant centers, petals, berries, or small container-cover seeds, and wait twelve hours before sealing the cardboard in the frame.

BOUTIQUE SEED HANDBAG

You can create a most unusual boutique handbag by applying a seed-flower design to a child's rectangular metal lunchbox, a very "in" reticule these days. These lunchboxes are sold in hardware, department and variety stores; they are usually covered with cartoon or nursery-rhyme characters in garish colors, and each contains a small vacuum bottle which for this purpose is expendable.

Fortunately, these lunchboxes have raised frames that are painted in solid colors: white, yellow, red, or dark blue. The first step in transforming the box into a bag is to cover its flat surfaces — top, bottom, and sides — with three coats of enamel to match or contrast with its raised rim. It is important to wait twenty-four hours between coats, so that the brush will not pull off or craze the paint already applied. Then the box should be lined, and this can be quickly done with self-stick felt or quilted plastic from the housewares section of a department store.

Apply the montage of seeds only to the lid, showing right side up when the box is carried by the handle. The techniques of positioning and gluing are the same as for seed-flower pictures on paper, but this design is framed by the raised rim of the box. When the seed flowers are finished, allow the glue to set for twenty-four hours before finishing the handbag.

So that the seeds won't be knocked off when the purse is carried, give them a tough, transparent protective covering. Use two coats of clear white shellac, applied with light strokes of a full, soft brush.

NUTS

Any acquaintance would be happy to share the harvest of hickory nuts, Chinese chestnuts, hazelnuts, walnuts or pecans from your own trees, but nuts are the most beautiful of all edible seeds, and have other great gift possibilities. To trail over the edge of an arrangement of autumn fruits, what could be handsomer than a bunch of "grapes" made of glossy brown pecans? For a brass candelabrum's winter dress, nothing is nicer than sprays of glycerin-treated leaves, joined with a cluster of mixed nuts.

For either decoration, the nuts must be individually wired. It takes a brave woman to bore a hole through a slippery nutshell with an electric drill, and fortunately this isn't necessary. All you need is a pair of discarded nylons, scissors, and a coil of hair-fine aluminum wire.

WIRING NUTS IN NYLON HOSE

Cut the fine wire in eight-inch lengths. Then, with scissors, cut the legs and feet of the stockings into four-inch squares; discard the reinforced tops, heels, and toes. Runs do not matter, but non-run invisible mesh hose are really better for the purpose. Center a nut on a square, and pull the fine nylon mesh very tightly up and around the nut, twisting the ends of the stocking material. Wrap wire tight around the stocking twist, as close to the nut as possible, and make several turns for firmness; twist the

Nylon-wrapped pecan "grapes", large fresh ivy leaves dipped in self-polishing floor wax, and a chunky candle (molded in a tin can and colored with wax crayon) to brighten someone's table. The holder is an inverted clay saucer.

wire several times, and leave the ends free. Now cut off the ruffle of excess nylon, but be sure to leave a quarter of an inch extending beyond the wire wrapping so that the stretched material will not slip its moorings.

The fine strands of the stocking mesh are nearly invisible against the shell of any nut, but the nylon covering will be even less noticeable if both light and dark shades are used. Peanuts, almonds, and hickory nuts have such pale color and rough texture that very light sheer mesh disappears against their shells. English walnuts' pebbled tan blends well with summer sheers, while pecans and hazelnuts call for medium shades. For Chinese chestnuts and brazilnuts, use darker-colored hose.

CLUSTER OF MIXED NUTS

For a candlestick decoration, use hair-fine wire to bind together the stems of two short sprays of glycerin-treated leaves. Then group several nuts of different varieties into a cluster with a twist of their own wire stems.

132

Arrange several clusters into a lavish bunch, and wrap their twisted wires with a spiral of brown plastic tape. Center the nut grouping over the joined stems of the foliage sprays, and wrap the nuts to the stems with all-purpose wire. Leave the ends of this wire long, for attaching the finished spray to the candelabrum.

PECAN GRAPES

To make a bunch of pecan grapes, you will need twelve to fifteen nylon-covered nuts. Begin at the bottom of the bunch with a single nut; cover the top half with two pecans, and twist all three wires together. Add three nuts above the two, and then a row of four. In this manner, the bunch may be made as large as you like. Adjust all the pecans to face in one direction so as to hide the mechanics of mesh and wire. Wrap the wires at the top of the bunch into a stem by covering them with a spiral of brown plastic tape; the grapes are ready to trail over the edge of a bowl of dried flowers or fresh fruits.

9.

Portable Topiary and

Plants In Pots

By definition, topiary is "the art of producing garden ornaments by cutting and pruning shrubs or trees in fanciful form." It was extremely fashionable in Ancient Rome, and during the late eighteenth century no formal garden in England, France or Italy was without cypress, yew or arborvitae clipped to stylized pyramids or trimmed to resemble animals, birds, or human beings. Obviously, such a rigidly controlled shaping was not achieved without constant care. In the twentieth century, stylized topiary has given way to well-clipped hedges, and trees or shrubs espaliered on walls are the most prevalent manifestations of the ancient technique of train and trim.

PSEUDO-TOPIARY

In recent years, a sort of pseudo-topiary has become very popular; it consists of training vining potted plants such as ivy or ficus over a metal framework. Artistic topiary frames, from simple pyramids to elaborate animal and bird forms, are available but cost a pretty penny. Similar effects can be obtained from such homely materials as umbrella frames, metal baskets, coat hangers, and chicken wire.

WIRE BASKET FRAME

For pot-plant topiary, fill a large clay pot or an attractive planter with a mixture of one part sand, one part garden soil, and one part leaf mold or peat moss; near its center, plant three young ivy plants or rooted cut-tings. It is well to start such a topiary in the fall, to allow the ivy roots to become well established. Early in the spring, before new growth starts, set in place a framework over which the vine will be trained.

A small and simple frame consists of a wire hanging basket eight inches in diameter, plus a straight eight-inch piece of black-painted coat hanger wire. Firmly imbed the coat hanger wire upright in the center of a nine-inch flower pot planted with ivy, and bind the new shoots loosely to the wire with pipe cleaners, which will not injure their soft stems. When the ivy has grown to the top of the wire, invert the metal hanging basket over it, allowing the rim of the basket to rest upon the soil in the pot. Train a single shoot of ivy along each of the basket's down-curved wires, to create an airy mound.

UMBRELLA PARASOL-FRAME

A larger variation of potted topiary begins as before with three ivy plants near the center of a container filled with sand, loam and humus. Choose a pot or planter twelve inches in diameter, and for a framework use a man's umbrella so worn that it is ready for the discard. Remove the cloth covering from its metal frame, and unscrew or cut away with a hacksaw the handle from the center shaft. With wire-cutters or a hacksaw, cut each long rib off two inches beyond the point at which its short supporting rib is attached. Raise the skeletal umbrella and make sure that the ribs remain permanently extended by covering the catch with liquid steel, which is sold in tubes at hardware stores. Now stand this parasol armature upright in the center of the pot and force its shaft down into the soil until the topheavy framework is securely balanced. As the ivy grows, guide it up the center shaft with encircling pipe cleaners; when it reaches the top, train its shoots over and along the metal ribs so that it forms a cascade of greenery like a weeping cherry tree in form.

UMBRELLA CONE-FRAMEWORK

For a pyramid frame, open a skeletal umbrella only partially, and imbed each rib tip in soil near the rim of a large planter after forcing the shaft of the umbrella deep into the center of the pot. Then plant a vigorous young ivy cutting near each rib tip, and train its new growth upward toward the apex of the cone.

CARE OF POTTED TOPIARY

Fortnightly feedings of liquid fertilizer (20-20-20) will greatly encourage growth, and the soil should be kept moist by regular watering. To avoid a daily check for surface moisture, you can make a self-watering planter out of any clay flower pot with a drainage hole in the bottom. Set the planted pot inside a larger leakproof container filled with water; the pot should be raised above the bottom of the container on empty thread spools.

SOILLESS TOPIARY (even pseudo-er!)

Another sort of portable topiary is not only self-watering but soilless. It consists of a rigid metal armature covered with sixteen-gauge galvanized chicken wire and stuffed with sphagnum moss. In the moss, plant rooted ivy cuttings or small plants of *Ficus pumila* (creeping fig), with a small ball of soil attached, and train their growth over the chicken wire to cover and hide the framework. Small-leaved ivy is far more attractive for topiary than the coarser common *Hedera helix*. Baltic ivy is extremely hardy and very rapid in growth, but star-shaped, variegated, and geranium-leafed varieties are especially pleasing.

PYRAMID

You can easily form a pyramid by covering the partially opened skeleton of a child's umbrella with galvanized chicken wire: cut a blunt-topped triangle of the mesh with wire-cutters, and shape it around the umbrella cone; the chicken wire will stay put if you bend the short stubby cut ends of one edge with pliers, hook them through holes of the mesh near the opposite edge, and then firmly clamp them with the pliers.

Soak approximately one bushel of sphagnum moss overnight in tubs of cool water to which you add soluble fertilizer in the proportion recommended by the manufacturer and stated on the label. Remove the moss from the tubs, and place it outdoors on the ground to drain for three hours. Then from the opening at the bottom stuff the cone with the sphagnum, forcing it into the tip of the cone with the handle of a wooden spoon, and packing each succeeding layer of moss tightly with the fingers.

When the cone is as fully packed as possible, cover the bottom of it with a circle of chicken wire cut two inches larger in diameter than the cone's base: pull the edges of this circle up around the cone and hook stubby wire ends into the mesh.

Small rooted ivy cuttings can be planted six inches apart over the whole surface of the pyramid to ensure quick coverage. You can push their roots through the mesh into a hole poked in the moss with a wooden spoon handle, and hold them in place by pulling moss over and around them with the fingers. Guide tendrils of ivy to grow over and hide the bald spots, and hold them in place with wire hairpins; wherever their stems are pinned to the moss, new roots will form.

Place the cone in a deep clay saucer that is kept filled with water; where it will constantly renew its own inner moisture. However, until the ivy has covered the surface of the cone, the outside layer of moss will dry out unless it is thoroughly sprinkled twice a week. Every two weeks, soluble 20-20-20 fertilizer should be added to the water in the saucer, and the recipient must be so instructed.

ARMATURES OF WIRE AND CHICKEN WIRE

Using stiff wire for an armature over which chicken wire is wrapped, it is possible to achieve a bird with feathery green plumage — no artistic talent is required, for this will be a frankly fanciful fowl. For a lifesize goose, procure from a hardware store three six-foot lengths of heavy galvanized iron wire, and a packaged coil of pliable all-purpose aluminum or copper wire. Bind the tips of the three stiff six-foot lengths tightly together by wrapping them with the soft wire — twenty turns to cover three inches of the tips, then fifteen turns overlapping the first layer. This is the bill

This ivy-feathered flamingo literally drinks water from a cup to keep his plumage green and growing. The topiary frame (see Sources of Supply in Appendix) is stuffed with sphagnum moss. (Made by Mrs. Ernest C. Newton.)

of the bird. Separate the stiff wires slightly, and curve two of them up and one down to shape the head; bring the three wires together again and wrap them loosely with soft wire to form a sturdy neck. Then separate the three wires widely; extend one wire horizontally for the bird's spine, and curve the other two wires downward in a semicircle, a foot apart, to outline a plump beast. Bring the three wires together at the back of the goose, securing them with a tight wrapping of soft wire. The stiff wire spine will be longer than the other two; bend it above the wrapped joint into a triangle for a stubby fan-shaped tail.

Covering this armature with a single sheet of chicken wire would be well-nigh impossible; first, cut the mesh into strips with tinsnips so that it can be molded over the framework with ease; overlap the strips, and interlock their cut edges by bending them with pliers. Cut three-inch strips to cover the head and neck, and six-inch strips for the body. Form the neck first of all: press soaked and drained sphagnum around the wires and cover it with a spiralled three-inch strip of chicken wire. Then cover the head with strips of chicken wire and stuff it by poking wet moss through the mesh with the handle of a wooden spoon; repeat this process for the tail. Cover the breast and sides with six-inch overlapped strips of chicken wire, but leave the top of the back open. Pack moss very tightly into the body cavity, pressing it down with the bowl of the wooden spoon. When the packed moss is level with the stiff wire spine, close the top of the bird's body with strips of mesh.

Ficus pumila, the "creeping fig" often used to cover conservatory walls, grows quickly and has small overlapping dark green leaves that will make perfect plumage for this whimsical goose. Plants grown in two-inch pots and placed six to eight inches apart will cover the framework completely in a few months. Cut holes in the mesh with wirecutters; plant the roots together with a ball of soil, and cover them over with moss to prevent leeching. Once the plants are in place, the new growth tendrils are guided in the right directions and held in place with small metal hairpins set astride their stems and hooked into the wire mesh at an angle. The goose should sit upon a "nest" — a deep clay saucer or a low, broad ceramic planter kept filled with water for self-moistening, and it should be sprinkled from above, thoroughly, twice a week.

All the above types of pseudo-topiary can spend the summer out of doors in a shady garden spot, but must be brought indoors before frost. They do not have to hibernate in a greenhouse, but will serve as a focal decorative point for a friend's enclosed terrace or covered loggia all winter long.

TEMPORARY TOPIARY

FLOATING SWAN

The same basic construction methods can be used to produce a temporary topiary, covered with instant foliage of cut twigs instead of with slow-growing plants. A magnificent, never-to-be-forgotten thank-you gift for the neighbor who generously shares her swimming pool would be a floating swan — a smaller version of the goose described above.

Make the armature with three four-foot lengths of stiff wire and cover it not with chicken wire but with hardware cloth; half-inch or quarter-inch mesh will hold the cut twigs securely. A child's styrofoam float, bought at a drugstore or a variety store, will be the platform for the waterfowl. Use all-purpose aluminum wire to lash the framework securely to the float: cut a twelve-inch length of wire, bend it, and press the ends completely through the styrofoam, one inch apart. Set the bird upright on the float, weave the wires in and out of its mesh and twist them firmly together. Repeat this step several times to hold the bird steady on his perch. Stuff the framework with soaked sphagnum moss, and cover the entire head and body with short sprigs of conditioned foliage by threading their stems through the wire mesh into the moist moss. Prick long sprays of foliage or fern fronds horizontally into the base of the frame, to cover the plastic float, and give the waterfowl a fine feathery tail of ferns or spiky flowers. Set the float adrift in a pool, and the slightest breeze will waft it across the water. Tell its owner to turn the float upside down once a day and let the swan swim underwater for an hour. In spite of sun and wind, this daily soaking of foliage and moss should keep the arrangement fresh for at least a week. The moss-filled frame will last for many seasons, and can be re-covered with foliage or flowers again and again.

TEMPORARY ROSE STANDARDS

A standard rose tree is a handsome gift, be it a growing plant for the garden or a topiary whimsy made of an old umbrella. Denude the metal framework of its cloth or plastic covering, and unscrew the handle or cut it off with a hacksaw. Clip off each long rib, with wire-cutters, just beyond the point at which its short support-rib is attached. Open the skeletal frame and secure the catch permanently with a few drops of liquid steel. The two sets of ribs will form a flattened orb. Fill a low, wide flowerpot with moistened ready-mix concrete, which is sold in small bags, with directions, at hardware stores. While the concrete still is wet, cover its surface with sand or small pebbles. Insert the shaft of the umbrella in the center of the pot and brace it upright until the cement has begun to set. Cover the wire framework at the top of the shaft with strips of hardware cloth, leaving an opening at the top. Fill the cavity with soaked sphagnum moss and add the final covering strip of mesh. Prick sprays of rose foliage through the mesh to cover the orb, and add accents of well-conditioned roses.

SPECIAL OCCASION TOPIARY FRAMES

In our calorie-conscious society, a heart-shaped box of chocolates is a sweet thought on Valentine's Day but a severe temptation. A better gift idea is a heart-shaped flower arrangement made like a topiary but in a metal

A *"temporary topiary" table tree made in a salad mold. Sprigs of conditioned small-leafed holly form the green background for red "berries" cut from half a yard of ball fringe; the denuded braid makes a flat bow for the base of the tree. A cookbook holder props the mold upright. The topiary star, for a place favor or an invalid's tray, is an individual salad mold filled with tufts of curred pine needles and sprays of red-painted privet berries.*

salad mold. Paint the outside of a large heart mold with dark green enamel, or cover it with stick-on felt or green foil — use florist's foil rather than Christmas wrap, which cannot be molded around an irregular shape because of its paper backing.

Lay the mold flat and fill it to the brim with soaked Oasis. To hold the moist foam in place, lay hardware cloth across it, allowing a two-inch over-hang of mesh on all sides of the mold. Bend the overhanging edges of wire mesh at right angles and push them down inside the mold — if they touch the bottom and press against its sides, tension will hold the cover firm.

Fill the mold with flowers — well-conditioned red or pink carnations, roses or chrysanthemums — by pricking their short-cut stems through the mesh into the damp Oasis. Edge the mold with conditioned sprigs of small-leafed foliage, their stems set in at an angle to make a flat green border.

To make this flat-backed topiary stand upright, as it should, brace it with a metal cookbook holder or a small easel from a hobby shop.

By using other molds, you can extend this idea to other occasions. For the Fourth of July, fill a star mold with red sweet William, daisies, and cornflowers. At Christmas, decorate a tree mold filled with boxwood twigs with sprays of holly berries or with tiny glass ornaments wired to the mesh. The cans that hold precooked boneless hams are large and egg-shaped; one of these, filled with mixed spring blossoms, would make a perfect Easter topiary and would need no easel because it balances upright upon the flat rim of its larger end.

LEMON TREE

No gift from the garden is more versatile than a topiary table tree. Its stylized shape adapts to any setting, from the formally elegant to the functionally informal, and it is long lasting to the point of semi-perman-ence.

Begin by rolling a double thickness of hardware cloth into a cone; layer-ing adds such stability that no other framework is necessary, and hardware cloth's half-inch mesh offers firm support to short-stemmed foliage. The stubby ends of the top layer of mesh should be hooked through the lower, and bent back with long-nosed pliers to hold securely.

Turn the cone upside down and pack it firmly with Oasis — any old bits and pieces, or crumbling blocks that have as many holes as Swiss cheese. Immerse the inverted cone in cool water for an hour; a deep kettle or a tall plastic or metal wastebasket is better for this purpose than the kitchen sink. Cover the bottom of the pyramid with a double layer of green florist's foil, bent up and molded around the mesh to form a leak-proof base.

Meanwhile, four-inch sprigs of small-leafed foliage should be conditioning in hot water. Shallow roasting pans or cake tins are ideal for this purpose; pack the twigs in so tightly that they support each other in an upright position. Strip the leaves from the lowest inch of each stem before inserting it in the water. Boxwood twigs are best, but if they are unavailable these can substitute: holly (*Ilex microphylla* or *Ilex rotundifolia*), privet, barberry, or cotoneaster.

It helps to wear a glove while pricking these conditioned sprigs into the tree shape. Begin at the base of the cone, and set each segment of foliage at right angles to the form; press the leafless stem end through the mesh into the moist Oasis. As the cone narrows toward the top, the right-angled twigs will slant upward more and more. Finish the top of the tree with an especially well-shaped, fully leafed bit of foliage. This basic tree will remain fresh for several weeks if the Oasis is occasionally remoistened. To do this, remove the foil from the base and set the cone in cool shallow water for an hour; then replace the waterproofing.

This is the basis of the ever-popular lemon tree that is a year-round gift par excellence. To add fruit trim, use green stiff florist's wire cut in eight-inch lengths. Force a wire entirely through a lemon, one-half inch from the stem end. Bend the ends of the wire toward each other, over the end of the fruit, and twist them together; then press this twisted "stem" through the foliage deep into the mesh of the cone. Because they last so long, lemons are the most practical fruits to use; for special color effects, however, try seckel pears, crabapples, pomegranates, limes, or kumquats.

To make such a tree bloom, prick into the Oasis the short stems of well-conditioned flowers — carnations and chrysanthemums will last exceptionally well. Come December, use tiny glass balls or bright bunches of holly berries to turn the pyramid into a table Christmas tree. For a truly gala effect, deck it with miniature packages — lumps of sugar wrapped in several colors of florist's foil and tied with gold cord; use hair-fine wire, threaded through the mesh and then through the cord, to attach them.

At any season, this tree should have a holder to raise it above the table-top. A compote works well, but the best base for gift-giving is a squat green candleholder, of the type intended to support a candle two inches in diameter. Attach the foil covering the bottom of the pyramid to the holder with four foam picture mounts.

FRANKLY FALSE TOPIARY

Permanent, carefree, and frankly false topiary standards and pyramids are made on green styrofoam balls and cones, or on white styrofoam covered with green florist's foil. Lifelike artificial boxwood twigs, artfully molded of plastic in Hong Kong, are available from florists and at specialty shops, but the quantity required to make a large cone would be quite expensive. Plastic pittosporum, yew, or pine (from a variety store) are also realistic, and these do an even better job of masking. Almost invariably, flat leaf clusters of artificial foliage are molded around a center hole, and have been pressed down over knobby protuberances on the plastic stem. With the index and middle fingers spread beneath such a foliage circle, a sharp tug will pull it up and over the hump. It is then an easy matter to attach the circle of leaves to styrofoam: a kitchen match is precisely the right size to fit the center hole, and the red or blue matchhead forms a colorful, unrecognizable bud that holds the cluster firmly in place.

Once the cone is completely camouflaged with greenery, the table tree is ready to burst into bloom. Strew its surface with cured flowers — daisies, zinnias or marigolds fitted with wooden toothpick stems that you can easily prick into the styrofoam. With minimal effort, you can also prick in longer lasting strawflowers that have been given wire stems before being air-dried. Pinecone zinnias in mixed bright colors will make this a truly memorable pyramid; bind two or three by their own short wire stems to a single wooden floral pick, prick them in as a cluster, and you'll cover the cone faster. The effect is natural and very pleasing.

The raised base of this long-lasting ornamental gift could be a compote or a candleholder, but you can also "plant" the tree in a flower pot or a cachepot filled with plastic wood or wallpaper cleaner that has been topped with pebbles or sand. Give the tree a trunk made of a wooden knitting needle: press the point of the needle up into the cone from the center of its base; imbed the head of the knitting needle in the middle of the container, pressing it down through the mastic material to touch the bottom of the pot. About one-and-a-half inches of the wooden needle trunk should show between the top of the container and the bottom of the cone.

STANDARD TOPIARY TREE

By the same method, you can make a standard topiary tree from a styrofoam ball. Use artificial foliage and real preserved or pinecone flowers; give it a long knitting-needle trunk and a cachepot planter. Create a facsimile of topiary's prestigious "poodle tree" with three styrofoam balls of graduated sizes: impale them upon a section of curtain rod. When you prick foliage into a styrofoam ball, begin with a horizontal row — the sprigs at right angles to the surface — encircling its equator. As you move toward the top of the ball, slant each row of sprigs more sharply upward; on the lower half of the sphere, slant them down.

HOUSE PLANTS

Don't overlook the gift potential of plants in pots. You can grow them from seed, but for quicker results, make stem cuttings of such plants as geranium, philodendron, English ivy, coleus, lantana, chrysanthemum, fuchsia, and Christmas cactus. Cut off the young tips and root them, in soil or water. *a*) Keep cuttings moist. Cover the rooting pot with a pane of glass, or tie a plastic bag around it to retain humidity. *b*) When roots have formed, transplant the cuttings into three-inch pots; you'll have several "little" gifts.

Another sure and fast way to grow your own gift stock is to root the trailing crown divisions of African violet (*c*) or runners of spider plant (*d*) in small containers. Secure a runner to soil with a hairpin until it roots; then cut it away from the mother plant. Even faster: lift young budded plants such as nasturtium (*e*) from the garden, and pot them up for indoor gifts.

Since pretty containers rarely have drainage holes, you must put a layer of pebbles in the bottom of a pot before adding your plant, to be sure that water does not stay around its roots. Then add a good potting soil mixture (page 134), insert the plant so that the top of its root is about half an inch below the rim of the pot and pack soil down firmly over it, add water, and your plant is ready for giving. Be sure to label it and give directions for its care.

Inexpensive small cacti require sandy soil; planted in a miniature strawberry jar, they are sure to be appreciated (*f*). Remind the recipient that cactus likes lots of light and little water. Buy small plants such as *Philodendron cordatum* (1); dracaena (2); peperomia (3); and dwarf palm (4) for a dish garden. Arrange them in a shallow bowl or planter, tall ones in the center (*g*).

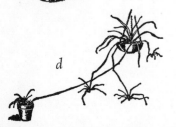

Children enjoy growing seeds and vegetables from the kitchen. Grapefruit, orange and lemon seeds should be soaked in warm water for several hours and then planted, pointed end up, in soil; cover with a quarter of an inch of soil, and keep moist in a dark place. When seedlings are two inches tall, move them into light (*h*). Sweet potato (*i*) and onion plants (*j*) can be grown in water: Balance half a potato or a whole onion on top of a jar; add water to touch the rooting end. Root an avocado seed the same way (*k*), with its wide part in water; when roots are about an inch long, transplant the seed in soil to cover (*l*).

Carrot, turnip, and beet tops can be grown by cutting off the lower tip of a vegetable and burying the top piece in pebbles; add water to cover all but the tip of the vegetable (*m*).

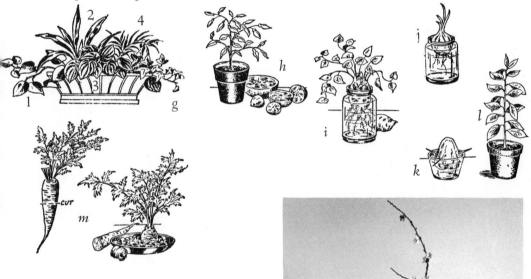

Wild plum branches with hemlock cone "blossoms" were cemented inside a hollow tree bole before a plant of baby's tears (Helxine soleiroli) was potted up in the cavity. Easy-to-grow houseplants in unusual containers are very welcome gifts. Do include plant care instructions: Helxine likes lots of light — fluorescent will do — but not direct sunshine; water roots sparingly, but spray leaves to keep moisture high.

10.

Herbs and Seasonings To Give

Herbs are the garden's oldest living inhabitants. We are told that they appeared on earth during the third day of the Creation (Genesis 1:11), and many varieties are specifically mentioned in the Bible: anise, coriander, cumin, dill, mint, mustard, rue, saffron, sage and wormwood. Archeologists have discovered that caraway seeds were used by the Lake Dwellers in Switzerland during the late Stone Age, and coriander seeds have been found in Egyptian tombs of the twenty-first dynasty. The recorded history of herbs began in the fourth century B. C., when Theophrastus wrote of the saffron and thyme that carpeted the hills of Greece.

Most of the herbs that are used in cooking actually prefer poor soil and are quite tolerant of drouth, and therefore can be grown where more demanding plants would fail. Herb gardening has great advantage where space is limited: a very few plants will provide seasonings for family use and for gifts as well.

GIFTS OF FRESH HERBS

Fresh and flavorful "kitchen" herbs are eagerly welcomed by good cooks. Snippets of dill stems and leaves add liveliness to potato salad. Minced chives give delicate onion flavor to cream or cottage cheese, and to sour cream topping for baked potatoes. Curly dark-green parsley is not only the world's favorite garnish, but is a valuable seasoning: melted butter liberally laced with minced parsley is an equally perfect sauce for broiled fish or for boiled new potatoes. Sprigs of mint trim the rims of frosty glasses of iced tea or fruit juice, and are the indispensible ingredient of mint julep. Bits of borage leaves add the flavor and aroma of cucumber to tossed and jellied salad, without the slightest risk of indigestion.

Pick herbs early in the morning, while their leaves still are wet with dew, wash them at once in ice water, and shake them free of surface droplets. Keep several sprigs standing upright in a glass of water in the refrigerator, ready for a gift occasion.

AROMATIZING VINEGAR

Flavored vinegars, aromatized with fresh herbs, are wonderful gifts for salad lovers. The method is simplicity itself. Wash several sprigs of tarragon (or dill, or spearmint) in cool water and shake off the droplets. Tie the stems together with white cotton thread, leaving an end of thread eight inches long. Lower the tarragon into a wide-mouthed quart-size glass jar with a screw top, keeping the long end of thread outside the rim. Gently pour in cold cider- or wine-vinegar to fill the jar to the brim. Seal the jar tightly, and store it in a cool dark place for two weeks. Remove the lid, and carefully lift out the tarragon by pulling on the thread. Decant the vinegar into small attractive bottles, and seal.

MOCK CAPERS

True capers are the unopened flower buds of *Capparis spinoza*, a thorny, straggling South American shrub. Very similar in taste (and more pleasing to many palates) are mock capers, which are nothing more exotic than the immature seed pods of the garden nasturtium. Gather the hard green pods early in the morning while the dew is on them; wash them in ice water and dry them between paper towels. Then pack them closely in tall, slender bottles; empty olive bottles are ideal. Heat distilled white vinegar to boiling, adding one teaspoonful of salt to each cupful, and pour it over the pods to fill the bottle to the brim. When the vinegar has cooled to room temperature, seal the bottle with a screw-on lid, and store it in a cool, dark place for three weeks. The "capers" are then ready for use in salads, as a garnish for fish, and in sauces (especially in mayonnaise).

MINT EXTRACT

It is almost indecently easy to make a flavorful mint extract. Wash freshly gathered sprigs of spearmint or peppermint in ice water, and shake off the surface droplets. Strip the leaves from their stems, and pack them in a measuring cup; measure two cups of packed leaves, and place them in a glass or ceramic mixing bowl. Bring two cups of water to a full, rolling boil, and pour it over the leaves. Cover the mixing bowl with a china plate, and allow the mint to steep for one hour. Strain the liquid through a triple layer of cheesecloth into a pyrex pitcher, squeezing the leaves in the cloth to extract all their juice. Add a few drops of green food coloring, and stir to distribute it evenly. Using a funnel, pour the mint extract at once into very small bottles, seal, and label it.

HERB SEEDS

Textbooks and garden guides advise that the seeds of herbs should be gathered "as soon as they are ripe, and before they drop to the ground," but this direction is almost impossible to follow. Instead of attempting to outguess the seed pods, most herb gardeners are content to surround each plant with a circle of plastic film cut from a drycleaner's bag, to catch the seeds as they fall; the circle should be slashed to the center on one side, fitted around the stem of the plant, and the cut edges overlapped. Herb seeds should be washed in cool water, patted between paper towels, and spread out on more paper toweling to dry overnight. They then are ready to be packaged and sealed. Clear plastic pill vials with snap-on lids, bought from a druggist, make splendid seed containers; labels may be glued to the lids or to the bottles themselves.

DRIED HERBS

DRYING HERBS

Leafy herbs should be gathered for drying just as the plants' flower buds are about to open, for this is when the leaves are richest in aromatic oils. Cut whole stalks early on a hot, clear summer morning, wash them at once in cool water, and shake them vigorously. Then strip the leaves from the stems. For centuries, herbs have been air-dried in a warm dim room, and many herb-fanciers insist that this traditional method is best (although many organic-food fanciers advocate sun-dried herbs). The leaves dehydrate much more rapidly on an elevated drying frame that allows air to circulate below as well as above them; you can make such a frame easily by placing a stock-size plastic window screen (from a builder's supply company) on bricks or books. Spread the washed leaves over the screen in a single layer; stir them each morning, and spread them out again. At the end of four days, they should be dry enough to crumble when pressed between the fingers, and ready for packaging in airtight containers (see below).

OVEN METHOD OF DRYING

The oven method of drying herbs appeals to impatient gardeners, for it prepares the leaves for use in hours instead of days. Arrange stripped, washed leaves in a single layer on a cookie sheet, and place them in the oven at 150°. After forty-five minutes, turn them with a spatula. Depending on their thickness and the amount of moisture they contain, the leaves will dehydrate to the crumbly stage in one-and-a-half to three hours. To avoid mingling of odors and flavors, only one variety of herb should be dried in the oven at a time.

CONTAINERS FOR DRIED HERBS

Save vitamin bottles throughout the year so as to have herb containers on hand when they are needed; the small clear glass or white china apothecary jars make attractive packaging for dried herbs. Olive bottles, mustard jars, and baby food jars with screw tops are other good ideas. Paint the lids sage green to cover up the original labels, and then paint on the name of the herb, or glue on typed labels. (Crumbled leaves of most herbs look much alike, so label the jars immediately, lest you forget.)

FINES HERBES

Instead of packaging each dried herb separately, it would be thoughtful to combine some into *fines herbes* as a particularly appropriate gift for an especially good cook, or for someone who wants to become one. Fines herbes are always a mixture or four different herbs in equal proportions, but the combinations vary according to the dishes they are to flavor. A good blend for seasoning cream or cottage cheese consists of chives, parsley, savory, and borage. Thyme, basil, savory, and chives add delicate flavor and aroma to omelettes. A plain butter sauce for baked or broiled fish is tremendously improved by the addition of chives, thyme, sage, and fennel. Very thin slices of whole wheat bread spread with basil, thyme, sweet marjoram, and parsley, mixed with soft butter make delicious tea sandwiches.

Begin a basic blend of fines herbes intended for general use with chives and parsley, and to these add any two of the following: basil, chervil, sage, savory, and thyme. Toss equal amounts of the dried herbs together

Gifts for the gourmet. Dried fines herbes (parsley, chives, savory and thyme), sage and dill seed are packaged in small apothecary jars that once held vitamin capsules; each hollow jar lid is filled with tiny dried starflowers in bright yellow, red and blue.

in a bowl until indistinguishably blended, and seal the blend in small jars labelled "Fines Herbes"; also, specify on the label the four herbs that constitute the mixture.

Unless the recipient of your gourmet-aid gift considers herself a cook of cordon bleu calibre, it wouldn't be amiss to include, with your herbal offering, a list of choice uses for the particular blend given, and a recipe (such as the fish sauce mentioned above) that actually utilizes it.

HARDY HERBS AND THEIR USE

The flavorful herbs listed below, all hardy in the temperate zone, are easy to process and are often used in cooking.

Anise, *Pimpinella anisum,* annual. Fresh leaves used in fruit salads or as a garnish. Seed used in cakes and cookies.

Basil, *Ocimum basilicum,* annual. Dried leaves flavor tomato dishes, soups, and stews. Sometimes cooked with peas, string beans, or squash.

Borage, *Borago officinalis,* annual. Fresh flower sprays used like sprigs of mint in iced tea or fruit punch; they have the scent of cucumber. Fresh leaves, chopped fine, add flavor of cucumber to tossed or jellied salads.

Burnet, *Sanguisorba minor,* perennial. Fresh young leaves in green salad. Sprigs
formerly were so often used to top tankards of ale that the herb is commonly
called "toper's plant".

Caraway, *Carum carvi,* biennial. Seeds used in cheeses, rye bread, potato salad.

Chervil, *Anthriscus cerefolium,* annual. Fresh leaves look like parsley, and are
used as a garnish. Dried leaves flavor soups, and often are an ingredient
of *fines herbes.*

Chives, *Allium schoenoprasum,* perennial. Hollow leaves, fresh or dried, give
delicate onion flavor to cream or cottage cheese, sour cream, butter. Can be
grown in pots on a sunny windowsill, or in a windowbox.

Cumin, *Cuminum cyminum,* annual. Seeds used to flavor bread, cheese, and
sauerkraut.

Dill, *Anethum graveolens,* annual. Fresh leaves and flowering tops aromatize
vinegar. Seeds flavor pickles, potato salad.

Fennel, *Foeniculum vulgare,* annual. Dried leaves an ingredient of *fines herbes.*

Mustard, black or white, *Brassica nigra* or *B. alba,* annuals. Seeds flavor sauces,
pickles.

Nasturtium, *Tropaeolum minus* and *T. majus,* annuals. Flowers as garnish.
Flower petals and young leaves in salads. Seeds, chopped fine, as pickling
spice. Immature seeds, in vinegar, called "mock capers."

Opium Poppy, *Papaver somniferum,* annual. Seeds *only* for flavoring breads,
cookies, cheeses, dressing for fruit salad. (Opium comes from the juice of
the unripe pods, but is not present in the seeds.)

Oregano—See Pot Marjoram.

Parsley, *Petroselinum crispum,* biennial. Fresh leaves as garnish. Dried leaves
in sauces, *fines herbes.* Can be grown in windowbox.

Peppermint, *Mentha piperita, perennial.* Fresh leaves and flowering tops flavor
drinks. Leaves make flavor essence for icings, ice creams, sauces, mint jelly.

Pot Marjoram, *Origanum vulgare,* perennial. Oregano. Dried leaves flavor
spaghetti sauce, pizza, meat loaf, tomato dishes.

Rosemary, *Rosmarinus officinalis,* perennial. Can be grown in pots or in windowbox. Fresh or dried leaves in soups.

Sage, *Salvia officinalis,* perennial. Dried leaves in stuffings for poultry, fish, and
pork. Used also in spaghetti sauce, meat loaf, stews.

Sesame, *Sesamum orientale,* annual. Benne seed. Seed in cookies, cakes, wafers.

Spearmint, *Mentha spicata,* perennial. Fresh leaves flavor fruit drinks, aromatize vinegar for fruit salad dressings.

Summer Savory, *Satureia hortensis,* annual. Fresh leaves in green or tomato
salads. Dried leaves in poultry stuffing, meat loaf, vegetable soup, dried
beans. Often a part of *fines herbes.*

Sweet Marjoram, *Majorana hortensis,* annual. Fresh leaves as a garnish. Dried
leaves season spinach.

Tarragon, *Artemisia dracunculus,* perennial. Fresh leaves flavor pickles, aromatize vinegar. Dried leaves in salad dressings, sauces for fish or lamb. This herb gives Dubonnet its distinctive flavor.

Thyme, *Thymus vulgaris,* perennial. Grows between flagstones, in rock wall pockets. Can be grown in windowbox. Dried leaves flavor soups, stews, stuffing for fish or poultry. Often part of *fines herbes.*

AROMATIC HERBS

In addition to these flavor enhancers, a second group of herbs is grown for scent rather than for taste. Most, but not all, of these aromatic herbs are hardy in the temperate zone. Their captured sweetness is valuable for sachets and perfumes, and the plants are all attractive additions to the garden.

Balm, *Melissa officinalis,* perennial. Lemon balm. Leafy tips top glasses of lemonade or fruit punch.

Clary, *Salvia Sclarea,* biennial. Clary sage. Dried and powdered leaves a fixative for more volatile scents in sachets.

Damask Rose, *Rosa damascena,* shrub. Petals scent sachet and potpourri. Attar (oil) of roses for perfume and cake flavoring distilled from petals.

Lavender, *Lavandula spica,* perennial. Dried flower buds used in sachet, cologne, perfume. Calyx of flowers yields oil for perfume.

Lemon Verbena, *Lippia citriodora,* shrub in southern states, pot plant north of Washington, D.C. Leaves flavor fruit punch, fruit cup.

Provence Rose, *Rosa gallica,* shrub. Same uses as damask rose. Scent slightly lighter and more delicate.

Rose Geranium, *Pelargonium graveolens,* shrub in deep South and on Pacific Coast, elsewhere a pot plant. Fresh leaves flavor jellies, blanc mange. Oil from leaves and petals used in perfumes.

Southernwood, *Artemisia abrotanum,* perennial. Dried stems and leaves used as a moth and ant repellent.

Sweet flag, *Acorus calamus,* perennial. Calamus root. Pulverized dried root used in sachets.

Wintergreen, *Gaultheria procumbens,* perennial. Berries steeped in brandy produce a flavorful, scented liqueur. Oil from leaves used in perfumes, and as a flavoring for candy and chewing gum.

AROMATIC HERBS IN A TUSSIE-MUSSIE ARRANGEMENT

In the Elizabethan Age, London's ladies of fashion followed the example of their queen and carried nosegays when they walked or rode abroad; the small hand-bouquets of sweet-scented flowers and aromatic herbs served to counteract the noxious smells of the city's streets. The tussie-mussie, a random combination of perfumed flowers and sweet herbs, was the indoor version of the nosegay.

Fresh aromatic herbs, combined with small flowers in a compote or a rice bowl, still please the nose as they delight the eye. Apartment dwellers, residents of retirement homes, victims of lengthy illness — all are cheered by the coolness of mint, the tart-sweet scent of lemon balm or lemon verbena, the spiciness of rose geranium, or the clean astringency of lavender. While you wait for the doorbell to be answered, bruise a few of the herb leaves between thumb and finger to release their aroma.

SEASONINGS

RED PEPPERS

In colonial days, a string of dried red peppers hung on the chimney breast above every yawning kitchen fireplace — a colorful decoration as well as a pungent seasoning. The idea, so old that it is new again, lends itself well to gift giving. String hot red peppers fresh from the garden — chili, long red, cayenne, or red squash — using a large needle and heavy white cotton thread. Leave a six-inch "tail" at the end of the thread. Tie several strings of peppers to the crossbar of a metal coat hanger, and hang them in a dark but airy closet until the skin of every pepper is shrivelled and dry to the touch. Finish each string with a bow of ribbon or thick colorful yarn, tied to the loose end of thread, and bestow them upon friends with wood-panelled kitchens.

PICKLED PEPPERS

The same varieties of peppers are easily transformed into hot pepper sauce, a man-pleasing condiment and a useful seasoning for soups, stews, and spaghetti sauce. Wash and dry freshly gathered hot peppers, and pack them whole in tall bottles, jars, or cruets, sterilized in the dishwasher. Heat one cup of distilled white vinegar with one teaspoonful of salt to the boiling point, and pour it over the peppers to fill the bottle to the brim. Cool to room temperature, seal, and set aside in a cool, dim cupboard for at least three weeks. The fiery-flavored vinegar is then used in the same manner as Tabasco sauce.

Milder pepper varieties — cone or banana peppers — can be pickled by the same method. Cone peppers (peperoncini), drained and chopped, are a delicious addition to green salad; banana peppers are served as pickles or added, chopped, to salads and sauces.

DRIED PEPPERS

The oven-drying method used for leafy herbs works equally well for dehydrating fresh green bell peppers, sweet red peppers, or small hot cherry peppers. Wash and dry the freshly gathered pods; cut off their tops, and remove the seeds and white membranes. Dice the flesh of the pods in quarter-inch bits, and arrange them in a single layer on a cookie sheet. Place the peppers in the oven at 150°, and stir them once each hour. Remove the sheet from the oven after three hours, and allow the shrivelled pieces of pepper to stand uncovered overnight before packing and sealing them in cool sterile glass jars. When you label gift jars of dried green pepper, do add directions for its use: Reconstitute by soaking for half an hour in ice water, and then use as fresh pepper in salads or in cooking.

A gift from the kitchen garden in Christmas red and green. The inexpensive tiered glass container from a variety store holds a triple gift of parsley, red hot pepper, and green sweet pepper gathered at peak of perfection and dehydrated in the oven.

OTHER DEHYDRATED SEASONINGS

Onions, too, can be dehydrated in the oven, though for best results they must be minced very fine. Two to two-and-a-half hours at 150° will find them hard and dry; they should be cooled to room temperature before packaging and sealing. Dried onion may be added to soups and stews just as it comes from the jar; for salads and sauces, it should first be reconstituted in ice water for thirty minutes. Many people actually prefer dried to fresh onion as a seasoning. The flavor is there, but it is less persistent and, some feel, more digestible.

Celery leaves, in a single layer on cookie sheets, dry even more quickly than herbs at 150°. An unsurpassed flavoring for soups, they go directly from jar to kettle.

Three small jars of dehydrated seasonings — one each of green pepper, onion, and celery leaves — add up to one great gift from your kitchen garden.

11.

Scented Gifts

When uncovered butter absorbs the smell of fish in the refrigerator, it is a minor domestic tragedy, but when lard can be made to smell of lilacs, the French call it "enfleurage." The secret of French floral perfumes lies in the ability of fats and oils to absorb the fragrance of flowers. By applying this principle to a simple home method of treating fresh flower petals, it is possible to preserve the sweet scents of the summer garden in pomade, cologne, solid perfumes, and bath oils that make delightful winter gifts.

POMADE

Pomade originally was intended to be used as a hairdressing. It is unsurpassed for smoothing an unruly lock or a recalcitrant eyebrow, and its scent is extremely long lasting when rubbed on the inner wrist or the crook of the elbow.

The basic ingredient of pomade (and cologne) is purified white lard which may be bought in vacuum-sealed cans at any supermarket. (Solid vegetable shortening is a poor substitute for lard in pomade making, for it neither absorbs nor retains flower scents as well.) Any one of the following flowers can be used to perfume the pomade:

Roses — dark red or crimson varieties are best; Cape Jasmine (or gardenia); tuberose; carnation or clove pink; hyacinth; lilac; lily-of-the-valley; night-scented stock; narcissus (and fragrant jonquil varieties); mignonette; magnolia *glauca* or *grandiflora*.

Gather flowers for pomade in the morning, as soon as the sun has dried the dew. (Stock is the exception to this rule; it is fragrant only at night and must be cut after the sun is down.) Gently pull the petals from each flower, and throw away the calyx and the stem.

Melt one cup of freshly opened purified white lard until it is just liquid, in a new aluminum pie tin. Pour it at once into a new aluminum grease container for the kitchen — the kind that has a tight-fitting lid and a re-movable perforated strainer fitting over the inner cavity. Let the lard stand, covered, at room temperature until it has solidified, and then score it all the way through with a knife in a checkerboard pattern; the cuts should be no more than one-half inch apart.

Cover the surface of the strainer with two layers of freshly picked flower petals. Put the lid on the grease container, and seal it with a strip of mask-ing tape; leave the container sealed for twenty-four hours. Then open the lid, remove the flower petals and discard them. Cover the strainer with fresh petals, and reseal the container for twenty-four hours. Repeat this step each morning for seven days, by which time the fat should have absorbed its full quota of fragrance.

Using a wooden tongue depressor, scoop the scented lard out of the container and pack it into small jars with screw tops. This pomade will keep its perfume for many months.

COLOGNE

To make floral cologne, begin with fresh pomade made by the method just described. Chop up the scent-impregnated fat into pea-size bits, and place them at once in a bottle or jar with a screw lid; fill the bottle half full of fat. Add enough grain alcohol to fill the bottle, seal, shake, and set it away in a dark, cool closet for at least three months. Shake the bottle occasionally during this waiting period.

Strain the alcohol off into a smaller bottle, and add a few drops of either oil of cedar or oil of sandalwood (procured from a druggist or a perfumer) which will serve as a fixative to keep the floral scent in the volatile alcohol. At least one drop of fixative should be added to each ounce of alcohol, but more of this secondary scent may overpower the floral perfume. It is of course important that the cologne be kept tightly corked.

SOLID PERFUME

Wax as well as fat absorbs odor, and the same method used to impermeate lard with floral scent can produce a solid perfume more acceptable to the many people who do not like the idea of rubbing even the sweetest smelling lard upon human skin.

157

Melt together slowly, over very low heat, one large, eight-ounce jar of white vaseline and one three-ounce block of paraffin. As soon as the two have liquefied, stir to blend them indistinguishably and pour the mixture immediately into a clean and odor-free kitchen grease-container. Cover and cool to room temperature, and then set the container in the refrigerator for an hour. The wax mixture will not be completely solidified, but will have the consistency of whipped butter. Score the surface of the wax deeply in a grid pattern, and place two layers of fresh flower petals on the grease-container's strainer. Cover, and seal the lid with masking tape. Replace the flowers with fresh petals every day for ten days.

Since wax is not so receptive to odor as fat, you may want to reinforce the scent of the solid perfume by sprinkling over each day's allotment of petals one-half teaspoonful of powdered orris root, which your druggist can procure from a wholesaler.

Just-right gift containers for solid perfume are pocket-sized pillboxes with tight-fitting lids. Transfer the scented wax to these little repositories with a wooden tongue depressor or a flat popsicle stick.

Flat aspirin tins, given two coats of solid color enamel and decorated with small gold rose decals, are equally efficient containers for solid perfume and cost virtually nothing.

BATH OIL

Delightfully fragrant bath oil is very easy to make, and once again a kitchen grease-container should be employed. Vegetable oils are best for this purpose. Coconut oil really is superior to the olive and safflower oil which are everywhere available in grocery stores, but unscented coconut oil must be obtained from an importer or a perfumer (see sources of supply). Two cups of oil can be processed at a time, over a ten-day period, by the same method used to permeate solid fats with floral scent. Use any attractively shaped bottle with a screw top or a tight fitting cork as a holder for the bath oil.

PERFUME ESSENCE

To make a very pleasing, long lasting floral perfume with an oil rather than an alcohol base, employ the same principle but a different method.

For a container, use a glazed cylindrical crock of pottery, stoneware or porcelain or a new, wide-mouthed glass jar. In the bottom, place an inch thick pad of sterilized absorbent cotton and saturate it thoroughly with any odorless oil — olive, safflower, cotton-seed, castor, or mineral. Over this il-soaked pad spread an inch-thick layer of fresh, fragrant flower petals, and over the petals sprinkle a dusting of plain (un-iodized) table salt — not enough salt to cover, but enough to show. Add a second oil-soaked cotton pad, being sure that it completely covers the petals and touches the sides of the jar. Cover it with another layer of petals sprinkled with salt, and repeat until the jar is seven-eighths full. Using a well-washed stone or a heavy glass paperweight, press the mass down in the jar as much as possible; leave the stone in the jar for a weight. Seal the jar and let it stand at room temperature for forty-eight hours.

Line a glass or china bowl with a large square of doubled cheesecloth. Remove the weight from the jar, and pour its contents into the bowl, on top of the cheesecloth. Gather the corners of the cloth together into a bag; lift the bag and squeeze it over the bowl until all the scented oil has been expressed. Pour the perfumed oil immediately into small, tightly stoppered bottles.

POTPOURRI

Originally, potpourri was made of dried rose petals and tight buds, spiced with rare perfumed oils. Many people still value this rose-and-spice mixture as a room freshener, but most gardeners make gift potpourri of rose petals only, and substitute kitchen spices for costly aromatic oils.

Gather fully open roses on a hot, dry summer afternoon. Medium and dark red roses are more richly and lastingly perfumed, and among the best garden varieties for potpourri are 'Crimson Glory', 'Etoile d'Hollande', 'General Jacqueminot', 'Mirandy', 'Rubaiyat', and 'Red Radiance' — plus, of course, the species Damask, Provence, Musk, and single Rugosa roses. The petals dry quickly, as herb leaves do, on a raised plastic window screen which permits free circulation of air below as well as above it. They should remain on the drying frame for twenty-four to thirty-six hours; they should feel dry to the touch, but not crumbly.

Potpourri can be made in a cylindrical glazed pottery crock or in a wide-mouthed half-gallon size jar. Put a half-inch layer of dried petals

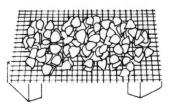

at the bottom of the crock and sprinkle the petals with half a teaspoonful of salt; then sprinkle on half a teaspoonful of mixed powdered cinnamon, cloves, mace, and allspice; add one-fourth teaspoonful of powdered gum benzoin as a fixative. Place a second layer of rose petals in the crock and top it with another sprinkling of salt, spice, and fixative. Repeat until the crock is filled, ending with spice. Sprinkle over the top of the last layer one teaspoonful of brandy mixed with five drops oil (or attar) of roses from a perfumer. To economize, mix half a teaspoonful of good rose perfume with the brandy instead of the rose oil. Cover the crock or jar with its lid, seal with masking tape, and store for two weeks in a cool, dark closet. Open the crock and stir its contents gently but thoroughly with a wooden spoon. Reseal the lid and store again for two months, stirring once a week. The potpourri is then ready to be packaged for gift-giving in attractive covered containers: candy, ginger or cookie jars, or small tureens. Flower-decorated china jars with perforated lids are made in England especially for potpourri, but the constant escape of fragance can be better ensured by packing the spiced petals in a pierced brass betel nut box or in a large incense burner. In any case, line the container with a double layer of nylon net, pour in the potpourri, and gather and tie the corners of the net; this see-through inner package will prevent accidental spills when the container lid is lifted.

ENGLISH ROSE POTPOURRI

Old English potpourri calls for: one quart of dried rose petals; thirteen ounces of powdered orris root; one-eighth ounce each of Oil of Rose and Oil of Sandalwood; one-fourth ounce of Oil of Rose Geranium; one-half ounce each of Oil of Bergamot and Tincture of Musk; one ounce of yellow sandalwood chips. (The ingredients are available from Caswell-Massey Co., Ltd, in New York, or from Hove Parfumeur of New Orleans, and the addresses are listed in the sources of supply.)

These constituents should be mixed together thoroughly and stored in a tightly closed wide-mouthed glass jar for four weeks. The contents of the jar should have a weekly stirring with a wooden spoon.

ENGLISH MIXED POTPOURRI

English mixed potpourri is easier to make and far less costly. It calls for three cups of dried rose petals, two cups dried lavender buds, and one cup of dried lemon verbena leaves, mixed with two ounces of powdered orris root and one-half ounce each of powdered allspice, cinnamon, cloves

Dried rose petals enhanced by spices can be packaged in a see-through plastic bag. For a more important gift, wrap the mixture in nylon net and present it in an English potpourri jar with perforated top, or in a pierced brass betel box.

and gum storax. It, too, should be tightly sealed in a glass jar and stored for four weeks (with a weekly stirring) before using.

PERSONAL POTPOURRI

Any dried perfumed flower petals or aromatic herb leaves may be included in a potpourri — balm, mint, rosemary, geranium, verbena, carnation, and mignonette, along with chips of vetiver or calamus root. If you dry and store flower petals and herb leaves separately, in glass containers, you can combine them with spices into a potpourri as individually yours as a fingerprint. Be sure to add a fixative to your mixture — powdered gum benzoin and gum storax are easiest to obtain unless you grow your own clary sage in the herb garden.

SACHETS

Materials for sachet also are dried on an elevated window screen in a warm dim room: the petals of roses or violets; leaves of rose-geranium, lemon balm, and lemon-verbena; leaves and calyxes of lavender. Spread the leaves and petals in a single layer on the drying frame, and gently

161

stir them each morning for four days; by this time they will be dry enough to crumble between the fingers. As a fixative for their delicate natural perfumes, add powdered gum benzoin, gum storax, or orris root (from a druggist), one-half ounce to a quart of dried material. (Dried and pulverized leaves of clary sage from the herb garden may also be used as a fixative.)

Sachets may be single-flower or mixed fragrances, and powdered spices may be added if desired — cinnamon to rose petals, mace to violets, allspice and cloves to mixed bouquets.

Attractively packaged sachet is a delightful all-occasion gift, and a little goes a long way if it is made up into no-sew handkerchief or lingerie sachets. It takes no time at all to construct a tiny sweet-scented pouch: cut a circle five inches in diameter from strong, finewoven but thin cloth which will allow the scent but not the spice-dust to escape. Good possibilities are cotton batiste, handkerchief linen, and organdie; contrast white material with a top layer of colorful nylon net or cotton lace. Place two tablespoonsful of crumbled sachet in the center of the circle; lift the edges of the cloth and tie them, just above the now mounded mass of sachet, with narrow colorful satin ribbon. There will be an attractive ruffle of material above the closure. Finish the small pouch with a spray of tiny pastel artificial flowers thrust through the knot of the ribbon bow.

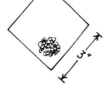

Only a teaspoonful of the spicy mixture goes into each of these rosebud sachets, to scent a stack of handkerchiefs. Make a rosebud from a three-inch square of white or pastel taffeta, or use three-inch-wide satin ribbon, cut in three-inch lengths instead; one yard of ribbon makes twelve sachets. Lay the small square of material flat on a table with one corner toward

Old-fashioned favorites in new dress: gifts of sweet-scented sachet made of rose petals and aromatic herbs. The transparent container at the left is a glass coffee percolator basket on a footed bill spindle; the basket on top holds pink artificial flowers. Rosebud handkerchief sachets of pink satin ribbon; each needs only a teaspoonful of crumbled sachet. For a green-and-white bridal shower gift, a metal coffee basket to hang on a closet rod.

you, and place a teaspoonful of crumbled sachet halfway between this corner and the center of the square. Fold the opposite corner down over the sachet, and fit it over the corner nearest you, forming a triangle. Pick up the left point of the triangle; fold it over and down upon these two corners. Then fold the right point in and down upon the other three. With the fingers, gather the flaring "wings" and press them against the layered points; secure all the material by twisting hair-fine wire several times around the base of the bud. Clip off the ragged edges of the cloth below the wire. Cover the wire, and make a calyx for the rosebud, with a tight wrapping of narrow green plastic tape. Now lay the rosebud on a stemmed spray of plastic roseleaves; with a second strip of green tape, bind the calyx of the flower to the short stem of the foliage, covering the whole stem for neatness with spiralled tape.

Perfect for bridal shower or engagement gifts, these small sachets also make most acceptable Christmas remembrances for teachers — kindergarten, day-school, Sunday-School, music or dancing — and for den mothers or Girl Scout leaders.

Larger amounts of sachet are required to fill containers that stand upon the linen closet shelf or hang from the rod in milady's wardrobe. Two very satisfactory free-standing holders can be made from a pair of tall square or round kitchen shakers; their perforated tops release the scent slowly, and the sachet will remain fragrant for a year or more. Cover the shakers with plain or quilted contact plastic, which will hide the raised or incised "Salt" and "Pepper" labels. Add a bow of narrow ribbon and a spray of matching or contrasting tiny plastic flowers, which are better for this purpose than your own dried or cured blossoms since they are shatterproof.

For a transparent container that allows the sachet to be seen as well as smelled, use the topless glass coffee-basket meant to be used in a pyrex percolator; these coffee-baskets are sold separately in department and large variety stores. Discard the removable metal stem, and make a stand for the round glass basket of a footed bill spindle from an office supply company: fit the slender center tube of the basket over the spike, and its perforated metal base will be securely balanced on the footed stand. Fill the basket with sachet, leaving the leaves and petals uncrumbled for better appearance in the see-through container. The plastic lid of a sour cream or cottage cheese carton, inverted to show its white inner surface, will be the right size top for this container. Cover the rim of the glass basket with white glue; bore a small hole in the center of the lid and force it down over the spindle until it rests upon the glued basket rim. An inch or more of the metal spike will project above the lid; you can quickly camouflage it by impaling upon it the sort of small lacy plastic basket sold in variety stores as children's party favors. Press floral clay (or wallpaper cleaner) into the basket around the spindle, and insert the short stems of pink or red miniature plastic roses. The basket of roses serves not only to trim the holder but also helps to hold the plastic lid in place. Since the perforated metal bottom of the glass coffee-holder is lifted above the shelf surface by the stubby feet of the spindle base, the scent will escape slowly and the sachet's fragrance will linger.

Coffee-baskets for metal percolators also are sold separately, and these make fine hanging holders for sachet. Such a coffee holder is of metal, and is perforated all over — bottom, sides, and removable lid. Once again, discard the metal stem. Paint the basket, on the outside only, with bright colored or pastel enamel; while the paint still is wet, reopen each tiny hole with the tip of a wooden toothpick. After the paint has dried, fill the cavity with sachet and glue the metal lid to the rim of the basket. Double a length of narrow white grosgrain ribbon and thread it through the slender tube in the basket center, from top to bottom. Tie the two ends together below the basket, making a knot so large that it cannot be pulled through the tube; then tie the ends of the ribbon into a bow. Glue tiny white plastic flowers to the lid of the basket, circling them around the loop of ribbon that protrudes from the top of the tube. A shower curtain hook, painted to match the basket, will serve to attach the sachet holder by its top ribbon to a closet rod; use the metal variety that fits over the rod and closes like a safety pin; it makes a better hanger than the rigid plastic type of shower curtain hook — the closed metal hook cannot slip off the closet rod, and the loop of ribbon cannot escape it.

For individual coat hanger sachets, large metal tea balls make very attractive and extremely practical containers. They are sold in summer at variety and department stores, and mail-order catalogs sometimes offer them in bell and egg shapes that are especially appropriate for wedding, Christmas, and Easter gifts. Like metal coffee-baskets, these tea-infusers are pierced on all sides; each of their screw-on tops is centered with a short chain ending in a small hook that will fit securely around the base of the large hook of a padded coat hanger. First paint the tea ball with white or pastel enamel, and reopen the holes with a toothpick. Then fill the ball with crumbled sachet and screw on the lid. Finally, tie a sprig of miniature plastic flowers to the base of the chain with a bow of narrow ribbon.

POMANDERS

Another source of spicy scent for linen, clothes or storage closets is the pomander, which has been popular for this purpose since the Elizabethan era. As their name implies, pomanders originally were made of apples selected for their natural perfume and their keeping qualities. In the nineteenth century, when railroads began to carry citrus fruits quickly to all parts of the United States, tart-sweet scented oranges, lemons and limes proved even more fragrant and long lasting than apples for making pomanders. Whatever fruit is used, the method is the same: its skin is covered completely with a studding of whole cloves and its natural fragrance is fixed and reinforced with pulverized spices and powdered orris (which is made from the lastingly aromatic root of the Florentine iris).

Select firm, ripe fruit, and pierce the skin all over with the tines of a fork, making a pattern of holes no more than one-fourth inch apart. In a small bowl, place three tablespoons of pumpkin pie spice; this delicious combination of powdered cinnamon, cloves, nutmeg, allspice and grated orange peel comes ready-mixed in a small tin from the supermarket's spice rack. Add three tablespoons of powdered orris root, procured for you by a pharmacist or ordered from a perfumer, and stir until the substances are thoroughly blended. Roll the pierced fruit in the spices and place it on a saucer. You'll see the perforations made in the skin as darker dots through the powdery coating. Using a thimble for comfort, press a whole clove into each hole; the tops of the cloves should touch, and the surface of the fruit should be entirely hidden. With a wire hairpin, attach the center of a length of narrow ribbon, which will serve as a hanger, to the top of the fruit.

Place the finished pomander on a wire cake rack, so that air can circulate freely beneath it, and allow it to dry out in a cool room for two or three weeks. The pomander is ready for use when it is rock-hard to the touch; by this time, shrinkage will have clamped the fruit-skin firmly about the hairpin hanger.

One full-size apple or orange pomander will perfume a medium-size closet. Smaller lemon and lime pomanders will permeate a deep bureau drawer with scent. Apples from your own trees and citrus fruits from potted houseplants will supply the raw materials for many fragrant gifts.

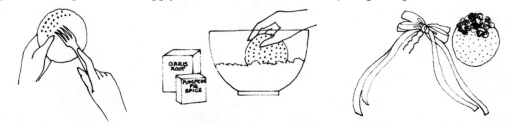

Different, and perfectly delightful for giving, are tiny pomanders made of crabapples or of the inedible fruits of the osage orange. One of these, attached with matching narrow ribbon, puts the finishing touch on a velvet-covered coathanger.

Ordinary wire coathangers can be inexpensively transformed into desirable gift items by slip-covering them with colorful velvet tubing bought from a needlework shop or a florist. With pliers, unwind the end of wire that is twisted around the base of the hook, and slip the hollow tubing over the wire to cover the whole hanger including the hook. Fold each cut end of the tubing back inside the tube and stitch the end closed. Retwist the now covered end of wire around the hook base, attach a small pomander or a tea-ball sachet, and finish the gift with a spray of artificial foliage and a velvet bow. (One and a half yards of tubing will be enough to cover the hanger and make the bow.)

STORING POMANDERS AND SACHETS

Sachets made in summer for holiday gifts will best retain their scent during the waiting period if they are kept tightly sealed in a tin box. Only one variety of sachet should be placed in the box, to prevent mingling of fragrances.

Each pomander, as soon as it is hard and dry, should be packaged in a plastic sandwich bag and sealed with a tightly tied ribbon bow. Several wrapped pomanders can then be stored in a cardboard shoe box sealed with masking tape.

Gifts for the boudoir. Clockwise: A "slip-covered" wire coathanger with artificial oak leaves, and a miniature crabapple pomander. A clove-studded orange pomander on a ribbon hanger. A sachet holder (salt shaker) covered with "Contact", with gilded hemlock cone "roses". A bath powder box (originally a refrigerator container) with seed flowers glued on.

12.

Waxed Flowers and Candle Crafts

In the 1840's, paraffin began to be produced in quantity as a by-product of the petroleum industry, and ladies soon discovered that they could preserve fresh flowers and leaves by coating them with this inexpensive, odorless and translucent substance. Bridal bouquets and funeral wreaths, wax-dipped and glass-covered, were favorite parlor decorations of the "Age of Sentiment," cherished for the memories they evoked.

FRESH PLANT MATERIALS FOR WAXING

Obviously, a coating of semi-opaque wax dims the natural colors of fresh blossoms, but white petals become whiter and attain a pearly luminescence; this explains the prevalence of white flowers in Victorian waxed bouquets. Flowers with hollow stems do not take kindly to this treatment, nor do heavy, many-petalled blooms such as double daylilies and chrysanthemums. Lilies of the valley, sweet peas, orange and mock-orange blossoms, fuchsias, daisies, calla lilies, waterlilies and (surprisingly) full-blown roses are among the fresh flowers that wax well; small but full-grown deciduous leaves and dark green ivy leaves are best bets for fresh foliage. Clusters of berries — holly, mahonia, hawthorn, firethorn, privet, pyracantha — also last well when waxed.

In selecting fresh colored blossoms for waxing, choose deep bright hues which will be lightened by the process: bright red becomes deep pink; orange alters to apricot; gold pales to yellow; purple usually fades to lavender but sometimes changes to blue or rose.

DIPPING FRESH FLOWERS IN WAX

Because of paraffin's low melting point, you can dip the flowers into the fluid wax without cooking them. In an old saucepan, melt together over low heat one pound of paraffin (from the canning supplies display at the supermarket) and a two-inch stub of a white candle. Use a candy thermometer to determine when the wax has reached a temperature of 130°; turn off the heat. Hold a flower by its stem and dip it into the liquid wax, which should be deep enough to cover its entire head; lift it immediately and shake it over the pan to remove excess droplets. Separate and straighten the petals, if necessary, with a flat wooden toothpick. Stand the flower upright in a narrow necked bottle until the surface of the wax has hardened; this will take from ten to fifteen minutes. Reheat the wax in the pan to 130°, to melt the skin that will have formed on its surface. Hold the flower faceup over the pan, and spoon wax over its stem and leaves; then return it to the bottle, and leave it undisturbed overnight. Use a separate bottle for each flower, to avoid smearing the wax as petals touch. If the flowers seem limp when viewed in the cold light of morning, cut their stems off short and re-dip the blossoms.

Don't be discouraged when some flowers have to be discarded; if sixty percent turn out well, the experiment was a success. Nor is the pan with its hard lump of solid wax a total loss. Set it in the refrigerator for an hour; the wax will shrink away from its sides and can be removed in one piece. Save it for another waxing project.

Exposed to the air, wax-coated fresh blossoms gradually lose their color. For a tongue-in-cheek adaptation of a Victorian parlor ornament, mound the waxed flowers on a flat tray and cover them with a clear glass bell jar of the sort used in chemistry labs. Seal the dome to the tray with household cement to make the protective covering air-tight, and present this nostalgic arrangement to the friend with a marble-topped table. The bell jar can be obtained from a company listed in the yellow pages of the telephone directory under *Laboratory Equipment and Supplies.*

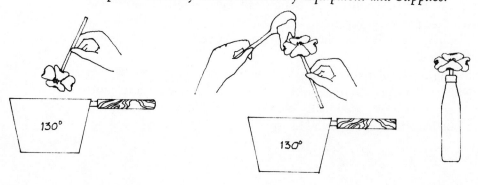

WAXING CURED FLOWERS

Instead of fading, the colors of cured flowers are stabilized by being sealed in wax. Red blossoms that deepened during dehydration to wine or mahogany are lightened by the warm paraffin to a softened version of their original hue. Air-dried everlastings are preserved in perpetuity by waxing, as are pressed green or autumn leaves. Those doubtful cures — the blossoms that are spoiled by the damaging moisture of the air — can be made permanent by sealing the surface of the flowers with wax as soon as they are removed from the drying agent. This is the answer for lilies — Bermuda, madonna, auratum, speciosum, milk-and-wine — and for day lilies!

Melt one-half pound of paraffin (two cakes) with a one-inch piece of white candle until the wax shows a temperature of 130° on a candy thermometer. Remove the pan from the heat.

This time, the wax should be applied like paint with a small artist's brush. Hold a stemless cured flower face up in the palm of one hand, supporting its petals with the fingers. Dip the brush in the pan and dribble wax over the center of the flower and the bases of the petals; then lightly brush wax over each petal. At 130°, the wax is not hot enough to burn your fingers. Hold the flower for a moment, until the paraffin becomes cloudy, and lay it on newspaper to harden for ten minutes. Reheat the wax to 130°, turn the flower over on your palm, and paint its back beginning with the stem stub and the calyx. Place it facedown on newspaper for ten minutes more. If the petals seem limp, brush another coat of wax on the back of the flower. Should a petal break, repair the crack with a brushful of wax on the back and a thin coat over its whole top surface.

These waxed cured blossoms need not be protected from air, and can be arranged on half-rounds of green styrofoam once they have been given stems.

Squeeze white glue into one end of a green cellophane drinking straw, and insert the stub of the flower's stem; balance the blossom in a narrow-necked bottle until the glue has set. Decide where a flower should be placed, and prick a wooden flower-pick into the styrofoam at this point; cut the hollow end of the straw to the correct length; then slip it over the pick and press it down to rest upon the surface of the styrofoam.

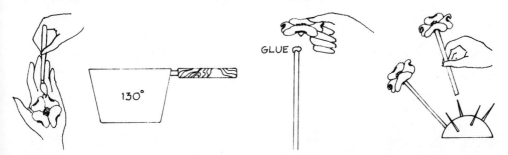

CANDLE CRAFTS

Candles, year-around ornaments for mantels and coffee tables as well as illumination for the festive board, are ever-welcome gifts. They are commercially made in all sizes from slim floral tapers to towering fat cathedral candles; they can be round, square, or intricately shaped and they come in a veritable rainbow of colors.

DECORATING CANDLES WITH WAXED FLOWERS

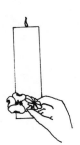

Waxed cured flowers are a most appropriate decoration for a wax candle. For an extremely acceptable coffee table arrangement, choose a squat round candle three or four inches in diameter, in sage green. It must have support, but this need not be a "proper" candle holder. In fact, the candle will be and will look much better-balanced on a flat base: a round trivet or a small metal tray; a wooden vase-base; even a slice of wood, with bark intact, from a lumber company. (As an example of something-for-nothing, the base might be the bottom of a large thirty-two-ounce tomato juice can; smoothly remove it with its rim by inserting the empty can sideways into a wall-type or electric can opener.)

Secure the candle in the center of its base by pressing it down upon a blob of melted wax dripped from a candle stub. The surface of the base that extends beyond the candle can support a circlet of stemless waxed flowers with accents of waxed foliage. Attach these, too, by settling each one upon a coin of candle-dripping and steadying it with the fingers until the wax has hardened.

ATTACHING WAXED FLOWERS TO A CANDLE

For a mantel ornament, a few waxed leaves and blossoms can be attached directly to a large candle. Lay the candle on its side, and dribble melted wax from a candle stub over the area the spray should cover. Quickly place the flowers, one by one, upon the soft wax, and add a waxed leaf or two. Then drip more wax over the flower stems and on it lay a pre-tied bow of velvet ribbon, holding it in position until the candle grease has solidified.

To support such a flower-trimmed candle, a turned-wood holder from a boutique or a candleshop would be perfect. You can make an acceptable substitute, however, from a five-inch clay flowerpot and its matching saucer. Brush both with latex paint that blends or contrasts with the candle color. Invert the pot, and cover its base with Epoxy cement; center the saucer, faceup or facedown as you prefer, upon the glue. Cement the candle to this holder, or anchor it with dripped candle wax.

WAX GRAPES

For a change of pace, decorate not a candle but its holder with a cluster of waxed fresh grape or ivy leaves and a bunch of grapes made of the melted paraffin left over after dipping the leaves. Allow the wax to stand until it becomes opaque and cool enough to handle. Coat the palms of both hands with mineral oil. Put a teaspoonful of wax in one hand and shape it into a ball by rolling it between the palms. Insert the tip of a short length of green florist's wire for a stem, and place the grape on a plate covered with waxed paper. When you have molded all the wax into balls, set the plate in the refrigerator for half an hour to hasten the hardening of the grapes. Then gather several grapes into a tapered bunch by twisting their short stems together; cover the twisted stem ends with green floral tape, and add a tendril made by spiralling green wire over a pencil.

CANDLE RINGS

Another good gift idea — an ornamental ring to be slipped over a candle and rest upon its holder — utilizes snap-on plastic lids that would otherwise be thrown away. The tops of individual ice cream cups, junior baby-food jars, or small yoghurt cartons will be right in size for standard tapers; for candles two inches in diameter, use plastic lids from quart-size frozen whipped topping, cottage cheese, or sour cream containers. Trace a circle in the center of the lid with a ball-point pen; make the diameter of this circle one-half inch greater than that of the candle. Heat the point of a paring knife over a candle flame, and cut a slit in the middle of the circle large enough to admit one blade of a pair of shears; cut out the circle neatly, leaving a flat doughnut of plastic with an outer rim.

Instead of waxed blossoms, use small painted pods or coneflowers to trim the wreath; attach them to the plastic with clear household cement, working from the inner edge of the doughnut toward its outer rim so that the hole for the candle remains unobstructed. Add one or two sprays of trailing artificial ivy, and finish the candle ring with a tiny bow of narrow velvet ribbon.

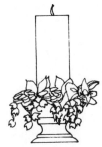

MOLDED CANDLES

Commercially-made candles are beautiful but by no means inexpensive, and many people find it fun to make such decorative gifts from scratch by molding their own candles. Because wax shrinks as it hardens, almost any hollow cylindrical or square container can serve to shape a candle. Round tin cans of all sizes, from two-ounce mushroom to thirty-two-ounce fruit juice, are splendid molds, and as every den mother knows, individual metal heart, flower, or star-shaped salad molds are fine for making candle-floats. The tall square tin that holds a pound of saltine crackers can be pressed into service, as can a cardboard milk carton or a square pint-size freezer container. Suitable, too, are hollow glass containers, either with straight sides or wider at the top than at the bottom: tumblers, vases, bowls and cigarette boxes, to name but a few.

Anyone who has ever helped prepare for a charity bazaar will testify that candle ends can be melted and remolded. Candles also may be made of pure paraffin or of paraffin combined with candle stubs. A battered percolator (or a doll-size teakettle borrowed from the playroom) is a better melting pot than a saucepan, and a small funnel helps guide the hot wax from pouring spout to mold. Make wicks of white cotton twisted cord.

COLORING CANDLES

An easy way to color candles is by melting wax crayons along with the paraffin; stir the wax as it melts, to distribute the color evenly. Wax also

Gifts for pennies. Left: *a white homemade candle wears a wreath of red deodar "roses" made on a plastic lid with cutout center.* Center: *the holder is two jar lids and a tin can top; the candle was colored with lipstick ends; the boxwood wreath is trimmed with red sprayed privet berries.* Right: *a candle to use wherever an open flame is prohibited (for example, in a nursing home). The tall "taper" is a cardboard tube covered with gold foil and glued on a round silvery hot-pad. The "flame" is a sprayed-red pointed pod. Fresh holly leaves and berries were dipped in liquid floor wax.*

can be tinted, after it is melted and removed from the heat, by stirring in lipstick ends or a few drops of artist's oil paint.

PERFUMING CANDLES

A lightly scented candle is delightful; as it burns, warm fragrance permeates an entire room. Several drops of oil of bayberry, oil of pine, or floral essence (procured for you by a pharmacist or ordered from a perfumer) will suffice, as will a small amount of a favorite perfume — this is a good way to use up the dregs of several bottles. Scented bath oil and solid stick cologne also work exceedingly well. Melted wax should be allowed to cool slightly before perfume is added, for in boiling hot wax the volatile fragrance evaporates at once.

MOLDING A CANDLE IN A TIN CAN

To mold a candle of a particular height in a tin can, measure the inside of the can in advance with a ruler and mark the proper level by scratching the tin with the point of a nail. Glass, plastic and cardboard containers can be marked with a laundry-marker pen.

When you use a tin can as a mold, first wash the inside with warm soapy water, rinse, and dry. Then rub the inner sides and bottom lightly with mineral oil, which will keep the wax from sticking to the metal.

Measure a wick of cotton cord: the height of the can plus six inches. Tie a curtain weight, a lead fishing sinker, or a small nail to one end of the cord and drop this weighted end into the center of the can. Tie the loose end around a pencil, lay the pencil across the top of the can, and wind the wick taut by turning the pencil.

Melt the paraffin and/or candle stubs slowly, over low heat, until the wax is fluid; at this point, if candle ends are used, their old wicks will float free and can be fished out with a long-handled fork or with kitchen tongs. Then add color with wax crayon, lipstick, or oil paint. Cool slightly, and add scent if desired. Pour the melted wax slowly through a funnel, which will prevent spills and splashes, into the can. Place the can mold in the

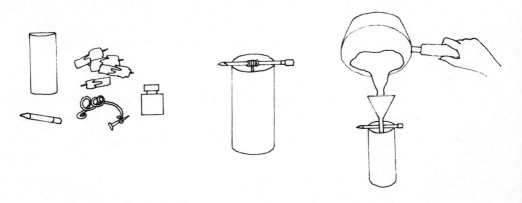

refrigerator for several hours — the length of time required for complete hardening will vary with the size of the candle.

As it cools, the wax will shrink away from the sides of the can and the candle is removed by turning the can upside down and shaking it. If the candle does not slide out, dip the can in a bowl of hot water for a few seconds, turn it over, and tap the bottom with a hammer. Then trim off the excess wick, and polish the sides of the candle with a soft cloth.

MOLDING A CANDLE IN GLASS

A glass mold must be rinsed in very hot water (to prevent cracking when the melted wax is poured in), dried, and lightly coated with mineral oil. The methods of inserting the wick, preparing the wax, and filling the mold are the same as for tin cans, but the glass container should be allowed to stand at room temperature for an hour before being placed in the refrigerator. Remove the candle by dipping the mold in hot water and pulling on the wick while the container is held upside down.

LACY CANDLES

The lacy candles sold in specialty shops can be copied by the following method: cut off the peaked top of a quart size cardboard milk carton, and stand a ten-inch white candle upright in its center. Pack cracked ice between the candle and the sides of the carton, using enough ice to hold the candle straight and steady. Pour melted wax (colored with crayon, lipstick, or artist's oil) over the ice to fill the container and cover all but the wick of the center candle. As the paraffin quickly hardens, the ice melts and leaves its outline in empty spaces. When the wax has shrunk away from the cardboard, the candle has set; turn the carton upside down and pour out the water. The candle should slide out with the water; if it does not, the cardboard can be carefully slit down each side with the point of a sharp knife, and pulled open very gently so as not to break the edges of the wax. When its wick is lighted, the center candle burns down inside the lacy lantern of its shell. This delicately patterned candle needs no other ornamentation than a circle of conditioned evergreen foliage around its base. To keep the greenery fresh, insert each stem into a water-filled corsage tube or a small block of moist Oasis wrapped in green foil.

EGG-SHAPED CANDLES

Egg-shaped candles are appropriate Easter gifts, and these can be molded in plastic eggs (from a variety store) that screw apart in the middle to be filled with candy. Come-apart eggs come in several sizes, and for this purpose they should be larger than hen eggs.

Take an egg apart and coat its inner surfaces with mineral oil. With the sharp point of a knife-blade heated over a candle flame, bore a hole in the center of the small end; this hole should be large enough to admit the tip of a very small funnel. Screw the egg together and stand it upright in a custard cup, a teacup, or a small bowl, depending on its size. Melt and color wax, and scent it if you like with floral perfume for a hint of Spring. Pour the wax through the funnel to fill the shell, and remove the funnel. Tie a metal bead to one end of a cord wick and drop it through the hole in the top of the shell; the weight of the bead will carry the wick to the bottom. Set the egg in the refrigerator for several hours, and then dip the shell in hot water for a few seconds before unscrewing it. Pull the two halves of the mold apart to release the egg-shaped candle and smooth away the lines around its equator with the flat of a heated knife blade. Place the egg on a saucer, and surround it with a wreath of pastel dried flowers.

BYZANTINE CANDLES

Paschal or Christmas candles decorated in the Byzantine style, with jewels and gold braid, are extremely handsome and will be treasured by their lucky recipients. A large round candle — white for Easter, red or green for Christmas — should have a brass or gilded holder. A no-cost candle-stand can be made of a plum-pudding tin opened at the large end with an electric or wall-type can opener. Gild the outside of this little tub with gold paint, invert it, and glue a gilded plastic lid to its solid top to serve as a bobeche. The candle can be cemented to the plastic lid or attached with melted wax.

A Byzantine-style candle, decorated with gold braid, pearls and motifs cut from a gold lace paper doily — all attached with sequin pins. The spray of miniature Easter lilies is made of white-painted columbine seedpods.

Begin by encircling the base of the candle with wide gold braid; overlap the ends of the strip and secure them with three pins pushed through both layers of cloth into the wax. Slender sequin pins are not apt to crack the candle; if you warm them for a few seconds between thumb and finger, they'll push much more easily into the solid wax. Use a thimble to press the heads of the pins down. One and a half inches above this wide strip, add a circle of narrow gold braid overlapped and pinned to the candle.

Between the two braid strips, pin on a row of jewel decorations: filigree flowers, round sequins, sequin stars or leaves, pearl beads. The pearls will show up best if each is pinned above a motif cut from a gold paper doily. Round or square decorative brass nailheads, with sharp points for attaching them to cloth or leather, can be pressed into the candle to substitute for pearls on Christmas candles. Above the narrow braid, add a scattering of nailheads, sequins, or pearls with paper motifs. Let restraint be your watchword, for too many jewels will give the candle a "loving hands at home" look. The decoration should cover only the lower two-thirds of the candle, so that it actually can be lighted.

Trim the bobeche of a Christmas candle with a wreath of gilded evergreen leaves interspersed with tiny hemlock cone roses dipped in gold paint. Finish an Easter candle with a spray of white flowers — dried, cured, waxed — or white painted pods. Miniature lilies, the seedpods of columbine or potentilla, are the perfect choice; a spray of five, dipped in white paint, can complete a bow of gold metallic ribbon anchored at the base of the candle with a heated wire hairpin.

Byzantine candles are especially suited to mantel decoration, for their tracery of braid and jewels can be seen to best advantage at eye level.

13.

Happy Holidays—
New Year's To Thanksgiving

EASTER

Since pagan times, the egg has symbolized spring's annual miracle of re-generation. In the Eastern Orthodox Church, Easter is not only the climax of the Christian year, but a joyful day when brightly dyed or colorfully patterned eggs are exchanged to celebrate the Resurrection of the risen Christ. Imperial Russia produced the ultimate in Easter gifts with eggs carved from semi-precious stones and ornamented with costly jewels.

SEED-JEWELED EGGS

Less valuable but even more symbolic of the season are eggs decorated with flowers made of naturally colorful seed. Empty eggshells can be used, and painted black, dark blue or maroon in imitation of favorite Balkan dyes.

Smooth china nest eggs, colored with nail polish rather than with paint to preserve their translucency, have the look of polished porphyry or onyx, and suggest the semi-precious eggs of czarist Russia. Unless you live in a poultry-producing area, china nest eggs are scarcer nowadays than hen's teeth. However, a farmer's co-op or a feed-and-seed store will order the eggs for you if you agree to buy several dozen. Since they cost very little, it will not seriously upset the household budget to buy them in quantity. These long-oval white eggs are very beautiful, with a look of fine trans-lucent porcelain; they are smooth, shiny, and practically unbreakable.

When applied to china, the various shades of red nail polish produce hues that range from royal purple to orange. Pale opalescent and metallic polishes give china eggs a look of quartz or mineral ores.

When cemented to colored eggs around a center of a single yellow mustard or black okra seed, the slender petal-shaped seeds of canteloupe and squash become orange, yellow or cream-colored daisies. A dogwood bloom evolves from four large white pumpkin seeds centered with a beet seed rosette. Small stylized blossoms are made by encircling a green or yellow split pea with round white petals of bell pepper seed. You can obtain a most striking effect by using a single large four-petalled flower as a crown on the rounded large end of an egg, or two large flowers on opposite sides. A scattering of daisies is very attractive, but most interesting of all is a "calico egg" whose surface is closely patterned with minute stylized flowers.

Be it a real or a china egg shell you ornament with flowers, it will seem a more important present if it is displayed upon a stand. This could be a gilded tripod or ring-shaped holder, sold in specialty shops as mounts for the popular alabaster eggs. It could also be a low brass candlestick or an inverted eggcup.

PRESSED FLOWER EGGS

In Austria and Switzerland, blown eggshells are ornamented with pressed flowers and gold braid for Christmas tree ornaments. These dainty decorations are even more fitting for an Easter tree made of a gnarled driftwood branch or a thorn-tree limb.

To make them, one needs empty eggshells, and despite the French proverb, there *is* a way to "make an omelette without breaking the eggs." Remove an egg from the refrigerator and let it stand at room temperature for an hour. Then pierce the center of the large end of its shell with the sharp point of a paring knife that has serrated edges. With a gentle sawing motion, cut out as small a piece of shell as possible — if you're lucky, the hole will be less than half an inch in diameter. To remove the contents of the egg through so small an opening, you must first break the yolk-sac: insert a skewer or a nutpick through the hole, stir carefully but thoroughly, and pour out scrambled yolk and white. Then rinse the shell with cold water poured slowly through the hole, and let it dry overnight before beginning to decorate it.

Once the shell is empty, the rest is easy. Choose small pressed flowers in bright colors — pansies, violets, geranium or primrose florets — and with white glue attach one or two to each side of the egg. For foliage, add a few pressed pine needles or a bit of fern. Glue a strip of narrow braid or ribbon around the egg from top to bottom; this covers the hole. Before pressing the tape down on the top of the egg, insert beneath it a six-inch length of gold cord which will serve as a hanger, and finish the top by gluing to it a flat ribbon bow or a tiny bird.

One egg, in a small glass keepsake dome of the type sold by jewelers for displaying an antique watch, makes an unusual all-season coffee table conversation piece.

EASTER EGGHEADS

For anyone who no longer believes in the Easter bunny, an "Easter egghead" makes a memorable memento, and one that will be enjoyed from year to year.

Make eggheads of shells emptied by the knife and nutpick method. Both the durability and the appearance of a thin white shell will be enhanced by a coat of flesh-colored paint; a tiny bottle of plastic paint, from the model car display at a toy counter, will cover two large eggs. The shells of brown eggs need no change of color, but should be brushed with clear shellac as a preservative.

To make the egghead a portrait bust, give it shoulders and a neck. Brightly colored plastic eggs that screw apart for filling make appropriate as well as balanced bases; each half of such an egg, open end down, becomes the shoulders of an egghead. White plastic curtain rings one inch in diameter are sold in packets of fourteen wherever cottage curtains are displayed. Four of these, glued one atop another with clear household cement, will form a hollow stack; cement it over the curved top of a plastic egg half, and the curved base of the egghead should be fitted down into the hollow neck and cemented in place.

The end of the egg that rests upon the stacked neck is of course the chin of the egghead. If the egg is small end down, the face will seem long and thin; large end down, the egg face will have plump cheeks and heavy jowls.

Anyone with a modicum of talent can paint features on this face, but those of us who were absent on the day drawing ability was handed out must resort to subterfuge. Large black or dark blue sequins, cut in half with scissors, make expressive egghead eyes. Squeeze a dot of clear household cement from the tube to the surface of the shell and lay the sequin, rounded side up, upon the dot of glue. Place the straight cut edge on top to give the face a downcast eye; the reverse will make a laughing eye. For a look of wide-eyed amazement, use whole large light blue sequins with centered small black sequin "pupils". Glue the small sequin at the upper edge of the large one to simulate surprise; glue it to an outer edge to make the egghead peer out of the corner of its eye. Form an upper lip from a small red sequin cut in half, the two halves glued side by side with the cut surfaces down; complete the mouth with half a red sequin glued below them, cut side up.

You can paint on hair, of course, but a three-dimensional coiffure will greatly improve the appearance of the egghead; it will also cover the blow-hole if the large end of the egg forms the crown of the head. Make fluffy hair of lamb's wool or absorbent cotton, untreated or dipped in ho diluted brown dye. Gold curly-metal pot cleaners make fine blond curls while steel wool is great for a gray pompadour; straight hair is most effec tively imitated with strands of embroidery floss. Doll wigs can sometimes be purchased at large toy stores and are always available at doll hospitals One of appropriate size would be most lifelike, and you can separate a large doll wig into several egghead toupees by cutting its rubber backing between the sewed rows of hairs, with kitchen shears.

Finding Easter bonnets for the eggheads is an exercise in ingenuity Snap-on bottle caps, to keep soft drinks fizzy after they've been opened are sold in supermarkets and variety stores, and sometimes come shaped like miniature jockey caps or sailor hats. Sometimes they are large daisies with raised snap-cap centers — these become egghead garden hats with wide scalloped brims. Little lacy plastic baskets (from a display of children's party favors) make high-crowned, narrow-brimmed hats when shorn of their handles and turned upside down. Oval shoe buckles, of white plastic or "simulated tortoise shell," curve just enough to hug an egghead as an Empress Eugenie creation. The screw-on plastic top of a pill bottle very logically serves as a pillbox hat; a round plastic tablespoon measure divested of its handle, becomes a skull cap. Without its stem, a pointed oval coffee measure can be tilted forward over the forehead to make an eighteenth century bonnet. A flat turn-of-the-twentieth-century "sailor' results when you glue a snap-on plastic bottle cap to the center of the snap on plastic cover of a babyfood jar.

Quarter-inch velvet or grosgrain ribbon, glued in place, is excellent for hat-bands, but you can make bows more easily to scale of satin baby ribbon. White and colored soutache or middy braid also works well for bands and bows.

Trim this miniature millinery with the tiniest florets from your hoard of dried flowers and painted seedpods: pastel Peruvian star flowers and statice; dyed pearly everlasting; forget-me-not-shaped pods of ironweed painted blue, white, pink, yellow or red. Attach them individually with dots of clear cement to the crown of a basket bonnet or the brim of a sailor hat. An Empress Eugenie derby demands a curled plume, made perhaps of a fluff from a feather duster, and three flat flowers to cover the end of the feather on the front of the hat.

For finishing touches, add: a mink-tail boa; a portrait scarf made of a circular plastic-mesh pot cleaner, or a knotted scarf of plastic mesh cut from an apple-bag; a veil of nylon net; a necklace of seadpearl beading or a collar of narrow gathered lace. Finally, give the little lady an orchid corsage for Easter by gluing a cured larkspur floret to her shoulder.

Equally attractive and much more durable eggheads can be made of china nest-eggs or ovoid simling gourds. China eggs make portrait busts that look like porcelain figurines. Elaborate period hats and hair-dos suit them well, and turn them into the most elegant of eggheads.

Unless you grow your own, simling gourds are in rather limited supply. Inquire about them at a farmer's market; if the name doesn't ring a bell, ask for darning-egg or nest-egg gourds. These are precisely the shape and size of a large hen egg and their pale tan color is often dotted with brown freckles. If they are very badly blotched, give them a coat of flesh-colored paint, but lightly freckled gourds are fine for boy or character eggheads. If you don't paint them, brush them with white shellac; thus protected, they are as indestructible as wood.

GARDENER EGGHEAD

An amusing full length figure of a gardener with a gourd (or an eggshell) head can be made on a bill-spindle from an office supply company. You will need two rubber balls — one two inches in diameter and one "jacks" size — for the gardener's body; pipe cleaners will form the arms and legs. Impale the large ball upon the point of the bill spindle, and push it two-thirds of the way down the spike. Push the small ball down the spindle to rest on top of it. Run a large darning needle completely through each ball from side to side — near the top of the small ball, near the bottom of the large one. Push a yellow or brown pipe cleaner into each top hole to make the arms, bending the exposed end of each cleaner into a circle for a hand. Use two paper lamp-chop frills for bell-bottom slacks, supporting each one with a pipe cleaner leg fitted into one hole in the large ball and bent at right angles into an oval foot resting upon the base of the spindle. The frill will be just long enough to reach from the bottom of the ball to the spindle base. For a flaring "topper," cut a half-circle of bright colored felt, with slits for armholes. Fit it over the pipe cleaner arms and lap the back; then "button" the back by pushing colorful round-headed pins through the material into the rubber ball. Give the gardener a doll spade to hold in one hand, and crook his/her other arm around a tiny flower pot. Then fill the pot with wallpaper cleaner and plant it with forget-me-nots made of iron weed pods.

Once the body is finished, add the egghead. Rim the hole in a real eggshell with glue and slip it over the top of the spike to rest upon the upper rubber ball. Pierce one end of a gourd head with a nail, before doing the face, to make a hole for the spindle.

THANKSGIVING

Ever since nomadic hunters settled down in one place and began to culti-vate plants for food, harvest time has been a season of rejoicing, but Thanksgiving Day is an All-American holiday. The traditional turkey, cranberry sauce, sweet potatoes, corn pudding and pumpkin pie are all foods native to this continent which New England's earliest settlers were devoutly thankful to find here, and the holiday decorations should in all conscience be equally germane.

GLITTERED PUMPKIN

"The frost is on the pumpkin," and you can transform this lowly vegetable into a sophisticated symbol of the season with diamond-dust glitter and spray glue. You can find both glitter and glue wherever artist's supplies are sold, but transfer the diamond dust from its own can to a kitchen salt-shaker for greater ease of application. Place the pumpkin on a widespread double layer of newspaper and spray its top with glue, holding the pressurized can about a foot above the surface. Use enough glue to overflow the top and trickle slowly down over the rounded sides. While the glue still is wet, sprinkle glitter liberally over the pumpkin's top and sides; most of the shiny particles will adhere to the glue, and those that slide off will be caught for re-use by the newspaper pad. Place the frosted pumpkin on a round tray, and surround it with brown beach leaves.

Dark green acorn squash frosted in the same manner are just as apropos and far more elegant. Mound them on a cakestand and border them with glittered evergreen foliage.

FRESH FRUITS AND NUTS

Fresh fruits and nuts need not be spilled from a cornucopia to look bountiful. Heap them in a footed wooden nut bowl for a holiday gift. Begin with a grapefruit or a firm cabbage head — either will do, because it will not show — anchored in the bottom of the container with a double-sided picture mount. Make a hole with a nail in the top of the grapefruit and insert the blunt end of a wooden floral pick; press a fresh pineapple down upon the pick until it rests upon the grapefruit. In like manner, cover the sides of the grapefruit with smaller fruits — apples, hard cooking pears, oranges, lemons and limes — but do not use highly perishable bananas or fresh grapes. No grapes? Grapes of course, but of a variety that will long outlast the rest of the arrangement: beautiful brown pecans.

Adding formality to such an arrangement begins with a change of container: spray an inexpensive glass or pottery compote with gold paint from a pressurized can. Then add a touch of gold to the pineapple and the citrus fruits (as these must be peeled before being eaten) by brushing on slightly beaten egg white and dusting it immediately with gold glitter. Then frost the pecan-grapes lightly with gold paint sprayed from a distance of six feet.

CHRYSANTHEMUM PINEAPPLE

The pineapple has for centuries been the symbol of hospitality. Since Thanksgiving is a time to gather family and close friends together, an unusual gift for this year's hostess would be a pineapple-shaped arrangement of the garden's last bronze chrysanthemums, stripped of their leaves and well-conditioned in hot water.

Begin with several long liriope leaves, tied together with a green chenille pipe cleaner about four inches from their tops; turn the leaves to curve up, out, and down like pineapple foliage. Select three small, long-stemmed chrysanthemums and circle them around the liriope, hiding the pipe cleaner; hold them in place by wrapping their stems to the foliage with another green pipe cleaner. Add a row of five medium-size blossoms, tied so close below the first three that their petals intermingle. Then tie on three rows of seven large blooms each; this represents the bulging center of the fruit. Last, add one row of five blossoms, wrapping all the stems together well. Cut the tied stems off half an inch below the lowest row of chrysanthemums and balance the pineapple on a candlestick; fill the candle-cup with water and insert the tied stems. As an alternative, cut the stems off even with the lower petals of the last chrysanthemum circle, and stand the pineapple upright, in a little water, on a deep saucer or a shallow compote.

14.

. . . And Merry Christmas

Long before the birth of Christ, the houses and temples of ancient Rome were ornamented with evergreens during the midwinter Saturnalia. The early Christians adopted this custom at the Christmas season, and consecrated it by attaching religious symbolism to the pagan wreaths and garlands: evergreen foliage became the symbol of immortality; the wreath, with no beginning and no end, exemplified eternal life; a wreath of holly represented Christ's crown of thorns, and its berries drops of His blood. As the centuries passed, the origin of evergreen Christmas decorations and their symbolism were almost obscured by the mists of time, but they became a lingering and well-loved tradition.

PINE ROPING

Roping of pine or laurel for today's mantels and stairways can be made in much the same way that the Romans made their garlands. Condition whole branches of foliage in hot water, and cut them up into sprays six to eight inches in length. Hold the stem of a short spray of pine in one hand and lay over it the needled tip of a second sprig; fasten the two stems together by wrapping them with a twist of green florist's wire. Hold the stem of the second sprig, cover it with another tuft of needles, and wrap with wire. Separate the foliage of each spray as it is added, and wire only the stems so that the needles will be free. As an economy measure, use green cord or twine instead of florist's wire: wrap the twine twice around the stems, pulling it very tight so that it won't stretch later, and tie the ends with a double knot. Be sure to don an old pair of gloves to protect your hands from scratches.

Anyone with a banistered stairway will bless you for a length of this roping; unless it is exposed to direct blasts of hot air from the furnace, it should hold its needles for at least ten days. Looped in swags along a banister, caught up with red ribbon and tied with clusters of cones, pine roping was a popular eighteenth century Christmas decoration.

LAUREL ROPING

By the same method, short conditioned sprays of evergreen laurel leaves can be tied or wired into garlands. Laurel roping is most effective swagged across an Adam mantel from corner to corner in the manner of the Classic Revival Period. At each end, the garland should hang down over the top third of the mantel's pilaster.

EVERGREEN WREATHS

Simple wreaths of fresh greenery are equally easy to construct. A wire coat hanger makes a wreath frame approximately eleven and a half inches in diameter, a suitable size for a front door or an overmantel. The best way to bend the stiff wire into a circle is to place the thumbs together on the inside of the coat hanger and push outward. Leave the hook attached; it will be a handy hanger for the finished wreath.

Cut conditioned pine, spruce, laurel, box or hemlock in short pieces. Beginning at the base of the hook, wire one sprig flat and straight upon the frame. Add a second spray, placing it so close to the first that it completely hides the stem tip; slant this second twig very slightly toward the center of the circle. Place and wire a third twig, this time angling it beyond the rim; the fourth twig, like the first, should lie straight on the wire frame. This makes a full, flat wreath. Continue until the circle is complete, tucking the stem of the last twig under the foliage of the first. Then wire on a bow of red weatherproof ribbon large enough to hide all but the curved top of the metal hanger.

A thorough spraying with colorless plastic will hold the needles or leaves of an evergreen wreath firmly in place throughout the holidays. This treatment will, however, make the foliage rather shiny.

DELLA ROBBIA WREATHS

With the addition of small fruits, this basic green wreath becomes a colorful della Robbia decoration. Little red apples, hard yellow-brown seckel pears, lemons, limes and kumquats can be attached with aluminum wire pushed completely through the fruit; bend the ends of each wire to encircle the frame, and twist them together several times for maximum security. The·effect is better if the fruits are grouped by twos and threes, for color; place the largest groupings first, and fill in between them with single apples, limes or kumquats. The fruit will last a great deal longer if it is given a coat of white shellac before being wired, but once again, the effect is unpleasingly shiny. Liquid self-polishing wax acts almost as well as a preservative, and produces a matte finish. For an antiqued effect, dip the fruits before wiring in brown satin-finish varnish.

WREATHS AND GARLANDS OF LASTING MATERIALS

WREATH-TOPPER

Beautiful though it is, a della Robbia wreath is destined to be discarded when the holidays are over. A splendid holiday gift idea is a wreath-topper of cones and nuts that can be added each year to a plain flat wreath of fresh greenery. Begin with an eleven-inch circlet; make it of galvanized iron wire or of a coat hanger untwisted and the hook cut off with wire clippers. Overlap the ends of wire, twist them together with pliers, and cover the joint with tire tape.

You will need about twenty small whole pinecones and thirty cone-flowers, each with a wire stem to cover this circlet, plus a one-pound bag of mixed nuts in their shells and a handful of unshelled peanuts. Reclaim torn nylon mesh stockings from the ragbag; cut their legs and feet into four-inch squares, discarding the reinforced tops, heels, and toes. Cover each nut with a square of mesh secured with a tight winding of hair-fine aluminum wire.

This slim circlet you are making would look skimpy without a green wreath backing, and it must therefore have a built-in means of attachment. As the first step in its construction, cut four strips of all-purpose aluminum wire, each ten inches long. Wrap the middle of each wire twice around the frame and twist the ends together to hold it in position; place these hangers at the four compass points of the circle.

Don't take the trouble to wire cones and nuts individually on the wreath; twist several stems together to form a cluster, and wind the cluster's twisted stem around the frame. Make some clusters all cone, some all nut, and some a combination. For emphasis, add an occasional grouping of dark-shelled nuts and break the symmetry of the circle with an irregularly shaped raceme of peanuts. Place the clusters very close together on the frame so that they brace each other and completely hide the wiring, and finish the bottom of the circlet with curved okra or long locust pods wired to resemble a bow-knot.

Separated by its supporting green wreath from the surface of a wooden door or a wood-panelled wall, this topper will be beautiful in its natural

A cone and nut wreath on a wire frame will last for many holiday seasons. Peanuts, almonds, chestnuts, hazelnuts, English walnuts, brazilnuts and pecans were wrapped in squares of nylon stocking mesh and wired to the frame in clusters. Huge flat coneflowers and deodar roses trim the top of the wreath, and tufts of glycerin-treated pine needles complete the design.

shades of brown. If you are making it for a more formal room or entrance, gild it lightly with gold spray paint. For a white house with a colorful door, or for a room with white panelling or pastel walls, spray the whole circlet stark white. Two or three coats of white spray enamel will be required for complete coverage.

Unless you plan to present the wreath topper in person and demonstrate its usage on the spot, be sure to include with it a note of explanation and directions for wiring it to an evergreen background.

CONE AND NUT WREATH

A more important gift, and one that is sure to become a family tradition at the holiday season, is a large cone and nut wreath made on a rigid background. Your florist will sell you a metal wreath frame of the sort he uses; these are made of four or more circles of stiff wire braced together, and come in assorted sizes. A nine-inch frame would make a wreath large enough for an average dining room table; the twelve-inch size would be right for a front door. Since these forms are designed with a deep groove in the center, it takes a great many cones and nuts to fill the frame and cover its wires completely; the finished wreath will be heavy, but handsome and very nearly indestructible.

First, group whole cones and large nuts in mounded clusters to fill the groove, and wind their twisted stems tight around the cross-support wires on the bottom of the frame. The easiest way to do this is to place the cluster and then turn the frame over and work from the back. Next, wire smaller, flatter clusters or individual cones to the two top rims of the groove, and cover the inner and outer edges of the frame with nuts and small coneflowers. Center the top of the wreath with a grouping of large flat coneflowers and deodar roses, and add a ribbon bow if you feel that one is required.

Sometimes such a brown wreath, though dignified, looks wintry rather than festive. In this case, tip the edges of the coneflowers' scale petals with gold to accent their outlines and bring the whole arrangement to life. This can be done with gold paint and a small artist's brush, or with rub-on gold applied with a fingertip. Exercise restraint. You can always add more gilding, but you can't remove an excess.

CONE-NUT WREATH ON A WOODEN FRAME

An equally attractive cone and nut wreath, and one that requires far less material, is made on a wooden backing. Cut a pattern for this frame from kraft paper or thin cardboard: draw a circle fourteen inches in diameter and within it a concentric circle six inches in diameter; between the two, there will be a circular strip four inches wide. Cut out this pattern, take it with you to a builder's supply company, and buy a thirty-six-inch square of pegboard which will be closely perforated with holes. Ask to have five copies of your pattern cut from the pegboard — one from each corner and one from the middle of the square. You may have to plead a little, and you *will* have to pay a small cutting charge. Bring home the five wreath forms and the five circles cut out of their centers — these will be the basis of another type of decoration.

Give each wreath a hanger of a twelve-inch length of all-purpose aluminum wire: thread the bent wire through two holes in the pegboard near the outside edge of the frame; twist the wires together, and leave the ends free. This hanger will mark the center top of the wreath.

This time, gather cones and nuts into flat, spreading clusters. Poke the twisted stem of a cluster down through one hole in the pegboard, bend it, and push it up through an adjoining hole. Flatten the tip of the stem to the top of the wreath form, hiding it beneath the clustered cones. In this way, cover the entire surface of the frame, marking the top of the wreath with large coneflowers or with an okra pod bowknot.

For neatness, and to make the wreath scratchproof, slipcover the back of the frame with self-stick felt. Use the same pattern to cut the felt, but allow an extra half inch on the outside of the circle. Remove the paper backing and press the felt to the underside of the frame covering the wires; trim the outside edge of the felt to fit the frame exactly.

CONE-NUT PLAQUE

The flat circle of pegboard cut from the center of a wreath frame can become a wall plaque, a table ornament, or a filler for the center of an evergreen wreath. For a plaque, add a long wire for a hanger near one edge. Then center the circle with a large flat coneflower or a deodar rose. Encircle the plaque with a border of large glycerin-treated leaves or short foliage sprays, their stems wired at right angles to the outer edge. Fill in the remaining surface with flat clusters of small coneflowers and nuts; the outer row should cover and hide the stems of the foliage.

CONE-NUT MOUND

Make a rounded table arrangement on a pegboard circle with round clusters of cones and nuts. Begin at the outer edge, and wire each row a little taller than the one before; end in the middle with a large cluster centered with a wooden rose. This will resemble a colonial bouquet. Backed with self-stick felt, it can be laid flat on a tabletop or balanced on a wooden candlestick. Add a finishing ruche of small glycerin-treated leaves by gluing their stems to the bottom of the frame before pressing the felt in place.

WREATH-FILLER

Without a foliage border, this mounded nosegay makes an intriguing centerpiece for an evergreen wreath. Add six long wires at measured intervals around its rim; these are to be threaded through the back of a green wreath and twisted to hold the center in place. Like the circular wreath-topper, this ornament may be more striking if it is sprayed with gold paint or with flat white enamel. Hung on a door or a wall, a wreath with such a solid center becomes a decorative medallion.

PEGBOARD SWAGS AND GARLANDS

England's famous sculptor, Grinling Gibbons, often ornamented wooden fireplace facing or panelled overmantels with swagged garlands of fruits, flowers, foliage, acorns, cones and nuts, in high relief. Gibbons' carvings were faithful copies of nature's handiwork; it is perfectly possible (and an interesting sort of double play) to imitate *his* designs with natural materials. Such a swag can be hung below the mantel shelf or on the wall above it, and for ease of workmanship and attachment it should be made in three separate sections: an elongated shallow crescent for the center, and two tapered falls to hang down from the crescent's tips. In many contemporary houses, the formality of such a classic swag

would seem pretentious and out of place, while a simple crescent would be a welcome adornment.

For the crescent of the three-piece swag, again use pegboard cut to your pattern at the builder's supply company where you buy it. This gift can hardly be a surprise, for you *must* know the measurements of the recipient's fireplace in order to cut the pattern to scale. For visual balance, a four-foot crescent should be at least six inches wide at its mid-point; the tips should be squared rather than sharply pointed and hence very apt to break off.

Let whole medium-size pinecones represent fruits; pinecone slices and deodar roses will emulate flowers, while nuts and acorns, nylon wrapped and wired, will simulate their own carved counterparts. For attaching glossy sprays of small glycerin-treated foliage or individual larger leaves you must add wires to their stems. Begin in the middle of the crescent with a cluster of large cone flowers and whole cones representing fruits; Grinling Gibbons' "trademark" was a single pea pod, so be sure to add one locust or okra pod to your creation. Above and below this grouping wire on flat sprays of foliage that extend beyond and cover the edge of the frame. Work toward the tips of the crescent with separated group ngs of cones and coneflowers in descending order of size; fill in between these materials with clusters of nuts and acorns, and add foliage accents. At each end of the swag, place a cluster of cones and coneflowers approximately one-third the size of the center of interest.

If your swag is to have a fall at either end, each pegboard back should be an elongated triangle. Cones and coneflowers should decrease in size from wider top to squared-off tip; at the bottom of each fall, one perfect coneflower of medium size should cover the stem of a spray of treated foliage.

The all-brown composition will have the appearance of a woodcarving, but, again, may seem rather sombre. Touches of gilt on some of the materials will greatly enliven the look. This eighteenth century swag will change its style to Empire if you gild *all* the materials before wiring them to the frame. Cover foliage, cones and coneflowers solidly with gold spray paint; for contrast, merely frost the nylon-wrapped nuts and acorns with gold spray.

CHRISTMAS TREES

CONE-NUT TABLE TREE

A miniature stylized Christmas tree — a twelve-inch styrofoam pyramid closely covered with acorns, nuts, and the small cones of hemlock, larch, or mugho pine — is a great gift and one that is easily made. Cut off the tip of the white styrofoam cone to make a flat top one inch across; frost the styrofoam very lightly with gold spray paint, or cover it with gold florist's foil. Wire the materials in clusters to wooden floral picks; for best support, push each pick into the foam at a downward angle. Prick the wire stems of single cones directly into the styrofoam to fill the spaces between the clusters. For a finial, add a sweet-gum star or a Chinese chestnut burr to the flattened tip of the pyramid. Spray the completed tree gold, and give it a candlestick or a compote for a base. One tree can ornament a coffee table or serve as the centerpiece at Christmas dinner; a pair would be perfect for a mantel, a buffet table, or a hall console.

ESPALIERED TABLE TREE

An espaliered table tree is a handsome decoration for a doctor's reception room or an executive's office. The easiest espalier has a trunk made of

For a bachelor's apartment, a doctor's waiting room, or an executive's office, here's a year round gift: a pyramid of coneflowers with an octagonal brown candleholder for a base. The wooden flowers have been colored with copper and patina rub-on metallic finishes; the blue-green patina enlivens the copper and brown. The raised design on each panel of the candleholder was touched with copper.

half a hollow brass curtain rod, of the type that extends from twenty-eight to forty-eight inches and pulls apart in the middle. For the branches, you'll need four feet of half-inch copper tubing from a hardware store or a plumbing company. Have it cut into two pieces, one eighteen inches long and the other thirty inches.

Mark the curtain rod (with chalk) eight inches from its knobbed top; mark again, ten inches from its open end. Flatten the midpoint of each length of copper tubing by pinching it flat with a pair of pliers. Then lay the tubes parallel on a table, ten inches apart, and cover the flattened centers with liquid steel from a tube. Hold the curtain rod at right angles to the parallel tubes, and fit the two chalk marks on the liquid steel, pressing the rod down firmly; the short tube should be nearest the knobbed top of the rod. Be sure that the rods are perfectly straight, and allow the steel to harden overnight before lifting the tree.

Paint an eight-inch clay flowerpot brown, and fill it with ready-mix concrete; cover the surface of the wet cement with coarse sand and press it down lightly. Set the espalier upright in the center of the pot,

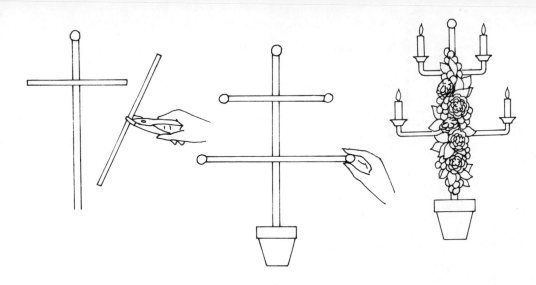

forcing its hollow curtain-rod trunk down into the concrete, and brace it until the cement has hardened. Spray the sand, which will have bonded to the concrete, with glue and add a light sprinkling of gold glitter.

Decorate only the trunk of this tree, with large glycerin-treated leaves, clusters of cones, and bunches of pecan grapes wired around the cross-rods. The copper branches can remain straight, and their ends can be closed and trimmed with small gold Christmas balls attached with clear cement. If you prefer, the branch tips can be bent upward at right angles, three inches from their ends, and topped with gold ornaments. You can convert the espalier to a candle-tree with four brass candle cups (which are sold separately in boutiques and candle shops) cemented to the upturned branch tips and filled with brown or gold candles.

WALL CHRISTMAS TREE

In a small apartment, where floor space is at a premium and all table surfaces are in constant use, the only place for a Christmas tree may be on the wall. Newlyweds or retirees would appreciate this flat stylized tree made of a fan-shaped metal trellis.

Unbolt and remove the length of pipe that would be driven into the ground, and turn the fan of round wires upside down. Thread corded picture wire through the bolt holes at the top of the flat stylized tree shape, so that it can be suspended from an existing picture hanger.

Cut, and condition with hot water, flat branches of evergreen foliage; hemlock is ideal for this purpose. Beginning at the bottom, cover each round white wire with foliage sprays, attaching their stems with a tight wrapping of white plastic tape, and overlapping the successive sprays so that all the taped stems are covered.

195

With ornament hooks, hang rows of bright unbreakable Christmas ornaments from the slanted wires and cross-supports of the trellis, and cover the joining stems at the top of the tree with a large star. Clamp the tips of the hanger-hooks tight around the wires with pliers, and secure the star with a wire passed through the bolt holes.

CONTEMPORARY TREE

A striking Christmas tree for a contemporary house is much less difficult to make. Select and cut a sycamore limb that is angularly branched and liberally twigged with round pendant balls. Paint a ten-inch clay flowerpot white, stop the hole in the bottom with a cork, and fill the pot with ready-mix concrete; sprinkle the top of the wet cement sparingly with diamond dust glitter. Force the base of the branch down through the wet concrete to touch the bottom of the pot, brace it, and leave it until the cement has hardened.

Fill a small paper cup with equal amounts of white glue and water, well-mixed; half-fill a second cup with diamond dust glitter. Hold the cup of glue under a sycamore ball and move it up until the ball is submerged; lower the cup and hold it under the ball until the glue stops dripping. Then at once, in the same manner, dip the ball in the cup of diamond dust; shake the ball over the cup to dislodge loose bits. This tree requires no other decoration, and is strikingly effective when placed on the floor before a window wall.

BARE-BRANCHED TABLE TREE

A table version of this bare-branched tree begins with a gilded five-inch flower pot filled with plastic wood. Prune a branching sucker from a hawthorn tree or a flowering quince shrub — thorns add interest to this stubby tree. Center the branch in the pot, pushing its end down through the wood filler to the bottom. In the crotch of the branch place a small abandoned bird's nest with three eggs in it — tiny red Christmas balls, oval red beads, or red pistachio nuts. Perch a jaunty feathered cardinal on a twig, and the tree is ready for presentation.

PINECONE TABLE TREE

Make a charming miniature green tree, suitable for a mantel or a table centerpiece, on a large well-shaped pinecone and mount it on a colorful flat plastic lid. Cut and condition short sprigs of evergreen foliage with very small leaves or needles — boxwood, microphylla holly, or Japanese

Small decorations that children enjoy making and giving. A pinecone Christmas tree, decorated with balls of colorful foil and mounted on a spray-can top. A flat cardboard basket with a taped wire handle, brushed with gold paint, holds sprigs of juniper and red holly berries. A pompon tree of green cellophane soda straws, each tipped with a red dried starflower. Small matchboxes slipcovered with self-stick material and trimmed with iron-weed "forget-me-nots", pressed leaves and painted privet berries, or gilded hemlock cones.

juniper. Dip the stem end of a spray in white glue and insert it between two rows of the pinecone's scales, pressing it back to the cone's center stalk. Cover and hide the pinecone with greenery in this manner, and then coat the tree with colorless acrylic spray-plastic which will keep the foliage green for three or four weeks. Decorate the branch tips with tiny glass Christmas ornaments and foil wrapped sugar-cube packages, and top the tree with a gilded many-pointed sweet-gum star.

APPLE PYRAMID

A universally popular holiday decoration in colonial America was a cone-shaped arrangement of red apples and fresh greenery. At colonial Williamsburg, where the apple pyramid is a yearly feature of the elaborate and beautiful Christmas decorations, this table ornament is made on a flat-topped wooden cone studded with rows of headless nails. An apple is impaled on each spike, and the pyramid usually is topped with a fresh pineapple. Short sprays of greenery tucked between and behind the fruits conceal the wooden base.

Most modest colonial homes did not possess a spiked cone, but our ingenious ancestors did not therefore feel underprivileged — they made their beloved apple pyramids on stacked cabbages! Any friend interested in American history would be complimented to receive such a decoration, made on a large plate or an inexpensive metal tray.

Select a wide flat head of cabbage for the base of the cone and trim off a slice, if necessary, to make it stand perfectly steady on the tray. A smaller, more spherical cabbage will form the mid-section, and half a small round head of cabbage will be the top of the pyramid. Stack the cabbages neatly, and hold them together with an aluminum knitting needle thrust down through all three layers. Choose red apples similar in size, polish them with a soft cloth, and push the blunt top of a wooden floral pick into the blossom end of each one. Beginning at the base of the cone, prick the apple-topped floral picks into the cabbages in rows so close together that the apples touch each other. To top the cone with a pineapple, use a skewer to pierce the thick bottom rind of the fruit in three places; insert the blunt ends of floral picks into the three holes, and press the points of the picks down into the cone until the base of the pineapple rests on the rounded top of the cabbage half. Cut conditioned evergreen foliage in short sprigs, and tuck these between the fruits to hide the cabbages completely. Surround the cone with more foliage, laid flat on the tray with stems tucked under the lowest row of apples.

APPLE HEAD DOLLS

In pioneer days, heads for rag dolls sometimes were made of apples peeled and placed in the sun to dry. As an apple's moisture evaporated and its surface began to shrivel, a nose and chin could be formed by pinching with the fingers and eye sockets could be pressed in with a thumb. Daily the features were pinched and poked until the flesh of the apple was wrinkled and dry and its color dark as tanned leather.

Then doll makers discovered that features carved upon a firm fresh apple shrank in drying; the finished face became a caricature of the sculptured original. A carved apple would dry in a warm room in about three weeks. In recent years, carved apple heads have been given only to character dolls — their wrinkled, weatherbeaten faces perfect for an ancient mariner, or for a toothless crone. Such a character usually is made on an armature — like the one described for gourd-head dolls.

It is possible to shorten the drying period of an apple head, and at the same time to stabilize its color. (Golden Delicious apples respond especially well to this treatment; their firm flesh shrivels less as it dries, and remains unblotched as it darkens from cream color to light brown.) Pare three medium-size apples with a thin sharp knife, so carefully that no ridges remain, and use the tip of the knife to carve eyes, nose and mouth on one rounded side below the stem. At this point you can glue tiny blue or black beads into the eye sockets, but this is optional. Dip each apple in fresh lemon juice — not frozen or reconstituted — or in a solution of one teaspoonful of powdered citric acid dissolved in one cup of water. Place the apples on a cookie sheet or an aluminum pie tin and set them at once in the oven at a temperature of 150°. Keep them at this low steady temperature for twenty-four hours; they should then be ready for mounting. If, however, an apple's surface still feels sticky, return it to the oven for an additional three hours. Often the eye sockets will shrink to slits and the cheeks become puffy; the tip of the nose may turn down, and a double chin may develop. One thing is certain: no two apple heads will ever look alike!

Male apple characters can be mounted on armatures like the one described for a gourd-head doll, or made on bill-spikes, like the egghead gardener, with trouser legs of hollow black electrical sheathing. For little old ladies, there is an easier way. Cut the tip off a six-inch styrofoam cone and slip-cover the cone with cloth to make a wide-skirted dress. Use featherweight bodice boning, available in black or white at cloth shops, for arms; cover it with sleeves of the dress material and finish the ends with hands cut from flesh-colored felt. Attach the arms in one piece on the back of the figure by sticking pins through the boning into the styrofoam; cover the mechanics with a shawl, a cape, a scarf or a collar. Use white lamb's wool or absorbent cotton, or gray steel wool for hair, and attach it to the apple head with liquid household cement. Then cement the head to the flattened tip of the cone, and finish the figure with a lace cap or a bonnet if you like. An apple-head doll is an unusual and amusing Christmas present for a collector or for a history buff, and the mummified apple will last for many years.

THREE WISE MEN WITH APPLE HEADS

Marvelous for Christmas gifts are Wise Men with apple heads and bodies of styrofoam cones — two ten-inch cones for standing Magi and one six-inch cone for a kneeling figure. If one apple darkens more than the others as it dries, so much the better since one of the Magi is said to have been black. To emphasize this point, you could dip two carved apples in the color-preserving lemon juice and leave one untreated.

Cut off the pointed tip of each cone to make a flat top one inch in diameter, and attach an apple head to this platform with clear cement. Cover a ten-inch strip of boning with sleeves of wide velvet ribbon folded in half and seamed together at the edges; secure the one-piece arms to the back of the figure with pins, one and a half inches below the platform neck. Each Wise Man should have a long robe and a flowing cape that covers the apple head and is topped with a crown; the robe of the kneeling figure should be as long as the others, and be folded back beneath the cone.

For a Wise Man's robe, use a circle of velveteen or felt slashed to the center on one side and with two small slits for armholes; sew a border of narrow gold braid around the perimeter of the circle to hem the gown. Overlap the robe on the back of the figure and secure it to the styrofoam with several straight pins. Finish the neckline with braid overlapped and pinned at the back. Cut a wide triangle of thin but opaque material that drapes well for the burnoose. Fold under the point of the apex and cement the folded edge just above the eyes of the apple head. Slip a rubber band over the apple to hold the hood in place, and adjust the material in folds. Then hide the band with a crown. Cut a strip of aluminum or gold foil eight inches long and four inches wide. Fold it in half, lengthwise, press the fold with a thumbnail, and fold the foil again into a one-inch strip. Cut one edge into points, with scissors, but be sure to leave a solid band one-half inch wide. Fit the strip around the apple head and cut off any excess beyond a half-inch overlap; glue the overlapping ends. Spread glue along the rubber band and press the crown down over it.

To indicate the gifts of the Magi, one figure might hold a lump of sugar wrapped in gold foil; the second a gilded "sampler" perfume bottle, and the third a "casket" that was once an ornate gold pill box.

The set of Three Wise Men would make a treasurable gift for a minister's family or for a Sunday School. A single figure, symbolizing the visit of the Magi, would be a meaningful Christmas gift to any home.

KISSING BALL

A Christmas decoration in use in England since the days of the Druids is the kissing ball. Originally, this was merely a large bunch of mistletoe suspended in a doorway, but by the mid-eighteenth century it had become customary to tie short sprigs of mistletoe, with ribbon, around a ball of wet moss, and to hang this round kissing ball from a chandelier.

Now that mistletoe has become a rarity, kissing balls usually are made of other small-leafed greenery with a single sprig of wax-white berries added to satisfy convention. With hardware cloth (preferable to chicken wire) cover a core of soaked Oasis or sphagnum moss, the basis of this ball. Insert stems of conditioned twigs of boxwood, cotoneaster, or round-leafed holly through the mesh into the moist center; they keep fresh for ten days to two weeks. Tie real or artificial mistletoe with red ribbon to the mesh at the bottom of the ball, and make a hanger of more ribbon threaded through the top of the mesh, knotting it for security.

DOUBLE-DUTY KISSING BALL

A double-duty gift is a kissing ball with a utilitarian framework that will long outlast its evergreen holiday dress: this can be a lacy cast-iron string holder, a large perforated aluminum rice ball, a planting basket for bulbs, or a wire basket used for washing lettuce. In any case, open the container and fill it with moist Oasis, close it, and seal it with a strip of green plastic tape. Then prick the stems of conditioned evergreen sprigs through the holes into the Oasis. Tie a bow of ribbon around the attached hanging hook, and the useful object is gift-wrapped in greenery.

BACK DOOR DECORATION

When the front entrance of every home in the neighborhood is decorated for the holidays, children still come in through the kitchen. They will appreciate a back-door decoration, and their mother will find its components useful all year long. At an office supply company, buy a wall-type metal bill spindle. This will have a back-plate that can be screwed to the outside of a kitchen door, and a vertical pointed spike. Purchase from a variety store a shiny metal dustpan; hold it handle down and pack Oasis into the pocket formed by the dust shield. Then stuff the hollow handle with cleansing tissue, and tie a large bow of red waterproof ribbon to the point at which the handle is attached to the pan. Then arrange a fan of conditioned evergreen sprays in the moist Oasis. Affix the bill spindle to the door and press the handle of the dustpan down over the spike which will imbed itself in the wadded tissue and hold the decorated dustpan upright and steady. After the holidays, the dustpan will find a home in the cleaning closet, and the spindle will be a handy holder for notes to the milkman.

BIRD FEEDER

Other gifts of awkward size and shape can be presented unwrapped but with seasonal decorations. A bird feeder need not be boxed if it sports a lavish bow of ribbon and supports a pair of bizarre birds made of nuts and pinecones.

Winged maple seeds that litter the lawn in early summer are shaped like feathers. If you bring them indoors as soon as they fall and place them on newspaper, they dry paper-thin and creamy tan. Choose a slender immature cone for the body of a bird, and give it spread wings and a tail of maple feathers. Cut away the maple seeds with scissors, and use white glue to attach each feather to the cone. Overlap the feathers for verisimilitude, and glue a pointed maple-seed bill to the stem end of the cone, which is now the head of the bird.

Select a large, grotesquely bent peanut for the body of a second feathered friend, and make its wings and tail of pinecone scales. One fan-shaped scale from a deodar cone will simulate a half-spread wing, but several short overlapping scales from a jackpine cone will serve as well. Make the tail of three curved scales from a cone of the long-leaf pine.

Just for fun, add to the bird feeder a bumblebee with an immature hemlock cone body, cherry-stem antennae, and maple-seed wings.

GREEN ROSES

If you're giving a vase for Christmas, don't wrap it. Instead, fill it with an arrangement of "evergreen roses" made of galax leaves. For each rose, pick two small, three medium and four large leaves. Roll up a small leaf from side to side into a cylinder, and wrap this cylinder with green floral tape just above the stem. The leaf will spread slightly above the tape. Wrap the base of the second small leaf around the cylinder and secure it with floral tape; this is the center of the rose. Fit the cleft base of a medium-sized leaf around the two stems, just below the tape; add the other medium leaves, and adjust them to overlap. Wrap tape around the bases of these leaves to hold them in a curved and over-lapped position. With another short strip of tape, wrap the five stems together. Now fit the cleft of each large leaf around the taped stems, and adjust these at right angles to their own stems like the outer petals of a full-blown rose. Tape the stems of the four new leaves around the others, and trim all the stems off evenly about five inches below the rose. Spiral-wrap the trimmed stems with tape to within one inch of their ends, and place the ends in water; this galax rose will last several weeks. Removed from water and air-dried, it becomes a silvery green and semi-permanent flower.

Lacking galax leaves, make the green rose of the rounded leaves found on old plants of English ivy. The ivy rose will remain green for a month or more, in water.

One of the large evergreen roses will make a budvase an exciting gift; five roses will fill a vase of moderate size. Fill a larger vase with gold sprayed evergreens, and add three galax-leaf flowers as a center of interest. These Christmas roses will convey a merry message!

DECORATED TELEPHONE DIRECTORY

An unusual and highly practical Christmas gift for any home or office is a simulated leather telephone directory cover with a montage of dried or pressed materials. Choose a rich dark shade of cloth-backed vinyl upholstery material — maroon, perhaps, or bottle green — and cut a strip to fit around the book, letting it extend half an inch beyond the upper and the lower edge; allow three extra inches at each end of the strip, to be turned back into a pocket-flap to hold the outer edges of the directory's paper cover. Cut a piece of clear plastic material exactly the same size. Turn back the ends of the vinyl and fit the cloth over your own directory; center on the top of the slipcover a montage of flat dried material — silvery discs of lunaria, sprays of sea oats, pine needles, leaves of grain or grass — or of pressed leaves and flowers, and attach each element of the design with white glue. Cover the montage with white typewriter paper, and weight it overnight with heavy books. Then remove the decorated vinyl from the directory and lay it flat; fit the strip of clear plastic over it, and machine stitch around the materials close to the edge. Fold back three inches at each end of the doubled materials, and machine stitch the top and bottom of each pocket. When the edges of a directory's paper covers are slipped into these pocket-holders, the material will fit smoothly over the book and the protected design will mark the front.

CHILDREN'S PROJECTS

Before the Hallowe'en treats have been consumed, children begin to count the days until Christmas. While they wait for the great day, they are easier to live with if they are allowed to take part in the holiday preparations. They most enjoy small projects that are quickly completed: favors for the Christmas dinner table; pinecone trees or decorated candles, for teachers and neighbors; decorated matchboxes for uncles and aunts.

TABLE FAVORS

The same sort of tiny baskets filled with greenery that make good place favors are also appropriate remembrances for elderly relatives or decorations for invalid trays. Small plastic baskets are sold in packages of twelve for children's party favors; these can be used as is, or painted gold. Fill each basket with floral clay, into which press the stems of short evergreen twigs. Scatter holly berries dipped in white glue over the twigs, and trim the handle of the basket with a bow of narrow red ribbon.

PINECONE TREES

A well shaped medium-size pinecone, glued to the top of a paint-spray can, makes a miniature Christmas tree; tip the outer edges of the scales with green or gold paint for a more festive appearance. To decorate this tiny tree, glue small balls of bright foil to the scales, and gild a hemlock cone for a tree-topper. Cut silvery aluminum foil from the kitchen or colorful florist's foil into one and a half-inch squares, and roll them round between thumb and finger — this is a project that appeals to every child.

DECORATED CANDLES

Lids of spray cans often have an inner ring that fits over the nozzle, and such lids make fine holders for decorated Christmas candles. Steady a short taper in the inner cup with modelling clay, and surround it with evergreen sprigs thrust into modelling or floral clay packed into the outer ring of the lid. Attach a bright ribbon bow with a wire hairpin slipped through the knot of the ribbon and then pricked into the clay.

POMPON OF CELLOPHANE STRAWS

Dexterous children enjoy making flower-decorated pompons of cellophane drinking straws, to be used as tree ornaments or turned into tiny "standard" trees. Cut five green cellophane straws into thirds for a total of fifteen short lengths. Gather the straws into a bundle, and wind wire so tight around the middle of the bunch that the straws are bent by the pressure into a pompon. Twist the wire securely, leaving ends about three inches long. With the fingers, separate and adjust the ends of the straws to make the pompon roughly spherical. Dip the end of each straw in white glue, and insert into it the short stem of a very small dried flower. Insert the wires into the top of a soft drink bottle to balance the pompon until the glue has set. The ball is ready to be hung on a Christmas tree, its wires crooked to form a hanger. For a place favor or a coffee table decoration, fill a small spray-can lid with floral clay and imbed a six-inch length of a green straw upright in the center of it; then straighten the pompon's wires and slip them into the top of the straw. Finish the standard with tufts of artificial pine needles and a bow of ribbon to match the dried flowers; attach the greenery and the ribbon to the floral clay in the "planter" with wire hairpins.

DECORATED MATCHBOXES

Boxes of wooden matches come in several sizes, and can be converted by child power into colorful place favors or small gifts. First, cover each box with self-stick material — plastic, felt, flannel, or burlap — leaving the striking surface exposed. Then decorate the top of the box with small cured or dried flowers, pressed leaves, painted privet berries, gilded hemlock cones, or painted pods, as the youthful artist fancies. Any of these preserved garden materials can be bonded with white glue to plastic or to cloth, and happily the glue will wash off clothing and fingers with soap and water.

15.

Made-In-Advance Package-Toppers

Any present worthy of the name deserves to be so pleasingly packaged that it lifts the spirits as it delights the eye. Make package-toppers, in advance, of garden-grown materials and store them away with wrapping paper and ribbon until needed; they can change humdrum parcels into presentation pieces.

SMALL PACKAGE TOPPERS

For a complete collection of toppers for year round use, include decorations for little as well as large packages. Salvage the makings of small package-toppers from leftover materials — for instance, a bunch of brown pecan grapes would dignify a man's gift, wrapped in natural-colored burlap. Wrap the stems of a few extra glass flowers together with green floral or plastic tape; they will look well on a small oblong box wrapped in pastel tissue paper, and unless you want a flat bow at the top of their wrapped stems, no ribbon is required.

MINIATURE ROSE CORSAGE

Tiny hemlock cones and beech pods, painted or stained with hot liquid dye, and stemmed with green-covered bell wire, can be arranged as a corsage of miniature roses; color the cones red, pink, lavender, or white, and the beech pods green for foliage. Wrap the package in pale green shiny shelf paper, and tie it with ribbon that matches the roses; wire the corsage to the knot of the ribbon before making the bow.

206

EGGHEAD PACKAGE TOPPERS

No decoration is more attractive for an Easter gift than an Easter egghead, but this fragile ornament must be attached with care. First, with clear cement, mount the plastic egg-half base on a small metal lid — one from a baby-food jar would be the right size. If there is lettering on the lid, paint it out with black or gold paint. Turn the lid upside down and cement the plastic egg-half base inside the rim. Wrap the box in smooth-surfaced, solid-color paper that matches the plastic base of the egghead and cement the metal lid to the top of the package.

THE GRADUATE

"The Graduate" eggheads are especially appropriate for graduation gifts. Hide the plastic egg-half base with an academic gown made from a circle of black felt slashed to the center, fitted around the egghead's neck, overlapped in front and glued in place. Make a mortarboard of a smaller circle of black felt: cut two half-inch slits and overlap their edges to form a shallow cap. Then cut a two-inch square of cardboard, and glue it between slightly larger squares of felt for the flat top. Glue the square on the crown of the cap, and finish the mortarboard with a tassel of embroidery thread, fastening it with a black-headed straight pin to the center of the square. As the finishing touch, roll a two-inch square of white paper into a diploma and tie it with white thread. Glue tiny dried flowers in the college colors to the rolled paper; then glue the diploma to the felt robe and cement the graduate to an inverted jar lid. Wrap the package in one college color and use ribbon of the other; instead of tying the ribbon, overlap the ends and tape them flat. Glue the bottom of the lid over this joint, and be sure it is bonded to the paper as well as to the ribbon.

EGGHEAD BRIDE

For a shower gift or anniversary present, dress an egghead topper as a bride. This time, cement the curtain-ring neck to a jeweler's box covered with white satin, or to a plastic ring box shaped like a tiered wedding cake. Glue a triangle of lace to the bride's hair for a veil, and give her a miniature bridal bouquet of cured flowers — a white rosebud tucked into the center of a flat head of Queen Anne's lace and anchored there with white glue. Wrap the gift in a remnant of white satin (or in shiny white shelf paper) and cement the base of the egghead to its top.

Egghead package toppers with sequin features. The graduate (her hair is gold fringe) in black cap and gown, clutches a diploma of rolled paper tied with dried starflowers in her school colors. The bride (in a doll's wig) wears a lace veil and a strand of pearls, and carries a bouquet of cured white flowers: a round bloom of Queen Anne's lace with a rosebud center, filled in with florets of white spirea and white crepe myrtle.

LARGE ALL-OCCASION TOPPERS

DRIED FLOWERS

Larger boxes call for toppers on a grander scale. Half-rounds of green styrofoam, intended for use with artificial flowers, usually come with a self-stick base which remains covered with brown paper until the time comes to anchor the arrangement in a container. This sticky surface will adhere equally well to wrapping paper, and the styrofoam will be a perfect support for a mound of dried flowers. Make holes in the plastic foam, with a small nail or a large darning needle, and dip the tip of each short flower stem in white glue before pushing it into a hole; the flowers should be placed so close together that they cover and hide the green foam. Dried strawflowers, globe amaranth, statice, celosia, and cockscomb are stalwart possibilities, along with dyed life everlasting, and short sprigs of brown dock or gray artemisia are good spiky accents.

Wrap a large square box in shiny solid color shelf paper, remove the paper backing from the styrofoam, and press the mound down firmly on top of the package.

CONEFLOWERS

Paint sunflower-size pinecone flowers to match or complement an unusual shade of crepe paper. Glue a single flower flat on a box top, give it a stem of heavy green twine and foliage of pressed leaves. To add height to a flat package, glue two giant cone flowers on edge to the crepe paper wrapping, and tilt them toward each other until their upper scale petals touch. Between the standing flowers, glue a long flat-looped ribbon bow. The advantage of crepe paper for a package design of this kind is that its slight irregularity of surface will bond better with glue to the wooden cones than would a smoother paper.

DYED CORNSHUCKS

To top a tall box, a tuft of colorful cornshuck is far more unusual and interesting than a rosette of ribbon. Choose solid color wallpaper for wrapping, and narrow ribbon in two colors; one should match the paper and the other should contrast.

Use three whole shucks of corn for this magnified topper: pull the husks back from the kernels all the way around and break off the ear, leaving the shuck attached to the stub of stalk. Wash the shucks to remove cornsilks, dust and insects, and place them outdoors in the sun until they are dry and bleached; this will take several days. Dilute liquid dye (or vegetable food coloring, for pastel shades) with boiling water in a large mixing bowl, to match the color of the wallpaper. Submerge a shuck completely in the hot dye, weighting it below the surface with a small sealed jar filled with water, and leave it for fifteen minutes. Remove this shuck to a thick pad of newspaper and let it drain while you immerse another shuck in the dye. Since the water will no longer be boiling hot, the second shuck will be slightly lighter in color than the first. Prepare another batch of hot dye, in the contrasting ribbon color, and plunge the third cornshuck into it. By this time, the first shuck will have drained sufficently to be handled, but rubber gloves should be worn to protect the hands from dye stains. Wind the long segments of husk, two or three at a time, on plastic hair rollers. Begin at the outside of the shuck and roll the strips outward; roll the last long strips inward to close and cover the center of the cluster. Place the shuck on newspaper, curlers up, and let it stand for six hours or so — the rolled husks should still be slightly damp. Remove the rollers and separate the strips; leave some tightly curled but smooth others out into gentle spreading curves. Replace the shuck on newspaper for twelve hours, by which time it should be perfectly dry and the dye will not stain hands or wrapping paper.

Cement the stubby stalks of the three shucks to a round snap-on plastic lid from a quart-size ice cream carton or a pint freezer container; set the clusters close together, upright, and arrange the curled strips to cover the rim of the lid and hide it completely. Wrap the ribbons around the box, one inch apart; overlap their ends and tape them to the wallpaper. Use three picture mounts, for balance, to attach the lid above the ribbon.

DOUBLE-DUTY TOPPERS

All these all-occasion toppers have one thing in common: they are themselves small gifts. The bunch of pecan grapes can be added to an arrangement of cones and seedpods; the cone corsage or the glass flowers, in a

Green and gold packages with unusual decorations. The flat box is trimmed with long-lasting "roses" made of galax leaves and air-dried to a silvery green. For a "pineapple", the symbol of hospitality, tips of a pinecone's scales were brushed with gold paint, and nested clusters of plastic podocarpus were glued to its top for "foliage".

small vase, will ornament a dressing table. An egghead can be placed on an occasional table or added to a collection of figurines. The mound of dried flowers is the right size to be displayed on a compote, and the cornshuck cluster can be balanced on top of a candlestick or laid flat on a coffee table. One or two giant coneflower daisies can be added to a design of dried flowers, or used as a center of interest in an all-green arrangement.

CHRISTMAS PACKAGE TOPPERS

Wrapping Christmas presents is great fun, but not if it must be done at top speed during the last minute rush. Haste means fumbling fingers, crumpled paper, and lopsided bows. This final frenzy can be avoided with prefabricated package toppers.

MILKWEED POD BIRD

For instance, a tan rough-textured bird perched upon a flat package wrapped in brown crepe or tissue paper might actually be noticed, examined, and identified by the man who received it — a distinction that few package decorations can hope for. Half a large milkweed pod and one whole small pod are all you need to construct this gamebird; the twig of the large pod will be the neck of the bird, and to it a large seed can be glued to form a head. Split the small pod into its two matching halves, and glue one on either side of the large pod for folded wings. Glue or tape a spray of brown dock, or a lichened twig, flat on top of the box, and let this serve as a perch for the bird which should be attached with glue. Use no ribbon, which would only detract from the masculinity of the design.

SMALL PACKAGE ON A SQUARE PLASTIC LID

Good things often come in packages too small to wrap well. Here is a most unusual way to gift-wrap a tiny square jeweler's box: cover the box with colorful paper and anchor it with a double-sticky picture mount in the center of a large *square* plastic lid from a quart or half-gallon freezer container. Surround the box with small dried or cured flowers, cemented to the rim of plastic; substitute gilded or painted seed pods for the dried materials, if you like.

MAKING A TOPPER ON A PLASTIC LID

Any topper with a plastic lid base can be attached to a wrapped package in the twinkling of an eye. First of all, remove the paper from one side of a picture mount, and press the sticky foam firmly on the flat top surface of a plastic lid; leave the paper backing on the other side of the mount. Turn the lid over to construct the topper on it; the lid's narrow rim will help to confine the materials within its edges. Even fragile dried or cured flowers can be used to decorate gifts, and will survive undamaged, if you attach them with liquid cement to a round plastic lid of suitable size. For packages to be sent by mail, use sturdier seedpods and coneflowers, and cement them, also, to the plastic.

Set the finished topper aside until it is needed. Then pull the paper off the bottom of the picture mount, and press the plastic lid down firmly on the top of a wrapped box.

SINGLE CONEFLOWER CHRISTMAS TOPPERS

Very simple, but very effective, is a single very large deodar rose (or one giant pinecone daisy) cemented to a small round lid with one or two short sprays of artificial foliage. Both the rose and the daisy should be painted Christmas red, and can be used to top a cube-shaped box covered with patterned paper or solid green foil.

GILDED CURED FLOWERS

Salvage cured blossoms that changed color in the drying medium or dried flowers that faded unattractively for Christmas package toppers by spraying them with gold paint and cementing them to a gilded plastic lid. Cover a box with gold foil, and wrap around it a band of wide blue velvet ribbon; overlap the ends of the ribbon on top of the box, and Scotch-tape them to the foil. Set two picture mounts in place, one on either side of the joined ribbon, and press the lid down firmly on them.

SILVERED HYDRANGEA

A single large hydrangea head, silvered with aluminum spray paint and cemented by its stem to a very small unpainted plastic lid, will be an airy and esoteric replacement for a ribbon rosette on a large box. Eschew the blue that looks so cold with silver. Wrap the box instead in pink or orange foil, and tie it with wide silver metallic ribbon.

Holiday luster from dried or cured flowers and metallic paint. A package wrapped in gold foil and blue velvet ribbon is trimmed with a cured, gilded dogwood blossom and sprigs of gold-sprayed privet berries. The inner rim of a spray-can top is the right size holder for a gold candle; the rest of the lid cavity was filled with floral clay to support airy tips of dried oakleaf hydrangea silvered with aluminum spray paint. A bow of silver lace completes the gift.

WREATH TOPPERS

A most effective decoration for a flat foil-covered package is a small evergreen wreath — especially one that can be made months in advance and can be kept for years. The basis of this circlet is a red rubber jar-ring, from a package of twelve sold at the canning supplies counter of a supermarket. Cut short sprays of diminutive foliage — box, cotoneaster, jasmine, round-leafed holly — but do *not* condition them; snip each sprig into flat pieces one and a half inches long. With green plastic tape, wrap the stem of a bit of foliage to the flat rubber ring. Angle a second bit very slightly toward the center of the circle, and tape it in place; the tip of the third sprig should extend beyond the outer edge of the rubber, and the fourth, like the first, should lie straight. In this manner, cover the ring with miniature greenery so closely overlapped that all stems are hidden; the green tape also will overlap on the back of the circlet, hiding the red rubber.

213

Now place the wreath face up on a one-inch layer of silica gel in a shoebox, and trickle more gel over it until every leaf is completely covered. After four days, remove the circlet and examine the leaves. Occasionally they remain green as they dehydrate, but usually they will have turned brown. If this is the case, dilute dark green liquid dye with boiling water and place the wreath in it, upside down, for fifteen minutes. Transfer the circlet to a thick pad of newspaper, and let it dry overnight. Then finish the wreath with a bow of red ribbon, glued to the thumb-hold that protrudes from one side of the ring. Cut a picture mount in two, and use both halves, on opposite sides of the ring back, to anchor the wreath on the package.

PACKAGE-TOPPER WREATH PINS

The same trick of dehydrating and dyeing evergreen foliage, applied to the minature needles of spruce or juniper, produces tiny package-topper wreaths that moonlight as lapel pins.

Begin with a cord-covered circular shade pull, green or white, from the window curtain display at a variety or department store. Cut small-needled evergreen sprigs in one-inch lengths, and sew them to the shade pull with green thread; overlap them as you sew to hide all the stems. Bury the circlet in silica gel for four days, and then soak it for fifteen minutes in dark green dye diluted with boiling water; drain and dry it overnight on a pad of newspaper.

Trim the tiny wreath by sewing on a few beads or little balls of bright colored foil, and add the smallest possible bow of narrow red or gold ribbon. Behind the bow, sew the spine of a small brass safety pin to the back of the shade pull, so that the wreath may be pinned to a dress or coat. Attach the wreath to the top of a package with a narrow strip of Scotch tape threaded through the closed safety pin and pressed down on the wrapping paper.

PRESSED FLOWER PICTURE ON A PACKAGE

A unique decoration for a large flat package, and one with a promising future, is a pressed flower picture made on self-stick green felt. Cut the felt to the desired size and shape, but do not remove its paper backing. Begin the picture by placing a "container" cut from plain white contact plastic. Use white glue thinned with water to hold in place a grouping of a few pressed flowers, and add a foliage background of pressed leaves glued above the flowers and on either side of them. Glue a leaf among

The edges of this oblong package wrapped in gold foil frame a panel of self-stick green plastic sprinkled with gold dots. A single spray of pressed blackberry roses with buds and leaves has been glued to the panel, and appears to be growing from the green felt planter. The picture is protected with clear colorless adhesive plastic.

the flowers, too, to tie them visually to the container.

Cover the picture with a sheet of clear transparent contact plastic cut the same size as the felt background. Wrap the flat package in gold foil, to give the picture a gilded frame. Center the picture on the top of the box and mark the position of the corners with chalk. Remove a small triangle of the paper backing from each corner of the felt rectangle; fit each gummed point carefully into its chalk marks on the foil, and press it down. Since you have glued the felt only at the corners, it will be easy to remove from the foil. Peel off the remaining paper backing, mount the picture on a sheet of cardboard, and mat it for hanging.

PRESSED FOLIAGE PACKAGE DESIGN

As a variation on this theme, glue pressed ferns or large pressed leaves upright, like a growing plant, on a long, narrow rectangle of white contact plastic. Cut a flowerpot from colorful self-stick plastic, and press it in place just below the tips of the leaf stems so that the foliage appears to be growing out of the pot. Once again, cover the picture with clear contact plastic, and stick it by its corners to a long, flat, gold-wrapped package.

215

CORNSHUCK ANGEL

Finally, let a package convey a wish for Peace, with a cornshuck angel as the bearer of Glad Tidings.

Peel the husk strips carefully away from the kernels of an ear of green corn and break off the cob, leaving the whole shuck attached to a stub of stalk. Wash the shuck under running water, to remove silks, dust and insects, and place it on a pad of newspaper; bleach it in the sun for several days, turning it each morning for even lightening of color.

Meanwhile, make the angel's arms and wings from another husk. For the arms, cut two strips of shuck six inches long, lay one on top of the other, and roll them around a five-inch piece of stiff wire. Close the two ends of this slim cylinder with a tight wrapping of wire and cover the wire by gluing over it a shred of shuck. Using a cardboard pattern, cut the wings from two outer and hence wider strips of shuck. Of necessity the wings will be narrow and pointed. Bleach the wings and the arms in the sun.

When the whole shuck has bleached to creamy tan, soak it for fifteen minutes in lukewarm water to make its strips pliable. Drain it on newspaper for half an hour and then separate it, just below its rounded top, into two approximately equal layered halves. Spread white glue generously over and around the mid-portion of the rolled cylinder and insert the roll crosswise between the separated shuck halves. Push it up close to

A little girl will love the gilded cornshuck angel with gold-star hands and a silver Christmas ball (without features) to reflect the recipient's own face.

the stalk stub, and press the shucks firmly over it; push a row of.three flat-headed straight pins through the back of the layered shuck and into the roll, to help hold it in place.

Now trim off the layered ends of the shuck evenly, and spread them over and around an inverted on-the-rocks glass to make them flare out. Allow the headless angel to rest overnight before sprouting her wings. Glue the wings to the back of the shuck body, covering the pins that hold the arms.

If all the shucks have dried evenly to a creamy beige, they will need no further treatment; if streaks or blotches show on the angel's robe, or if the arms and wings do not match the robe in color, you can mask these deficiencies by spraying the whole figure with gold paint. Do the painting before adding the head and hands.

Select a silver Christmas tree ball of appropriate size, remove its wire hanger, and cement it to the angel's stalk-stub neck. Glue crossed shuck strips, like a collar, over the joined ball and stalk. You do not need to paint features on the ball, for whoever looks closely at it will see her own face reflected in its shiny surface. Dampen two large gold notary's seals and fit them together, back to back, to form a halo; glue the lower half of the halo to the back of the angel's head so that its indented rim, seen from the front, will frame the silver ball. Make hands of four gold stars, dampened and fitted together in pairs; glue a star at each end of the rolled-cylinder arms.

Coat a gilded plastic lid generously with white glue, and stand the angel upright on it. Attach the lid with three picture mounts to the top of a package wrapped in gold foil, and then bend the arms of the angel upward and forward in a gesture of benediction.

Sources of Supply

TOPIARY FRAMES
> Merryvale - Antiques and Gardens, 3640 Buchanan Street, San Francisco, California 94123
>
> Fifield's Folly, Orford, New Hampshire 03777

PLASTICS: materials and molds for casting, spraying, and laminating
> Lee Ward's, 840 North State Street, Elgin, Illinois 60120
>
> American Handicrafts Company: 115 shops across the continent. If one is not listed in your telephone directory, write for catalogue and list of stores to: 1001 Foch Street, Fort Worth, Texas 76107

FUSED GOLD
> Miles Kimball Company, 41 West Eighth Avenue, Oshkosh, Wisconsin 54901

PERFUMERS: fragrant oils, rare spices, and fixatives
> Caswell-Massey Company, Ltd., 518 Lexington Avenue, New York, New York 10017
>
> Hove Parfumeur, 723 Toulouse Street, New Orleans, Louisiana 70130

List of Anniversaries

First—Paper	Tenth—Aluminum, Tin
Second—Cotton	Fifteenth—Crystal
Third—Leather	Twentieth—China
Fourth—Fruit and Flowers	Twenty-fifth—Silver
Fifth—Wood	Thirtieth—Pearl
Sixth—Iron	Thirty-fifth—Coral
Seventh—Wool or Copper	Fortieth—Ruby
Eighth—Rubber or Bronze	Forty-fifth—Sapphire
Ninth—Pottery or Willow	Fiftieth—Gold

Methods of Preserving Flowers and Foliage

Ageratum	Cure face down in silica gel
Alder cones	Cut green, air-dry upright
Allium (onion, garlic)	Air-dry, hanging upside down
Amaranth	Air-dry hanging
Artemisia	Air-dry hanging
Astilbe	Air-dry right side up
Azalea	Right side up in silica gel, deep box
Baby's breath	Air-dry hanging, by single stalks
Baptisia	Blue-black seed pods dry on stalk; dip in shellac and alcohol
Bayberry	Dip in thinned shellac
Beauty-berry (*Callicarpa*)	Dip small bunches in thinned shellac, spray long wands with acrylic plastic
Beech leaves	Press, air-dry upright, or treat with glycerin
Bittersweet berries	Dry naturally on vine, or air-dry upright; dip in thinned shellac
Black-eyed Susan	Face down in sand or cornmeal-borax
Bluebell	Press; cure horizontal in silica gel, reinforce stem with wire
Boxwood	Submerge twigs in glycerin
Butterfly-weed	Air-dry right side up; cornmeal-borax
(*Asclepias tuberosa*)	
Caladium leaves.............	Iron between sheets of waxed paper
Carnation	Cornmeal-borax; silica gel
Cat-tail	Cut before fully ripe. Air-dry upright; dip in thinned shellac
Celosia	Air-dry, right side up
Chinese lantern	Air-dry hanging
(ground cherry)	
Chrysanthemum	Silica gel
Cockscomb	Air-dry, right side up
Coleus	Iron leaves between sheets of waxed paper
Columbine	Silica gel
Corn leaves and husks........	Dry naturally on stalk; soak in lukewarm water to shape
Corn tassels	Dry naturally, or air-dry upright
Daffodil	Upside down in silica gel or cornmeal-borax
Dahlia	Silica-gel, cornmeal-borax, sand
Daisy	Cornmeal-borax, silica gel, sand
Dock	Cut at right time for color (green in spring, rose in summer) air-dry upright
Dogwood blossoms	Cornmeal-borax
Dogwood foliage	Turns dark green in glycerin (two weeks)
Elder flowers	Silica gel
Eleagnus	Treat foliage with glycerin; dip berries in thinned shellac
Eucalyptus	Air-dries in arrangement, no treatment
Euonymus berries	Dip in thinned shellac

Euonymus foliage	Stand shrub branches in glycerin; submerge sprays of climbing and trailing varieties in glycerin
Ferns	Press, or dry in cornmeal-borax
Feverfew	Air-dry hanging; cornmeal-borax
Galax	Press, or submerge in glycerin
Geranium	Upright in silica gel, deep box
Ginkgo foliage	Press; iron individual leaves between sheets of waxed paper
Gladiolus florets	Upside down in silica gel
Gladiolus leaves	Air-dry flat, on paper
Globe amaranth	Air-dry hanging
Globe thistle	Cut before fully open, leave top leaves on, air-dry hanging
Goldenrod	Cut before upper florets open; air-dry right side up
Gourds	Pierce both ends; dry on paper, turning daily and wiping away moisture
Heather	Dries naturally in arrangement; color better if air-dried hanging
Hibiscus (and Mallow)........	Cure individual florets upside down, in silica gel
Hickory foliage	Press or cure in cornmeal-borax
Holly	Treat foliage in glycerin; spray berries with acrylic plastic
Hollyhock (and Althea).......	Cure individual flowers upside down, in silica gel
Hosta	Iron between sheets of waxed paper
Honeysuckle berries..........	Dip in thinned shellac
Huckleberry foliage..........	Air-dry, press, or treat with glycerin
Hydrangea	Pick for desired color (pale green, white, pink, dusty rose); air-dry upright
Iris	Cure individual blooms in silica gel; air-dry foliage flat, on paper
Ivy	Cure in cornmeal-borax, or submerge in glycerin (six days)
Joe-Pye Weed .... (*Eupatorium purpureum*)	Cut just before buds open to retain color; hang single stalks to air-dry
Larkspur (and delphinium)....	Cure horizontal, in silica gel
Laurel foliage	Treat with glycerin
Liatris	Air-dry hanging
Lilac	Upright in silica gel, deep box
Liriope	Press foliage; dip seed stalks in thinned shellac
Lunaria (Honesty)	Cut after seed pods mature, air-dry upright, peel off husks and seeds
Mahonia	Dip berries in thinned shellac; treat foliage with glycerin
Magnolia foliage	Glycerin mixture: two days for green, then air-dry hanging; ten days for brown
Magnolia pods	Dip in thinned shellac to retain seeds
Maple foliage	Press, or cure in cornmeal-borax
Marigold	Sand, cornmeal-borax, silica gel
Meadow rue	Cornmeal-borax
Milkweed pods (*Asclepias*)....	Cut green, split to remove silk; air-dry hanging (sage green outside, yellow within)
Mullein	Gray rosettes dry naturally in field

Nandina	Dip berries in thinned shellac; iron leaves between sheets of waxed paper
Narcissi	Silica gel, cornmeal-borax, sand
Oak leaves	Press, air-dry, or treat with glycerin
Okra pods	Air-dry, upright or hanging
Pampas grass	Cut when fluffiest, arrange without water
Pansy	Press; cure in silica gel
Pearly Everlasting	Cut just before maturity; air-dry hanging
Peony	Silica gel. Single varieties cure best
Pink	Cornmeal-borax, silica gel
Polygonum .... (bamboo, knot-bush)	Cut as soon as tiny flowers turn red; strip leaves, arrange at once, then spray with acrylic plastic
Pomegranate	Pierce both ends; dry on paper in dark room; turn daily, wipe away moisture
Poplar alba (silver-leaf)	Air-dry right side up, or cure in cornmeal and borax
Poppy	Press leaves; cure flowers in silica gel
Privet berries	Dry dark blue on bush, or cut green, dry hanging. Dip in thinned shellac
Pyracantha berries	Dip in thinned shellac or spray with acrylic plastic
Pussy-willow	Curve with fingers when freshly cut; arrange without water. No treatment
Queen Anne's lace	Silica gel, cornmeal-borax
Ragged robin	Cornmeal-borax, silica gel, sand—face down
Rhododendron flower	Right side up in silica gel, deep box
Rhododendron foliage	Air-dry upright; treat with glycerin
Rhubarb foliage	Air-dries on plant
Rose	Silica gel, cornmeal-borax
Rose foliage	Press, or cure in sand, cornmeal-borax
Salvia (red or blue)	Cut fully matured. Air-dry hanging, or cure horizontal in cornmeal-borax
Scotch broom	Air-dry upright. Tie to curved coat-hanger to change shape
Snapdragon	Horizontal, in silica gel, cornmeal-borax, reinforce stem with wire
Stock	Horizontal, in silica gel
Strawflower	Cut before fully open, air-dry hanging
Statice	Air-dry hanging
Sumac	Air-dry red fruits upright; press or iron leaves
Sunflower	Face down in sand or cornmeal-borax
Sweet-gum leaves	Cut before frost. Press or iron. Leaves keep color in glycerin (three days)
Sweet pea	Horizontal, in silica gel, cornmeal-borax
Tansy	Cut when blossoms mature, air-dry hanging
Violet	Press. Cure in sand, silica gel
Vinca minor	Submerge in glycerin solution
Vitex	Press foliage; dip seed stalks in thinned shellac
Winged Everlasting .... (*Ammobium alatum*)	Air-dry hanging
Yarrow	Air-dry hanging
Zinnia	Silica gel, cornmeal-borax, sand

INDEX